Black Space

The American Campus

Founded by Harold S. Wechsler

The books in the American Campus series explore recent developments and public policy issues in higher education in the United States. Topics of interest include access to college and college affordability; college retention, tenure, and academic freedom; campus labor; the expansion and evolution of administrative posts and salaries; the crisis in the humanities and the arts; the corporate university and for-profit colleges; online education; controversy in sport programs; and gender, ethnic, racial, religious, and class dynamics and diversity. Books feature scholarship from a variety of disciplines in the humanities and social sciences.

For a list of all the titles in the series, please see the last page of the book.

Black Space

*Negotiating Race, Diversity,
and Belonging in the Ivory Tower*

SHERRY L. DECKMAN

RUTGERS UNIVERSITY PRESS
NEW BRUNSWICK, CAMDEN, AND NEWARK,
NEW JERSEY, AND LONDON

Library of Congress Cataloging-in-Publication Data
Names: Deckman, Sherry L., author.
Title: Black space: negotiating race, diversity, and belonging in the ivory tower /
    Sherry L. Deckman.
Description: New Brunswick, NJ: Rutgers University Press, 2022. | Series: The American
    campus | Includes bibliographical references and index.
Identifiers: LCCN 2021011644 | ISBN 9781978822528 (paperback) | ISBN 9781978822535
    (hardcover) | ISBN 9781978822542 (epub) | ISBN 9781978822559 (mobi) |
    ISBN 9781978822566 (pdf)
Subjects: LCSH: Kuumba Singers. | Harvard University—Students. | African American
    college students—Massachusetts—Cambridge. | African Americans—Education,
    Higher—Social aspects.
Classification: LCC LD2166.K88 D43 2022 | DDC 378.008960744/4—dc23
LC record available at https://lccn.loc.gov/2021011644

A British Cataloging-in-Publication record for this book is available from the British Library.

www.rutgersuniversitypress.org

Manufactured in the United States of America

For my parents, Helen Deckman and the late Walter Long

"*And if the word* integration *means anything, this is what it means: that we, with love, shall force our brothers to see themselves as they are, to cease fleeing from reality and begin to change it.*"

—James Baldwin

Contents

Foreword

Black Space: Negotiating Race, Diversity, and Belonging in the Ivory Tower arrives at a consequential moment in the beautiful struggle toward racial justice, and a time of reckoning for historically white colleges and universities. We are immersed in a period of protest and yearning for social justice, with the attention of the nation, and the world, fixed upon us. At the same time, a regressive movement dismissive of the value of Black lives—an aspect of American society since 1619—vilifies, demonizes, and otherwise persecutes Black bodies and minds. Where, then, might one find a thoughtful examination of how Black students create spaces of support and validation—what bell hooks terms the homeplace, particularly when heated rhetoric and skewed portrayals are the dominant narratives?[1] I would submit that Sherry Deckman's ethnographic portrayal of the Kuumba Singers of Harvard College, a Black and multiracial student organization, provides that nuanced and respectful perspective sorely absent from the existing polarized discourse. As a scholar engaged in how Black people resist and persist in these spaces I am enthused that Sherry's book is advancing this important discussion.[2]

The concept of "safe space" has been pilloried and ridiculed by commentators on the right as the most recent and tortured aspect of "political correctness," a scourge they have been fighting since the 1980s. So often, however, these perspectives either ignore or dismiss the lived experiences of the students resisting to exist, surviving to thrive in predominantly white spaces. *Black Space* introduces the concept of the "safe Black space" which is a validating, affirming, self-authored space that embraces the membership and welcomes all. Deckman immerses the reader in the sites of resistance and struggle, and challenges the incomplete and clichéd notions that student of color organizations are sites of balkanization and separatism. Rather, such student organizations are where Black art and culture are embraced as a means to derive inspiration and work toward progress. Further, if one recognizes the centrality and beauty of Black creativity and spirituality, it is a space where those who identify as white, Asian, or Latinx, among other races and ethnicities, are welcomed.

Black Space also situates the Kuumba Singers in the context of other Black organizations—too often, observers overlook the variance in mission, intent, purpose, and goals within this community. Particularly, we are provided insight into how the Kuumbabes support a sense of belonging and embrace—and into the complexity of Blackness, again highlighting how nuanced aspects of identity, such as ethnicity, immigration history, and socioeconomic status break apart a monolithic ascription. Faculty, administrators, staff, and members of the campus community will appreciate this deeper understanding of the Black and multiracial student experience. Ultimately, we are granted the opportunity to understand how the Kuumba Singers' professional director, Sheldon K. X. Reid, leads, fosters the development of members, and continues the traditions of the previous organizational leader while educating students as they navigate multiple identities as members of the organization within the context of Harvard College, and in the (inter)national sociocultural context as well.

Deckman's ethnography beautifully blends history, sociological analysis, and a careful reading of the post-Bakke, post-Grutter, post-Fisher legal and policy milieu.[3] *Black Space* is an engaging volume, providing insights of value to students of higher education, postsecondary educators and researchers, and commentators who desire depth beyond the cursory and shallow analyses that populate social media and the blogosphere. As a scholar-administrator who cares deeply for the souls of Black students, I found myself engrossed with Deckman's storytelling and intrigued by the Kuumbabes' voices.[4] This volume is a strong companion to Beverly Daniel Tatum's *Why Are All the Black Kids Sitting Together in the Cafeteria?* and brings clarity to the vital issues pertaining to how students of color chart a path of resistance in college.[5] I eagerly anticipate the discussions and opportunities for engagement that *Black Space* will initiate. This is an ideal book club text, and practitioners in a range of historically white institutions will find it engrossing. I trust you will enjoy reading this as much as I did.

Richard J. Reddick
Professor of Higher Education Leadership and associate dean for Equity,
Community Engagement, and Outreach, College of Education,
The University of Texas at Austin
Faculty co-chair, Institute for Educational Management,
Harvard Institutes of Higher Education

Black Space

Introduction

HOW DO YOU LIFT *EVERY* VOICE?

Sing a song full of the faith that the dark past has taught us,
Sing a song full of the hope that the present has brought us;
Facing the rising sun of our new day begun,
Let us march on 'til victory is won.
—*James Weldon Johnson, "Lift Every Voice and Sing"*

The crowd was sizable, and on their feet, and uproarious. Kuumbabes—as members of the Kuumba Singers of Harvard College referred to themselves—were filing slowly onto the stage and radiating pride.[1] They wore black cocktail dresses, a few evening gowns, and tuxedos. My friend Ashley, who was attending her first Kuumba concert, turned to me wide-eyed and said, "People are acting like they are really famous!"

Ten minutes later, by the end of the second song—the Negro spiritual "Wade in the Water"—Ashley was in tears. Like the rest of the audience, she too realized this was a special occasion; it was the spring of 2010, the fortieth anniversary of the organization that was started in the wake of Martin Luther King Jr.'s assassination. During that era, much like our present, great social upheaval and unrest swept the country as Black Americans and their allies participated in the civil rights and Black Power movements.[2] The Ivory Tower was not immune to these forces of change as universities like Harvard found themselves embroiled in conflicts between students demanding progress and administrators who were unready for such.[3] Kuumba, which means "to create" in Swahili, arose then out of protests by Black students demanding a "safe space," meaning a place where they could be freed from anti-Black racism and racialized expectations from non-Black peers, faculty, and staff that pervaded campus.[4] Given the limited numbers of Black students enrolled at Harvard at the time and the racial animus that was felt throughout the area, Kuumba founders also envisioned the organization as a safe space for Black undergraduates in the greater Boston community.[5]

For the many audience members who were Kuumba alumni, the performance was a celebration of an organization that validated their existence at this Ivy League institution. Kuumba had made the hallowed halls of Harvard a little more tolerable, if not comfortable, during their time here. While many alumni returned year after year for either or both the Kuumba Christmas and spring concerts, this concert recognized a particularly momentous occasion: the organization had not only survived, but thrived, for forty years, despite shifting attitudes and policies regarding race and student organizations on campus and within Kuumba. And thus, hundreds and hundreds of eager listeners, gathered in Harvard's historic Sanders Theater, roared with excitement and waved their hands high, as if—drawing on my friend Ashley's sentiment—world-famous celebrities had just entered the building.

THE FOUNDING OF KUUMBA AND THE RECKONING OF RACE

The concert began with a somber power, both joyful and recalling a painful past. Eighty-two voices, strong and melodious, reverberated off the austere arches and dark-stained wood of Sanders's ceiling. *"Lift every voice and sing // 'Til earth and heaven ring // Ring with the harmonies of Liberty."* Audience members, some as if by instinct and others clearly following suit, rose to their feet. We stood out of respect for what many refer to as the "Black National Anthem," James Weldon Johnson's poem written in 1899 and set to music by his brother, John Rosamond Johnson. The hymn was first performed as part of a celebration of Abraham Lincoln's birthday by five hundred children at the segregated Jacksonville, Florida school where James Weldon Johnson was the principal.[6] The moment amazed me and raised questions. Here we were, a roomful of both strangers and old friends, Black and white, Asian and "Other"; we were young and old, we were multigenerational Americans and new arrivals to the country, and we were all joining together and intoning words of struggle and hope about the Black American experience on the campus of one of the country's—if not the world's—most elite, and consequentially white, institutions. And we were being led in this effort by a group on stage that was equally diverse in ways both seen and unseen. I wondered to myself, did all those who sang along understand the message of Black liberation and the call to action implied in the lyrics?[7] How was this organization contending with what struck me as an inevitable dilemma: Given the legacy of white supremacy and anti-Blackness, in what ways could white and non-Black students of color participate in a designated Black space without reproducing the power dynamics of our broader culture that often alienated and disenfranchised Black communities?

In much of the United States—and frankly, even across much of Harvard's own campus, at least prior to the Black Lives Matter protests of 2020—such a display of racially diverse people joined together in any activity was shockingly rare. What was more notable about Kuumba, a choir that did not require auditions, but accepted everyone who chose to join, was not just the racial diversity of the group, but that the group was diverse even while maintaining its mission of "being a safe space for black students on Harvard's campus, and a cultural mecca [sic] for all those who desire to celebrate Black creativity and spirituality in all its forms."[8] Historically and presently, marginalization of Black students at Harvard and other elite educational institutions has been well-documented, and when diversity or integration are spoken of in such contexts, it is almost always meant to describe incorporating Black (and brown) bodies into white institutional spaces.[9] In Kuumba, it meant just the opposite.

In fact, Kuumba was recognized by campus officials as both Harvard's oldest Black student organization as well as Harvard's largest multicultural organization.[10] David Evans, a popular admissions officer, recently retired, who had worked at the school since 1970 and had been recognized for his efforts to recruit and admit Black applicants to Harvard well before diversity statistics added to institutions' cachet, commented on the diversity and mission of the group. Evans observed, "Although [it] began as an African American vocal group, Kuumba has become one of the largest and most diverse organizations on campus. No other group depicts so vividly the 'New Harvard' as does Kuumba and this has not gone unnoticed."[11] Before attending the spring 2010 concert, I had gone to at least a half dozen other Kuumba performances and was struck repeatedly by the group's seeming ability to navigate being a self-proclaimed safe space for Black students while maintaining a multiracial membership. That ability was remarkable, considering that when Kuumba began, just forty years earlier, Harvard was a world apart from its current "New Harvard" manifestation and was not a likely place to find such a diverse group. But the ability to maintain a multiracial space was even more remarkable given that even today at elite college campuses across the country, students are most likely to be friends with same-race peers, and Black students report feeling less connected to members of other race groups, in part due to an unspoken racial hierarchy that relegates Blacks to the bottom.[12] Sociologists Wendy Laybourn and Devon Goss, who studied the experiences of non-Black members of Black Greek letter organizations, have written, "The concept of whites integrating into Blackness remains unorthodox, incomprehensible, and confusing to many. Moreover, when discussion is about other marginalized racial groups, such as Asians or Latinos, integrating into Blackness, it is conceived of as downward assimilation, or as evidence of the failure of the ability of these racial groups to integrate successfully in society."[13]

Historically, Harvard—like many other predominantly white colleges—has had a complex relationship with race, and the position of Black students in particular. It took over two hundred years from the university's founding in 1636 for the first Black undergraduate, Richard T. Greener, to receive a degree in 1870.[14] Around that same time, the university also graduated some of its most prominent early Black male alumni, all of whom were African American civil rights activists, including sociologist W.E.B. Du Bois, who was the first African American to receive a PhD from Harvard in 1895. That same year, journalist and businessman William Monroe Trotter completed his bachelor's degree and was the first Black person to be elected to Phi Beta Kappa at Harvard; and historian Carter G. Woodson, who founded Negro History Week in 1926, followed in Du Bois's footsteps, becoming the second African American to receive a PhD at the university in 1912.[15] The numbers of Black students were paltry at the time, though, and the situation did not improve in coming decades. The admittance and graduation of Black undergraduates at historically white institutions broadly remained a rarity well into the twentieth century.[16] Prior to the legally mandated efforts at desegregation in the 1950s, less than 1 percent of beginning first-year students at these schools identified as African American.[17] Thus, Harvard's decision to include Black students in the 1800s, even if just a handful, could be viewed as progressive compared to other institutions of higher education.

Yet, while Black male students were present on campus from the late 1800s, explicit discrimination persisted well beyond that time. For example, in the late 1820s Harvard professors like anatomist John Collins Warren taught courses on theories of racial difference that used "science" to demonstrate the superiority of whites and inferiority of Blacks.[18] Even Du Bois described a resigned acceptance of social exclusion from the white majority of students while at Harvard, writing, "I sought no friendships among my white fellow students, nor even acquaintanceships. Of course, I wanted friends, but I could not seek them. My class was large, with some 300 students. I doubt if I knew a dozen of them. I did not seek them, and naturally they did not seek me."[19] Similarly, one moment in Harvard's history that exemplified unequivocal discrimination was the 1922 decision of Harvard President A. Lawrence Lowell to exclude Black undergraduates from living in freshman dormitories among white undergraduates (a detail that is glaringly absent from most readily available official documentation).[20] This decision was quickly overturned a year later by the Harvard Board of Overseers—one of the university's governing bodies with an unseemly name.[21] Nonetheless, that there was such a decree in the first place illustrates the tenuous position of Black students on campus. This was also just one year after the Harvard branch of the Ku Klux Klan was founded.[22] Harvard was decidedly not a safe space for these students historically. The same could be said of the greater Boston area, which while often boastful of its abolitionist roots, is still characterized by residents as unwelcoming to Black people.[23]

Like many swaths of the country, Harvard of the late 1960s and early 1970s, around the time Kuumba was founded, was characterized by racial unrest. There was a small but growing number of Black students on campus—the number of Black freshmen doubled between 1968 and 1969 from 52 to 126—and they led protests to demand a Third World Center and an Afro-American Studies department.[24] Campus race relations were such that Kuumba, as an organization, decided only Black students would be permitted to attend the first concert in the spring of 1971. Hubert E. Walters, the first director of the Kuumba Singers, recalled,

> There was a great deal of excitement and tension on Harvard's campus the night of our first performance. Students placed black cloth around the eyes of white statues in Sanders Theater and around the campus. On the night of the performance, black students stood at the door of Sanders Theater and would not allow any white person to enter. This was not, in my opinion, a malicious act on the part of the students. They were simply trying to establish an authentic identity and unity among themselves and to make a statement about their presence on the campus and the contribution they would eventually make to the music life at Harvard.[25]

Given Kuumba's prioritization of creating a safe space for Black students and the campus racial divisiveness of the 1970s, it wasn't until the 1980s and 90s that Kuumba began having non-Black members in any significant numbers.

It is not entirely clear when the first non-Black member joined the choir. Sheldon K. X. Reid, Kuumba's professional director who first joined Kuumba in 1992 as a freshman at Harvard, said that for as long he had been affiliated with the organization, anyone had been welcome.[26] He suggested that it was actually white students who likely didn't feel "comfortable" joining Kuumba "when it was almost all Black." However, according to one alumnus, initially the decision to permit non-Black members was met with controversy, causing some Black members to leave the organization and for Kuumba to have a majority non-Black membership for a period in the 1990s. It is not entirely clear, though, how much of a choice it was to permit non-Black members—perhaps it was more about being welcoming—given that in 1985, Harvard adopted a university-wide anti-discrimination policy that prohibited organizations from barring members based on race.[27] Since then, the group has been comprised of students of various racial and ethnic backgrounds in different proportions each year, all the while maintaining a commitment to be a safe space for Black students.

Clearly, much has changed over the decades regarding race and race relations on Harvard's campus, and within Kuumba. Today, for instance, Harvard boasts the admitted class of 2025 as one of the school's most diverse, comprised of 15.9 percent (over three hundred and sixty) African American students, a percentage that roughly mirrors that of the U.S. Black population aged eighteen to twenty-four.[28] Kuumba has also gone from not permitting white students to attend performances to having white students take on leadership roles within the organization. Some of this is attributable to the current Harvard policies forbidding student groups from restricting membership based on race. However, there is a difference between the theoretical mandate of inclusion and the enactment of such policies so that everyone feels welcome in a group or entitled to participate, as students consistently have claimed they do in Kuumba.[29] This is a difference that may partially explain why at UCLA only 1.2 percent of white undergraduate students participate in ethnic—traditional "minority"—organizations (a rare example of such data).[30] Though the data is scarce, this tiny fraction of white students in "non-white" groups is likely the case for many colleges.[31]

Indeed, throughout much of U.S. higher education, students form relationships and participate in activities divided along race lines, with white students participating in majority-white organizations at higher rates than any other racial group and with only 3 percent of Latinx and 1 percent of white and Asian undergraduates at elite institutions participating in Black organizations.[32] Thus, the sustained sense of Black rootedness makes Kuumba's consistently integrated membership all the more unique. And it means that Kuumba provides both a rich and a rare site for exploring the meaning of multiracial community and safe spaces, particularly salient at the present time when debates rage, for instance, between those proclaiming, "Black lives matter" and those countering that "all lives matter." Kuumba demonstrates the complexities, paradoxes, and possibilities of a way forward.

Discovering a Safe Black Space

I am the daughter of a white mother and Black father. My siblings and other relatives self-identify with a number of different racial and cultural groups, from Black to white and Puerto Rican to American Indian and Pennsylvania Dutch. I suppose it is no surprise, then, that I have always been interested in how people navigate cultural and racial difference—and sameness, for that matter. I am interested in how people relate to those they perceive as being from a background they do or do not share.[33] These negotiations played out in my own family, as they do in so many others. My maternal grandparents rejected my father as an inappropriate partner for my mother, for reasons they never felt the need to articulate, since that was just the way things were. Even until their deaths, I cannot recall my grandparents ever speaking a word to my father, nor he to them. Being from a Black multiracial background influenced my decision about where to attend college as an undergraduate in the late 1990s. After participating in various campus recruitment events aimed at "minority" students during my senior year of high school, I became troubled by the racial dynamics that seemed to prevail. Where would I find belonging and feel affirmed at the predominantly white colleges I was considering?

At home in my small Pennsylvania town, my friends were from multiple backgrounds. But visiting these colleges I heard my hosts describe hostile climates, where the Black students kept to themselves and the white students did the same. Several of my Black hosts criticized interracial dating, suggesting it was a violation of one's commitment to their own community. Looking back, I can understand where this sentiment arose from, especially given the antagonistic race relations at some of the schools I was visiting. At the time, as a product of just such a relationship, I worried that I would not fit in nor be accepted on campuses where race was a volatile issue, and the division lines were forcibly drawn. It seemed it would be challenging to navigate the predominantly white institutional setting as a student of color—though my mother is white, phenotypically I am commonly read as, and identify as, Black—and I further wondered if I would be accepted by the Black community given my white lineage.

This concern about where one might fit in was one I heard repeatedly throughout my research with non-white Kuumbabes, particularly the Black participants. Like me, some of these students came from multiracial families or attended elementary and secondary schools primarily with non-Black peers, a scenario that is typical of Black students at elite colleges.[34] They, too, wondered if and where they might find a place they could just be themselves—acknowledged for their racialized lived experiences, but not essentialized by them. They found that place in Kuumba.

As for me, I ultimately attended the University of Pennsylvania, where my closest circle of friends couldn't have been more diverse: we were from Pennsylvania and New Jersey, and Thailand and Korea and Sweden; our parents included refugees from Cuba and Vietnam, as well as those who came to the United States as highly skilled South Asian immigrants; one of us even had grandparents who had escaped the Holocaust. We became a polyglot family, and amid all the usual quarrels of young friendships, we felt enriched rather than divided by each other's differences. As a graduate student years later, that family we made together was still central to my life. I admired our undergraduate naivete, and also the sincerity with which we listened to each other, bonded with each other, supported each other. But as I decided to focus my studies on this same navigation of race and culture and safe spaces, I realized just what a small group we were at University of Pennsylvania and in the larger United States. I wondered, by contrast, about how such dynamics played out in a bigger group, or in an organization, how these intimacies across differences were being reproduced in a more formal way, especially where Black people and communities were involved. The acceptance and support I received from my friend group was central to my college experience. I was curious, given racial tensions on many campuses, about the role higher educational institutions and organizations could have in fostering meaningful connections between students, in the power they might have to ultimately disrupt America's pernicious racial caste system—and in the role that higher education plays in maintaining that system.[35] And then I found Kuumba.

In 2008, a couple of years prior to the fortieth anniversary concert, I saw Kuumba perform for the first time. I was a second-year graduate student at Harvard, attending Cultural Rhythms, a food festival and performance showcase that had become the largest annual event on Harvard's campus.[36] At that event, a friend and I happened to notice several groups, including Kuumba, that had members who appeared not to be of the racial or cultural background of the group itself. For example, we noticed white students in the South Asian dance troupe. My curiosity was piqued. What was it like to be a member of an organization dedicated to a racial or cultural group with a multicultural and multiracial membership on a historically white campus? Given the legacy of anti-Blackness on historically white campuses, what about when the organization was dedicated to Black culture and heritage? How did such organizations maintain their focus on a particular heritage group while also making space for others who did not self-identify with that group to participate? What drew members of different backgrounds to these organizations? I wondered, was there a kind of entitlement to other cultures that one must have, to decide to participate in an organization focused on a heritage with which one does not identify? Or was there, I considered, a different dynamic at play at Harvard that made this acceptable?

I wanted to understand more about the process by which the students who were not Black found these organizations and chose to join. I questioned how this small bunch of students thought about race, and how that perspective shaped their decision to join the group. At the same time, I wondered how "the group" as a whole—primarily those who identified as Black—decided who could be members and whether there should be any limits on membership or privileges, spoken or not, based on a student's background. Might such Black student organizations, I pondered, offer insights on how to foster multiracial spaces that could be affirming and transformative for participants of various backgrounds?

My interest in Kuumba and the potential of such multiracial communities was also the result of my personal experience with student organizations in graduate school. One organization was dedicated to promoting the interests of students of color broadly. Each year the officers of this organization, of whom I was one, would privately debate the extent to which "white allies" could participate.[37] It was usually decided that white students could volunteer and participate with the group, but would not be permitted to hold officer positions. White students were seen at best as allies, auxiliary to the organization's mission, and at worst, a threat to focusing on the interests of students of color.

With the groups I watched perform at Cultural Rhythms, students from various backgrounds were not just members, but were publicly performing the culture of a race or ethnicity not their own.[38] This added component of performance seemed especially important. With the organization to which I belonged, in which anyone could volunteer, the commitment was not as visible since there was no public or performative aspect. As an audience member, students who appeared not to be members of the cultural background of the performing groups stood out to me; they were noticeable. These students stood out to others as well. During a more recent Cultural Rhythms showcase, I heard students in the audience make similar and very vocal observations about groups that included members of diverse racial and ethnic backgrounds. At one performance, a group sitting behind me narrated their views on who "belonged" in each group, questioning, in one instance, who "the awkward white girl in the middle" of an East Asian dance troupe was.

At the top of my mind was also the issue of cultural appropriation. Though this was before popular music artists like Katy Perry and Ariana Grande were called out for insensitive at best—and offensive at worst—incorporations of Asian, Black American, and South Asian symbols, style, and cultural referents, debates about who can represent whom and in what ways have been going on for time immemorial.[39] At issue in these debates is often the concern that members of the dominant culture can "play" or "mimic" the Other as convenient or entertaining, obscuring the harms of discrimination and systemic racism. Such issues have been central to a spate of recent incidents—extreme, but not uncommon—across U.S. colleges in which, for instance, white students have hosted "ghetto-themed" parties, drawing on racist stereotypes and in some cases, inspiring partygoers to don blackface.[40]

Furthermore, in my experience with Harvard undergrads, as a Race Relations resident tutor—charged with implementing residential, diversity-related programming for students—and through working on a separate project related to students' views of diversity, I heard many describe racial divisions on the campus.[41] Students frequently described the seating at Harvard's dining halls as divided along race lines, mirroring the title of psychologist Beverly Daniel Tatum's book *Why Are All the Black Kids Sitting Together in the Cafeteria?*[42] During my time on campus, I felt a persistent tension between the ideal of celebrating diversity—which usually was defined broadly as the presence, and potentially the intermingling, of students from different racial and ethnic backgrounds in a common space—and the embrace, in certain parts of campus and in certain organizations, of clear divisions along race lines. The university's overall apolitical approach to race allowed the institution to maintain the same structures and practices that had been put in place for the historically, predominantly white student body, while adding some people of color, rather than questioning the racial structures on which the power of the institution rested. Black students were regularly vocal with me about feelings of exclusion. Therefore, a group as diverse as Kuumba, performing dance and music from, to use the group's framing, the African diaspora, stood out from the typical dynamics elsewhere on campus, not to mention American culture as a whole.[43] I became convinced that Kuumba could provide insights on building bridges across divides of difference and anti-Black racism that have characterized much of American social life.

Kuumba, as I would learn, had the added dimension of focusing on Black "spirituality." It was not a Christian student organization, as students told me repeatedly. Nor was it even a religious organization, per se, and members ranged from Christian to Muslim to Jewish to agnostic to atheist. But, given founding members' religious backgrounds and owing to the role of Christianity in the music traditions the group performed—such as gospel and Negro spirituals— and in line with other historical movements focused on pursuing racial justice for Black Americans, many of the organization's practices and ideologies had roots in Black church traditions.[44]

As I came to know the group and individual Kuumbabes better over the course of this project, I became increasingly curious about how Kuumba created what members of all backgrounds described simultaneously as "a Black space," or a safe space specifically for Black students, and as "a safe space" for everyone. They used "space" to describe actual physical locations, the organization broadly, and to refer to any gathering of two or more, and they intended that wherever Kuumba was and whenever Kuumbabes gathered the intention would be to include all, but the focus would first and foremost be on the needs and interests of the Black participants. Kuumba seemed to be doing what proved impossible elsewhere on campus—bringing together students from diverse backgrounds in a community they found affirming and transformative, in which they could take up difficult conversations about identity and racial power dynamics. I wanted to understand how Kuumba as an organization addressed race, ethnicity, and diversity in ways that made this possible. I also wanted to understand how individual students in the organization navigated race, ethnicity, and diversity, and the many tensions—and potential benefits—therein. How was Kuumba able to invite everyone in while prioritizing Black ways of knowing and being? What dynamics and processes allowed Kummba to be a safe Black space— combining their uses of "safe space" and "Black space"—for everyone?[45] Or, in the end, would Kuumba's embrace of members from all backgrounds demonstrate a move towards sanitizing a once radical, Black movement?

Though I never performed onstage with Kuumba, I spent time across three academic years as a participant observer with the group (including one full year attending rehearsals, meetings, and performances), exploring these questions throughout. Living among Harvard undergraduates at the time, I spoke informally to Kuumbabes innumerable times and conducted nineteen one-on-one, in-depth interviews with student members and two one-on-one, in-depth interviews with Sheldon. I also pored over historical documents at the Kuumba office with the assistance of the group's librarian, and collected and analyzed other artifacts, including concert programs and group email communications.[46]

The results of my time with Kuumba have been revelatory for my own understanding of race in the United States. Based on its mission, composition, practices, and in particular, its adamant focus on the needs of the Black community; and its unapologetic, circumscribed inclusion of non-Black students, Kumba could be seen as a separatist organization. And yet it was touted by members as one of the most welcoming places on campus—a safe space—for students of all backgrounds. Even amid Harvard's proclamations of embracing diversity, and the larger moment of Barack Obama's election and our supposed postracial future, students were adamant that this safe space was essential. Kuumba had made this seeming contradiction possible: the organization had purposefully defined and enacted what it meant to be a safe space for Black students, all the while embracing a multiracial membership.

If we see Kuumba as a Black space that is more largely a safe space for all students, then we gain a deeper understanding of how a space can be inclusive while taking a decidedly race-conscious approach. In the field of higher education, as we seek to understand the effectiveness of so-called diversity initiatives, or how to quell the resurgence of racial violence on campus, or address increasing divisiveness of students from different social groups, this understanding is essential. Given the history of Black exclusion on predominantly white campuses—and in the history of this country—the perspective the case study of Kuumba provides has for too long been left out of the conversation. Yet Kuumba's approach may indeed be the only way to be inclusive of students from racially underrepresented and marginalized backgrounds at historically white institutions. In the words of activist Fannie Lou Hamer, "Nobody's free until everybody's free."[47] Hamer was speaking to the white-dominated National Women's Political Caucus, calling attention to the contributions of Black women in the women's liberation movement. Thus, the multiracial safe space—the safe Black space—Kuumba offered might only have been possible because the organization worked tirelessly to protect the interests of the Black students in the context of predominantly white higher education, which is otherwise mired in a history of anti-Blackness.[48] Showing what this entailed and the processes by which this happened—including the challenges and triumphs—is the focus of this volume. A primary purpose of this book, then, following the tradition of ethnographic research, is to *show* how the safe Black space functioned, including the conflicts and challenges that arose. Thus, this work is largely descriptive.

The Story Is a Song and the Song, a Story

The story this book aims to tell is about the Kuumba Singers as an organization. This story of the organization is told through the voices of individual students and Sheldon. Their voices are united as in song, a song steeped in history, representing and revealing trends and patterns present in the larger data set. Also, given the importance of context to this study, the actual name of the organization and the director's name are used with permission (though some details have been obscured to protect participants' privacy). All student and most alumni names are pseudonyms, as are names of most other Harvard student organizations mentioned.[49]

To borrow the words of Lauren Washington, a senior Kuumbabe, you must *see* and *hear* Kuumba to understand Kuumba. To help readers hear Kuumba, I drew on the sociological method of portraiture with grounding in both art and science.[50] Portraiture focuses on revealing "the complex dimensions of *goodness*" of social phenomena, and in doing so here I rely on rich, evocative, ethnographic description and metaphor in describing my findings.[51] I also hope I have offered "brave descriptions" of the participants so that you will be able to *see* them as well as *hear* them.[52] This methodology parallels the process between artist and audience that is central to Kuumba's practice as a choir and to their creation of a safe Black space.

In keeping with portraiture's focus on artistry and metaphor, the central metaphor of this book is a song. Consequently, the book is organized metaphorically as parts of a song. Chapter 1 serves as a prelude, situating Kuumba within the history of racial diversity and the ongoing debates over safe spaces in historically white higher education. Chapters 2 and 3 act as song verses, seeking to tell parts of the story. Here that story is about what "Black" meant within this organization and on Harvard's campus. Chapter 2 presents students' responses to what made Kuumba a Black student organization even while having a multiracial membership. In this chapter, we learn what Black meant to Kuumbabes and how that definition was, while grounded in the history of African diasporic peoples, dynamic, multifaceted, and collective in such a way as to account for the variety of lived experiences Black members brought to the organization. Chapter 3 continues this exploration; however, the focus shifts to considering norms and practices—and related rationales—put in place within Kuumba to ensure the Black space remained Black. This included parameters of participation based on members' racial backgrounds, focusing recruitment on Black potential members, and reserving certain leadership positions for Black students. Chapter 4 serves as the bridge, and like a bridge in a song, this chapter offers contrast to the verses. Here, we turn our attention to the experiences of the non-Black students who participated in Kuumba. We learn what brought them to the organization and what kept them participating, despite and because of dilemmas related to race that they faced in Kuumba and elsewhere on campus. Chapter 5 acts as the chorus and expresses the main theme of this work. In this chapter, I describe the practices deployed in the group to foster an environment where all members felt as though they belonged, the organization's "curriculum of care."

This is the heart of Kuumba's song. Here, I show how students learned how to care and be vulnerable, which they described as a radical departure from the high-intensity, competitive, invulnerable campus culture, and how this was a key component of making safe space particularly for Black students. Chapter 6 concludes the book with a coda—a discussion of the lessons from the safe Black space.

Given the central importance of song and music to this work, selected snippets of song lyrics are included in the text and endnotes. It is my hope that you will look up songs as they are referenced, and listen along as you read to fully understand the connections and reverberations across time and place of the origins and ongoing work of the safe Black space.

Prelude

(UN)SAFE SPACE AND RACIAL DIVERSITY
IN THE IVORY TOWER

"The fact that Harvard was started as an institution for white men is a really big deal."
                                        —*Claire Senai, Sophomore*

"Well, in the very beginning it was a place that Black students could come and get together and just be strong, because it was right after Martin Luther King Junior was assassinated. Of course, non-Black people wouldn't know, necessarily, how to deal with that, especially if they had to relate to Black students . . . So Kuumba back then, I would imagine, was a necessity. It's something that needed to happen." First-year Kuumbabe Jason Thomas said this to me as we met in my seven-by-seven-foot basement office in Adams House, the undergraduate dormitory where I lived and worked as an advisor. I had just asked Jason to tell me what made Kuumba a safe space for him. Given Jason's focus on Kuumba's origins, I wanted to know if the safe space Kuumba provided during the late 1960s and early 1970s was still important in the 2010s. Jason took his time responding, speaking slowly, pausing to reflect. His tall, thin frame bent slightly forward in his chair, his deep, burnt-umber hands folded in front of him, Jason continued, "I think it is . . . because Black students especially still need to know that there's a place where they can come and just be accepted." Decades after its founding, Jason, who many times expressed feelings of isolation as a Black student at Harvard, deemed the safe space of Kuumba was once again—or had never stopped being—"a necessity." Yet, at least for the past couple decades, it now included non-Black members. Did they know "how to deal with" the racial antagonism and violence facing Black communities? Did the space still feel safe with these non-Black members in it?

By all accounts, Kuumba of the 2010s was a safe space for members from all different backgrounds. Though "safe space" is generally an ill-defined term, not always agreed upon, Kuumbabes described the organization as a "family," a place where they felt "comfortable" and "comforted," and in the words of Asian American first-year student Daphne Han, free from the "epic judging" that characterized other spaces and organizations on campus. Daphne contrasted the safe space of Kuumba with the broader milieu of Harvard, which she unsurprisingly described as "competitive." Kuumba, instead of letting interpersonal issues fester, or allowing covertly nasty or conniving attitudes among peers, was a safe space because, Daphne said, "If you have an issue with someone [in Kuumba], like you'll talk to them." Similarly, Asian American sophomore Sei Matsuura put it this way: "I guess, safe space, knowing that I can share my thoughts, and I won't be immediately judged—like it's about clarifying, and not necessarily about judgment. So it's just that they're willing to listen . . . actually listening and thorough listening . . . willing to push back without being hurtful or, like everything they say, it never comes out from a negative space . . . [or a] distrustful space. It's more like, 'This is what I think, and you can take it how you will, but also know that I'm not trying to hurt you.'" African American senior Lauren Washington summed it up, "Kuumba really is a safe space where like I said, your batteries are recharged when you leave. . . . We share with each other things that we wouldn't necessarily tell people in our lives that are really close to us. . . . Some of the most intimate things that those people are experiencing right now, and just to feel like Kuumba is a space where not only will you be acknowledged, not only will you be recognized, but people will actually care."

The overwhelmingly positive ways in which students describe the safe space of Kuumba belied the contentiousness of the conversation around safe spaces on historically white college campuses in recent years. On the one hand are those who call for and define safe spaces as actual physical locations or more nebulously, gatherings, where students from marginalized backgrounds can come together as a refuge, to be themselves outside of the racialized expectations of the broader campus, to "get together and just be strong," to use Jason's words.[1] On the other hand are those who define and critique safe spaces as separatist and antithetical to the diversity goals espoused by many U.S. colleges. Contradicting Sei's and Daphne's characterizations of the safe space provided by Kuumba, Jay Ellison, Dean of the Students in the College at the University of Chicago and former Harvard College administrator, sent a letter to incoming students in the class of 2020, in which he infamously condemned safe spaces as places "where individuals can retreat from ideas and perspectives at odds with their own."[2] In a sense, safe space debates are about how we interact and connect across difference and promote belonging, how we negotiate diversity, and about the goals and hopes we attach to these actions and interactions. These debates provoke questions: Safe for whom? To what end? And how? These are questions that become more complicated to consider given the current racial diversity efforts in U.S. higher education and the historical legacies of racist exclusion, particularly of Black people, at elite, historically white colleges and universities.

In this chapter, I situate conversations about safe spaces at elite, predominantly white colleges and universities within the larger racial contexts of these institutions. I suggest that while in recent years Harvard and others have actively engaged in campaigns to racially diversify their campuses, given the historical legacy of racial exclusion and anti-Blackness, such efforts may in fact serve to stabilize the dominance of whiteness, thus undermining efforts to achieve safe space for Black students. There is an embedded assumption that these campuses operate in race-neutral ways and that safe spaces, when they are grounded in a distinct racial perspective, undermine the idealized goals related to pluralism and diversity that colleges and universities seek.[3] Yet very little empirical research has been done on so-called safe spaces in which white students are present and are in a minority. Instead, the primary focus has been on spaces for students of color with no mention of white participants, or seemingly race-neutral safe spaces, such as classrooms, or LGBTQIA organizations and centers that have been shown to tacitly prioritize the perspectives of white participants.[4] Therefore, debates about safe space have largely taken for granted the whiteness of institutional contexts and reified whiteness as normal.

The Promise of Campus Diversity

To understand the salience of the safe space debates in higher education, it is important to first understand the hopes Americans invest in schools to right societal wrongs and build social cohesion.[5] This is no less true for higher education than it is for elementary and secondary education. However, given U.S. patterns of residential segregation and the re-segregation of elementary and secondary schooling, colleges and universities have become some of the likeliest locations in our country for young people to come into meaningful contact with those from backgrounds different than their own.[6] This has not been overlooked by higher education's leaders, who have taken up the charge to harness the potential of campus racial diversity to shape our democracy and promote social transformation.

The narrative that elite colleges and universities should serve as benevolent sentinels of democracy and promoters of social transformation has a long and deep history.[7] Extolling the importance of this assumed role, Carl A. Fields, the first Black administrator at Princeton in the 1960s, wrote, "If *total democracy* is to be translated from theory into practice, it will be done first in our *educational institutions* rather than in our *political system*. The college or university in particular, must bear the burden of this task."[8] The current Harvard College mission statement also reflects this purpose. "Through a diverse living environment, where students live with people who are studying different topics, who come from different walks of life and have evolving identities, intellectual transformation is deepened and conditions for social transformation are created. From this we hope that students will begin to fashion their lives by gaining a sense of what they want to do with their gifts and talents, assessing their values and interests, and learning how they can best serve the world."[9] The connection to democratic values and political engagement is implied, if not made explicit, in Harvard's mission statement, where students are referred to as "citizens" and "citizen-leaders."[10] Here, the university connects "divers[ity]" with "social transformation," and frames it as ultimately informing how students learn to "best serve the world," that is, how they can be active in our democratic society.

Though elite colleges and universities were inarguably founded on a legacy of excluding individuals based on, for example, social class, gender, religion, and race, over the last fifty to sixty years historically white colleges have increasingly granted admission to students of color in the avowed pursuit of supporting social transformation and democratic ideals.[11] In fact, colleges have come to be evaluated by would-be students and outside organizations based in part on "ethnicity/diversity" metrics (i.e. numbers of non-white student bodies on campus).[12] Consequently, across the Ivy League, the enrollment of Black students went from around 2.3 percent of students in 1967 to 5.7 percent by 2006.[13] Presently, the numbers are even higher, with Harvard boasting 15.9 percent African American students in the admitted class of 2025.[14] Much of the initial gains were owed to student protests in the aftermath of Martin Luther King, Jr.'s assassination in 1968, protests similar to those taking place today. At that time, as now, students at several Ivy League institutions, including Harvard, pushed administrators to address the sparse numbers of Black students on campus.

By complying with demands and increasing racial diversity, Harvard and similar elite institutions were able to reaffirm their commitment to democratic ideals. First, admitting students from underrepresented racial backgrounds was and is conceived of as increasing opportunities for those from disenfranchised backgrounds, laying the groundwork for social transformation.[15] Second, as Harvard's mission statement promises, fostering a diverse student body was and is seen as a way to foster cross-racial relationships that can render learning opportunities and momentum that brings about societal change.

However, the tensions and conflicts this framing inspires, particularly with regard to the debate over safe spaces on elite campuses, are both counterproductive to the espoused goals and dehumanizing to students from underrepresented backgrounds who are positioned as receiving access to exclusive educational opportunities in exchange for providing learning opportunities.[16] When, for example, Harvard makes a commitment to providing the context for "learning from our differences," racial minority students are often tacitly, if not explicitly, positioned as providing that difference from which to learn.[17] To put it even more plainly, Black students become part of the informal curriculum on campus from which their white classmates have the opportunity to learn. By marrying democracy and diversity in this way, predominantly white higher education institutions reinforce the racial hierarchy that white elites have long deployed for political benefit.

Yet, institutional commitments to cultivating a "diverse" student body for the sake of learning are matched by demand from students, especially white students, who have also come to view the presence of students of color as a curricular enhancement meant to enrich their educational experiences.[18] In research including perspectives from undergraduates at Harvard and Brown Universities, this was one of the most common benefits of a diverse campus that students noted, a trend that has been captured in other studies of elite educational institutions.[19] These students often pointed to the presence of students from different backgrounds on campus as offering varying points of view from which they could learn and grow, in effect using this as a justification for race-conscious admissions practices (i.e., affirmative action). Students of color at times, too, see themselves as "diversifiers" who can—and should—educate white peers.[20]

Even beyond the ivory tower, the value of diversity as contributing to learning has cachet. This was essentially the only justification for affirmative action in the form of race-conscious admissions policies deemed permissible by the last couple of decades of U.S. Supreme Court decisions.[21] In the recent Fisher I and II cases, two white women who were rejected from the University of Texas at Austin sued the school for racial discrimination. In Fisher II, drawing on the rationale from prior cases (Grutter and Fisher I), the Court reiterated, "Enrolling a diverse student body 'promotes cross-racial understanding, helps to break down racial stereotypes, and enables students to better understand persons of different races.' [. . .] Equally important, 'student body diversity *promotes learning outcomes*, and better prepares students for an increasingly diverse workforce and society.'"[22] In the majority opinion for Grutter, one of the precedential cases, Justice Sandra Day O'Connor penned the phrasing that would be used for decades to come, referring to the "educational benefits" of diversity as a "compelling interest." Justice O'Connor wrote, "The Equal Protection Clause does not prohibit the Law School's narrowly tailored use of race in admissions decisions to further a compelling interest in obtaining the educational benefits that flow from a diverse student body."[23] Though the higher education institutions in question have in some cases identified the need to address historical discrimination against groups like African Americans and Latinx people as motivations for their admissions policies, the popular discussion of the cases has been around the extent of the learning benefits of diversity vis-à-vis what some consider a discriminatory practice against white applicants.

This rationale of learning from a racially diverse student body was also invoked recently when Harvard was sued for discrimination against Asian American applicants.[24] The case was brought by Students for Fair Admissions, led by Edward Blum, a white, "anti-race conscious admissions activist."[25] In response to that lawsuit, President Lawrence Bacow reiterated what we might consider the democratic purposes of cultivating a racially diverse student body. "Diversity of all kinds creates remarkable opportunities and complex challenges," he said. "If we hope to make the world better, we must both pursue those opportunities and confront those challenges, motivated always by humility, generosity, and openness. The power of American higher education stems from a devotion to learning from our differences. Affirming that promise will make our colleges, and our society, stronger still."[26]

While few would argue in favor of limiting students' opportunities, treating racial diversity as a good or a commodity that can be deployed in the interest of white students is an example of interest-convergence at play. As interest-convergence theory suggests, Black Americans are afforded rights and opportunities only when their interests converge with those of white Americans.[27] In this case, granting exclusive educational access to students from underrepresented backgrounds is offered in exchange for providing learning opportunities, primarily for white students.[28] These "learning opportunities" are further parlayed into a kind of currency for white elites who are rewarded for displays of cultural omnivorousness and dexterity.[29] A prized marker of the educated elite includes valuing and being able to learn from texts as disparate as *Beowulf* and *Jaws*.[30] Mixing highbrow and lowbrow culture and showing familiarity with cultural forms identified as non-white becomes a sign of privilege in that only those from elite backgrounds have ready access to this range; those from less privileged backgrounds are less likely to encounter the more esoteric and rarefied forms and experiences. Further, by embracing learning from difference, elite students—particularly white students—have been able to develop and assert identities as non-racists, which is necessary for them to fully realize their place among the elite.[31] As sociologist Natasha Warikoo points out, though, this is very much an individual project for students, focused on the benefits they receive from racially diverse educational contexts and not, say, about advocating for human rights or social justice for historically oppressed groups. Nonetheless, this predilection makes elite higher education uniquely suited for a study of this sort, as it is possible that such schools may be likelier places to find, say, non-Black students interested in participating in Black student organizations with any sort of regularity.

While students of color are positioned as members of groups from which learning about diversity can happen, coming to be viewed merely as parts—or representatives—of a group, with little regard given to their individual lived experiences, white students are often treated as individuals by institutions and peers.[32] In my own research with secondary school teachers, I have documented how this dynamic plays out in the ways teachers talk about classroom management. In one study teachers spoke of Black students as a group or as nameless actors, as in "the Black girl" or "my Black students," while they spoke of white students by name and never by race until prodded to do so.[33] That being said, scholars who focus on equity in higher education have increasingly called on practitioners and administrators to recognize the differences among Black students, particularly in predominantly white institutions, and to use that to better support students.[34] Indeed, the Black student populations at elite institutions are perhaps the most heterogeneous in U.S. higher education.[35] One thing these scholars point out is that in a seemingly paradoxical situation, some Black students at highly selective colleges and universities are encountering a critical mass of same-race peers for the first time in their schooling.[36] Being part of a university where they were encountering more Black peers than at any other time in their prior education—all the while in the midst of a majority white campus—can require Black students at historically white institutions to not only navigate expectations of the majority culture on campus, but also new and tricky relationships with their fellow Black students.

Nonetheless, Black students continue to be treated as part of a homogenous group with a shared racial identity, which contributes to Black students' experience of elite campuses as unsafe space for several reasons. First, Black students regularly receive competing messages. They're told that they have earned their spots among the ranks of the educationally privileged because of what they can contribute to campus diversity as a member of a race group and, simultaneously, that individualism is prized, which suggests a need to dissociate from race groups. Sociologist of race and higher education Carson Byrd has described this dynamic. "Elite college students withdraw their connections to racial and ethnic groups to remove any deterministic logic of why they, as individuals, are in the positions they are currently in or could possibly find themselves in later in life."[37] At the same time, these students who may have had friends of various racial backgrounds prior to college find themselves closed off from social opportunities with peers of other race groups. In Byrd's large-scale, quantitative, cross-campus research at twenty-eight of the most selective colleges and universities in the United States, he found Black students were the most likely to be segregated from others.[38] Thus, despite strides in race relations in the United States over the last half-century, we can draw on the words of famed Harvard grad W.E.B. Du Bois to describe the position of students of color at historically white institutions as "in" but not "of" them.[39]

Perhaps more insidiously, while the increase in students from underrepresented backgrounds in elite higher education has expanded opportunities, a focus on "those who 'look different'" has obfuscated the workings of white privilege.[40] In her writing about the work of diversity practitioners in higher education, cultural studies scholar Sara Ahmed suggests that this misplaced focus allows institutional inequality and hostile campus climates to persist. "If diversity is what individuals have *as* individuals, then it gives permission to those working within institutions to turn away from ongoing realities of institutional inequality."[41] Meanwhile, those prized Black students, who contribute to the informal curriculum for white peers and add to the prestige of the university in terms of diversity metrics, may themselves struggle to find social belonging—or worse. Students of color often encounter microaggressions and negative environments that impede their participation in campus academic and social activities.[42] Consequently, what on the surface began as part of an effort towards inclusion and supporting democratic ideals has at times contributed to campus contexts that alienate.

Colleges and universities have not entirely ignored the possibly damaging consequences of focusing on discourses of diversity that can lead to experiences of marginalization for students of color. To the contrary, recognizing this dynamic has prompted some historically white colleges and universities to attempt a shift to a focus on discourses and practices of "belonging" and "inclusion."[43] Whereas diversity necessarily focuses on difference, belonging and inclusion intend to focus on points of connection and ways to navigate difference by bringing people together. In 2016, Harvard even convened a task force on inclusion and belonging, whose charge included the following framing: "For nearly 400 years, Harvard has steadily—though often painfully slowly—opened its doors, as it has welcomed groups previously excluded from its faculty, staff, and student body. But, as recent events both here and elsewhere have reminded us, much work remains to be done [. . .] It is essential that we bring together a diverse community. To realize the community's full promise [. . .] we must also work affirmatively and collectively to advance a culture of belonging."[44]

While initiatives such as Harvard's Task Force on Inclusion and Belonging can represent a move towards fostering campus environments where more spaces might be counted as "safe" among Black students and students of color, others caution that inclusion as a framework has limitations. Among the drawbacks is that inclusion, like diversity, continues to center whiteness.[45] It is the privileged—the white elite in the case of historically white colleges and universities—that host students of color as newcomers and guests. To maintain their contingent welcome, students of color are expected to comport themselves according to the already-established practices and within the existing structures, which again, are regulated by sociohistorical power relations, grounded in white supremacy.

Consequently, due to the historical legacy of exclusion on elite, predominantly white campuses, environments are created that impede efforts aimed at unconditional belonging, leading Black students to seek what we might call "safe spaces" with other students with whom they share a background.[46] This becomes problematic when considering universities' goals for diversity and democracy, and interest-convergence. There is the sense that safe spaces deprive the broader—normatively white—campus community of the opportunity to learn from those who are different. Black and brown students are expected to "belong" in an oppressive white space as opposed to asking white students to relinquish their monopoly on safety, comfort, and belonging. It is this tension that provides context for understanding how scholars and educators have conceived of and taken issue with the idea of safe spaces.

SEPARATISM, INCLUSION, AND SAFE SPACES

When people in higher education speak of safe spaces, the ideas that come to mind are legion and can be incompatible or contradictory. Some use the term to denote classroom contexts that encourage meaningful discussion in which all students feel heard and valued. Others envision advocacy- and movement-based organizations that bring together students from historically disenfranchised groups both for the sense of belonging felt by being with others who share similar life experiences and for working together for social change.[47] The latter definition encapsulates Kuumba's origins during the Civil Rights Movement and campus protests of the 1960s and 70s.

Proponents of race-specific safe spaces for students of color at predominantly white colleges and universities generally argue that these spaces are necessary to help students cope with racism, discrimination, and isolation they might experience elsewhere on campus. Safe spaces of this sort often take the form of racially-focused student organizations and have at times been referred to as "counter-spaces" to indicate the relief they provide from the white dominance of the rest of the college experience.[48] In turn, these kinds of organizational safe spaces have been associated with a host of positive outcomes for students related to academic persistence and achievement, comfort with integrating into the larger campus community, and senses of cultural connectedness and preservation, particularly for Black students at predominantly white institutions.[49]

One reason racially-focused organizational safe spaces contribute to positive outcomes and experiences for students of color at predominantly white institutions has to do with supporting students' sense of belonging.[50] Research has found that participation in such student organizations can help students feel more integrated into the ethnic community—associated with the group they're participating in—on campus.[51] As a result, students then feel more comfortable immersing themselves in the wider campus environment. Racially-focused organizational safe spaces for Black students can also help connect Black students from predominantly white home communities, not uncommon among elite institutions, to African American culture.[52] Students who find a community of same-race peers, research suggests, will feel more secure in navigating and integrating into the larger campus community. While the focus remains on students of color "integrating" into the majority white campus setting instead of vice versa, these organizational safe spaces can nonetheless be affirming for students of color.

Though some view safe spaces as ways to promote inclusion through supporting the sense of belonging of students of color, many opponents of safe spaces
in elite higher education excoriate them as separatist spaces where students iso-
late themselves with others with whom they share similar beliefs and identity
backgrounds, such as race. This critique gets at the perceived tension between
safe spaces and freedom of speech leveled by opponents, which in turn reveals a
tension about the role of campus racial diversity. In this view, safe spaces are
insular communities where like thinking is reproduced and where nonconform-
ing speech is sanctioned.[53] Those in opposition contend that if safe spaces are
meant to be protective of students from specific, identified backgrounds, any
speech that counters the assumed beliefs of that group—not to mention that
no so-called group is completely homogenous—would be shut down, making
impossible what these critics see as an open exchange in the marketplace of ideas.
As Michael Roth, president of Wesleyan University, has written in describing "safe
enough spaces," "Tensions between diversity and free speech arise on campus
when talk about diversity tends toward inclusion and talk about free speech tends
toward the harm that speech can cause."[54] Indeed, advocates of safe spaces have at
times focused on the harm that speech can cause, for example when speech is
experienced as racist.[55] At issue is lack of a shared definition of what should constitute free speech versus harmful or hate speech and, therefore, what type of
speech should be permissible in safe spaces—or, really, anywhere on campus—in
order to foster an inclusive environment where most students feel they can thrive.

Conceding that safe spaces might serve a crucial purpose and still wanting
the envisioned educational benefits of open dialogue on a racially diverse campus, some have called on schools to make available both safe spaces and "brave
spaces."[56] For example John Palfrey, former Harvard faculty member and Head
of School at the elite preparatory school Phillips Academy, defines safe spaces
as "environments in which students can explore ideas and express themselves
in a context with well-understood ground rules for the conversation. For instance,
a school or university might create a safe space for LGBTQ students in which
students know they can discuss issues of sexual identity or gender and will not
be made to feel marginalized for their perspective or exploration."[57] Brave spaces,
alternatively, are described as "learning environments that approximate the
world outside academic life. Brave spaces include classrooms, lecture halls, and
public forums where the rules and social norms for expression might in fact follow the doctrine of the First Amendment or something close to it, as set by the
school or university at large. Brave spaces are those learning environments in
which the primary purpose of the interaction is a search for the truth, rather
than support for a particular group of students, even insofar as some of the discussions will be uncomfortable for certain students."[58]

While Palfrey's proposition seems to offer a productive way out of the
safe spaces versus freedom of speech debate, by framing "brave spaces" as

opportunities to "search for the truth" and "approximate the world outside academic life," it nonetheless relies on a similar logic. Such a conception suggests that safe spaces are bound by a specific aspect, or aspects, of participants' marginalized backgrounds (e.g. safe spaces for LGBTQ students, to use Palfrey's example), and that brave spaces—or simply non-designated safe spaces on campus—are neutral ground where students from diverse backgrounds can come together and debate the truth. This conception suffers from a failure of imagining more transformative spaces where students from racially marginalized backgrounds might feel validated while engaging in rigorous intellectual debate, to use that example, with students from dominant backgrounds. It also neglects to take into account the monopoly white men have on hegemonic truth-making.[59] Consequently, "brave spaces" fail to account for the atmosphere of an anti-Blackness and entrenched white supremacy that pervades these institutions and U.S. society more generally.[60]

Northwestern University President Morton Schapiro offered a counterpoint to the false choice between group validation and inclusion and open communication, arguing, "Students don't fully embrace uncomfortable learning unless they are themselves comfortable. Safe spaces provide that comfort. The irony, it seems, is that the best hope we have of creating an inclusive community is to first create spaces where members of each group feel safe."[61] For Black students at predominantly white institutions, having such a space could be particularly salient given that their experiences are sometimes ignored, denied, or refuted, accompanied by the additional challenges of regular attacks on their racial identity.[62] This is what makes Kuumba such an interesting case: it provided a safe space, first and foremost, for Black students and, in so doing, for members of all backgrounds. In turn, Kuumba became an inclusive space in which "uncomfortable learning" could happen. The organization offers an illustration of Schapiro's argument in favor of a seeming contradiction in action. In the case of Black students at historically white colleges and universities, policies and practices that seem exclusive might be necessary in order to encourage inclusivity. The question arises as to how Kuumba was able to realize that vision.

UNSAFE WHITE SPACE

As we have seen, predominantly white colleges and universities have been admitting increasing numbers of students of color in an avowed commitment to democratic values, while at the same time calling attention to "diversity" in ways that typecast underrepresented minority students. This seemingly contradictory process is the result of the entrenchment of white norms and ideologies that persist on campuses, despite apparent diversification. Since the Civil Rights Movement, Black people in the U.S. have been granted presence in and access to previously closed-off locations, but predominantly white public spaces and institutions remain. Even spaces that seem "integrated" or "diverse" to white people can be experienced as "off limits," uncomfortable, or hostile to Black inhabitants.[63] This sense of disquietude has to do with the actual demographic composition of the people occupying the space (i.e., the numbers), as well as the feeling that pervades the space due to contextual considerations and what some might refer to as the culture.[64] In this way, institutional spaces can be racialized, and predominantly white colleges and universities are prime examples of "white spaces" in which Black students may feel of liminal status, as outsiders, or as holding a type of (precarious) guest status.[65]

In explaining why predominantly white institutions do not have to be openly racist to develop a hostile environment, scholars and educators have pointed to a number of factors that coalesce around the historical contexts, current policies, nature of cross-racial student interactions, and subtle signaling that contributes to the campus environment, as well as the beliefs and ideologies that undergird all of the above.[66] For instance, critical race theorist and sociologist Wendy Leo Moore identified four characteristics that contributed to the development of "white institutional space" at elite law schools, including Harvard Law School. First, these institutions have a history of racist exclusion both in terms of students and people in positions of power. This is evident, for instance, in the number of faculty from underrepresented backgrounds, which at Harvard is 125 out of nearly two thousand faculty members, or just 6 percent.[67] Second is a white frame—including conscious and unconscious ideologies, ideas, actions, and so forth, grounded in a view of white superiority—that organizes the logic of the institution. In thinking of the composition of the Harvard faculty, hiring practices that result in such demographics are likely influenced by a white frame that holds in higher regard, for example, canonical research that is more typically in line with the scholarly agendas of white academics.[68] Third is a curricular model historically set up to favor the thinking of white elites. Here, we might recall the so-called "great books" courses and curricula that advance and esteem the work of white scholars, but Moore also points to expectations about how students should interact, in class and with professors, that can exemplify the thinking models favored by white elites.[69] Finally, Moore names the assertion of neutrality and impartiality unconnected to power relations, which comes up repeatedly in safe space debates.[70] The white institutional space is subsequently reinforced through demographics and distribution of power, racialized practices and discourses, legal and political frames that protect whites, and hidden signifiers of white privilege and power. These signifiers may be ones that many hardly give a passing thought to, such as building names and portraits that adorn the halls, yet they can send powerful and repeated messages about who belongs in the space and who does not.[71]

Elite educational institutions are thus imbricated with whiteness and white supremacy; they are also entangled in a legacy of anti-Blackness. Historically, these institutions have been integrally involved in the production and promotion of "scientific racism" in the form of eugenics, and their exploitation of the labor of enslaved Blacks for their own gain and advancement.[72] Lest we imagine that this is all in the past, anti-Black rhetoric and action continues in the present. Moore, for one, recounted an incident in 2002 when a white Harvard Law student emailed a Black classmate asserting his right to use the word "n*gger."[73] (He wrote the actual word, multiple times, in the message.) And in 2015, Black law professors' portraits were vandalized in Harvard's Wasserstein Hall.[74]

Being and becoming elite requires being white, or in the case of students of color, approximating whiteness, argue Rubén Gaztambide-Fernández and Leila Angod, critical scholars who study issues of power and privilege in education.[75] Given that Black students will never be able to completely approximate the markers of whiteness—as they will never *be* white—Gaztambide-Fernández and Angod suggest that when they and other non-white subjects are "invited into eliteness," belonging is always contingent and tenuous. Further, approximating whiteness requires students of color to distance themselves from their own racialized histories and realities. This all matters as safe spaces are conceived, given that, as Gaztambide-Fernández and Angod write, "Whiteness demarks bodies, but it also demarks gestures, modes of speech, and behaviours, as well as the rules by which elite spaces are inhabited and constituted as safe."[76] In other words, safe spaces in elite educational settings do not operate in racially neutral ways, but are instead grounded in white racial ideologies; thus, so-called safe spaces might not actually feel that safe to students of color.

The alternative to the white space would be the Black space, though not as it is often construed and depicted from a white-centric lens: full of danger, violence, and foreboding.[77] Rather, a Black space might conjure what scholar and cultural critic bell hooks calls a "homeplace." She describes a homeplace as "a safe place where black people could affirm one another and by doing so heal many of the wounds inflicted by racist domination."[78] These are places where Black folks "can recover ourselves" from the indignities suffered in the white space.[79] However, when a Black space functions within a larger white space, what are the implications and limitations? For that matter, what happens when white and other non-Black members also participate in that space, as is the case with Kuumba?

While Black students may experience the whiteness of elite institutional environments acutely, white students may be oblivious to practices and policies that prioritize their own interests over those of students of color. White students are often unaware of and do not understand racism and its history in this country, and at times actively avoid learning about the history and present state of racism in order to maintain their own positive self-image.[80] Yet, to promote the type of cross-racial interaction and learning that universities and many of their students hope for requires attending explicitly to, and dismantling, the whiteness of the space.[81] What, then, would creating a multiracial safe space for Black students at such an institution entail?

A Note about Institutional Context

Individual colleges and universities have unique cultures, norms, and values that influence who students feel they can be(come) on campus, the types of activities they find appropriate to engage in, the views they deem acceptable to express, and the ways in which they express them.[82] Elite colleges and universities have sordid histories with race, grounded in white supremacy and Black exclusion. These are institutions where students of all different backgrounds struggle to find belonging and safe space, given institutional origins set up for serving the interests of the wealthiest of white, gentile men. These are also places where students are told they are the "best of the best" in the country (and the world), and they are taught that as the best of the best, they should exhibit and prize intellect, civility, and rationality.[83] That is, certain types of provocations in discussions are shunned, namely discourse styles that seem too emotional or not suitably intellectual. In this context, given the volatility of conversations related to race in the United States and the differences in lived experiences of racism between white and Black students, related conversations often run the risk of positioning Black students as too angry or upset. Further, research has shown that Black women in elite higher education are expected to engage in emotional neutrality.[84] It is this context that gave rise to, necessitated the creation of, and provided the parameters for Kuumba's safe Black space.

The safe Black space of Kuumba is a specifically Harvard phenomenon and Harvard, further, has a documented history of taking an apolitical, integrationist approach to racial diversity.[85] This is evident in university policies and practices, such as the antidiscrimination policy that requires organizations like Kuumba to not prohibit membership based on race, which means even in situations where students from an underrepresented background might seek to create a place of refuge apart from the whiteness of the campus, they may not do so in any way deemed to be exclusionary, or else risk the organization being shut down. Harvard's stance on racial diversity could also be said to support the cultural omnivorousness of (white) elites by focusing on cultural showcases and celebrations, given that at the time of this research, the largest annual event on campus each year was Cultural Rhythms, which consisted of an ethnic food fair and afternoon and evening performances by racially- and ethnically-focused student groups.[86]

However, while Harvard is often imagined to occupy a strata all its own in terms of elite higher education, in a number of ways, the University's history mirrors, and is intertwined with, that of the larger United States. Harvard's founding by and for affluent, white, Christian men, for example, parallels the country's broader history. Anti-Blackness also permeates both the national and the university contexts in subtle and overt ways. The overlapping should hardly come as unexpected, given the influence that the elite have and have historically held over major U.S. financial and cultural institutions. Therefore, while Kuumba's safe Black space is undeniably a phenomenon anchored in place and time, it is one that can provide valuable insights that might resonate in other places and at other times.

Verse I

BEING BLACK

"Skip Gates always says that there are four hundred million ways to be Black . . . I think to a certain extent that's true because even though your skin may be the same, your experience of what that color means to you, what that color means to people outside of yourself, what that color means to people within your community, is very different. So, I think that Kuumba tries to recognize many different layers of Blackness." —*Lauren Washington, Senior*

The only sound in Harvard's Memorial Church came from the steady staccato of director Sheldon Reid's hands—*dap-dap-dap-dap-dap*—against a djembe drum. Then, "*Iyo-oo-oo-ooooo.*" The intertwined voices of seventy members of the choir broke through the palpable excitement of the audience. Heads turned as the people tried to locate the singers. Tenors and basses continued, "*Iyo-oo-oo. Iyo-yo-yo,*" accompanied by the beat of the drum, *dap-dap-dap, dadyada-dap-dap-dap.* Two by two, choir members moved down the aisles from the back of the nave as all voice parts joined in. Their voices were sweet, but with a building force.

Iyo-yo hlonolofatsa Iyo-yo hlonolofatsa Iyo ka lebitso la ntate
Iyo-yo ka lebitso Iyo-yo ka lebitso Iyo ka lebitso la ntate.

The effect of the conjoined voices could be described as the sound of people rising up together. If you closed your eyes and relied solely on auditory clues, you could imagine being in colorful Cape Town on a warm day instead of Cambridge, Massachusetts, in the dead of winter, in an understated church, with blue-grey walls and unadorned, white wooden pews.

Kuumbabes began their performance with this traditional South African song, "Hlohonolofatsa," which translates to "Bless" in Sesotho and belongs to the repertoire of the Soweto Gospel Choir. The repeated lyrics speak of the protection provided through faith in God, and perseverance through hard times bolstered by that faith.[1] This song choice, which was grounded in Kuumba's organizational focus on Black peoples' overcoming struggle, seemed appropriate, if not ironic, considering Black men and women singing in the sanctuary of a monument built to memorialize the 372 Harvard men, presumably mostly white, who died in World War I. These men's names loomed above us, inscribed in gold lettering high up on the church's walls, an ever-present reminder of the church's original purpose—and Harvard's.[2] As Kuumba members walked down the aisles, passing under these names, the juxtaposition was striking. Kuumbabes and concertgoers were almost certainly the largest group of Black people to fill up the church for this performance each year. Elsewhere on campus, I had personally experienced how any more than a few Black students gathered could arouse suspicion and, in one instance, resulted in campus security being called.[3] It wasn't that Black people were unwelcome at or absent from the church, though. In fact, at the time of this concert, Peter Gomes, a nationally renowned African American preacher, was the minister of Memorial Church.[4] Still, Kuumba embodied groups that had been historically, systematically—and more recently, subtly—excluded, in one way or another, across generations of Harvard scholars.

The choir all wore "dressy black"—black slacks and button-down shirts for the men; blouses and slacks or skirts below the knee for the women—and kente cloth stoles draped over their chests, representing the group's pan-African connections. They moved rhythmically down the aisles, pumping their fists in front of their chests while stepping side to side, tossing their hands in the air, and then rapidly clapping—clap, clap, clap—in choreographed motions as they made their way to the front of the church. The eleven basses, all men, led; they were followed by the eleven tenors, mostly men; and then the forty-nine altos and sopranos, all women; and together they filled the risers in the chancel.

As this group of choir members processed, three other Kuumbabes danced at the front of the sanctuary. These lithe, barefoot "praise dancers" whirled and swooped their bodies to the rhythm of the drum and song. One of the three, a man, wore a blue-and-brown patterned dashiki with white pants. Two were women dressed in long-sleeved blouses and flowing, ankle-length white skirts accented by blue-and-brown chitenge fabric worn in an obi-style at their waists. The white garments highlighted the light-brown of their skin as they bobbed side-to-side in a wide-legged stance that recalled Nigerian writer J. P. Clark's poem, "Agbor Dancer": *See her caught in the throb of a drum.*[5] Eventually the choir members and dancers stood together in tight rows on the stairs and risers at the front of the church. The song sped up, as the *dap-dap-dap* clapping got faster and faster, and then slowed for the song's final line, "*Iyo ka lebitso la ntateeee*" ("Bless in the name of the father"). The voices gradually came to a hush. The audience cheered. Through the dance, music, and attire of the choir, all

grounded in the mission of the organization, as we shall see, we were being sym-
bolically transported from the "Harvard space" to the "Kuumba space"—from
a tacitly "white space" to an intentionally "Black space."

In the five years I watched Kuumba perform, I saw them use at least half a
dozen opening numbers, but all had this same essential setup, with the choir
singing and filing in, often down the aisles of the venue through the audience,
making the would-be spectators an essential part of the action. Indeed, a focus
on action—collective action, as in jointly performing a song—was a key feature
of Kuumba's safe Black space. Entering the concert venue from outside also
worked to demarcate the boundaries of Kuumba from the broader Harvard campus. Likewise, Sheldon often began rehearsals by calling for a moment of silence,
during which choir members were directed to "Leave your day behind"—surely
intended to include the stresses and expectations of the predominantly white
campus—to be fully present with Kuumba. And at the end of each rehearsal,
the choir would "circle up," holding hands in an unbroken chain to share collective "praises" and "prayers" before going back out to face the demands of their
daily lives, officially closing the Kuumba space before reentering the wider, whiter,
world.[6] Thus, the organization took care to ritualistically mark the entrances to
and exits from the safe Black space. It is the related questions of what "Black"
meant in this context, and how the "Black space" was further delimited, that
I explore in this chapter and the next.

Just as it is with many songs, the two verses of this book—this chapter and
the next—sound quite similar, but ultimately reveal different things. These first
two explorations of the inner workings of Kuumba both share a focus on Black
"authenticity," and how the ideas of what it meant to be a Black organization and
a Black individual were taken up, how members learned—and were instructed
on—what this meant and came to espouse a shared view, and ultimately how
they maintained these ideas through organizational practices and discourses.
In the first half of this chapter, that leads us to see how Kuumba grappled with
what it meant to be a Black organization—a Black space—in the midst of a white
institution, and how Blackness was framed as something dynamic, multifaceted,
and collective, grounded in the history of African diasporic peoples. This was a
definition that assumed, as curriculum theorist Esther Ohito and the Fugitive
Literacies Collective write, "Blackness comes into being *through* the body, suggesting that one becomes seen and known (even to oneself) as Black because of
others' readings of the phenotypically legible body."[7] Therefore, Kuumbabes
never debated who was Black or what made someone Black. In the second half
of the chapter, we see how Kuumba's expansive view of Blackness accounted for
and was inclusive of the varied backgrounds and experiences of Black Harvard
undergraduate students. Kuumba's embrace of the various experiences and
expressions of what it meant to be Black was what African American senior Lauren Washington was getting at when she said, drawing on the words of Harvard

Professor Henry Louis Gates Jr., "There are four hundred million ways to be Black," concluding, "Kuumba tries to recognize many different layers of Blackness." This embrace had the effect of creating the space for Black students who felt tenuous in their Black identity to feel like it was okay to join Kuumba in order to develop deeper connections to that identity.

In the next verse, chapter 3, what we find is that to maintain the group's conceptualization of Black authenticity, that is, its legitimacy, Kuumba focused on recruiting and cultivating Black membership and leadership, and placed limits on the ways non-Black members could participate. In both chapters, I consider the inherent limits and challenges to this audacious vision of Kuumba's safe Black space. Therefore, while this whole book is about conceptualizing Black space, and safe Black space specifically, this chapter focuses on what Black meant within that conceptualization, how that was communicated organizationally, and why this mattered.

Born Out of a Struggle

"How do you—either yourself or as part of the group—celebrate Black spirituality and creativity?" I posed this question to Daphne Han, a petite Asian American freshman with shoulder-length, coal-black hair whose measured gait revealed her training as a dancer. Earlier in our conversation, Daphne had named Kuumba as a Black student organization because of its focus on celebrating Black spirituality and creativity. In her answer to my question, Daphne drew on the narrative of the organization's founding: "This was an organization born out of a struggle. It was begun in 1970. . . . It was for people to have . . . a safe space at Harvard." Daphne's framing of the organization sounded very similar to the mission statement that was written in most concert programs. "Our mission remains the same as the time of founding—to celebrate Black creativity and spirituality and serve as a safe space for Black students."[8] By the time I met with Daphne, after many one-on-one conversations with Kuumbabes, I was no longer surprised when a member offered the mission and history of Kuumba, typically unprompted, during an interview. Indeed, nearly *every* Kuumbabe used the phrase "safe space" in describing the organization and mentioned the focus on Black students.

I had assumed that mission statements were largely a symbolic gesture. It was only after working at Harvard for a full five full years that I first read the College's mission statement or was even made aware that the College had one. But then I started working with Kuumba. The organization, I quickly realized, was living its mission statement and carrying on the legacy of its history; both were invoked at every performance. Further, not only were the mission and history repeatedly recounted, they were typically tied to the broader narrative of the struggles and perseverance of Black people—specifically on Harvard's campus, and more generally across the diaspora. The "celebrating" of Black spirituality and creativity in Kuumba was very much tied to acknowledging, teaching, and learning the history of diasporic Black struggle and perseverance, and formed the core of what it meant for Kuumba to be a Black organization.

This commitment was evident when I asked Claire Senai how she would describe Kuumba to me if I knew nothing of the organization. Claire was a sophomore who identified as "mixed," with a white mother and a father who emigrated from East Africa. We both laughed at the obviousness of her first statement: "I'd tell you that it's a choir—" She went on, after taking a deliberate pause, to share a description very consistent with Daphne's: "—that was founded in 1970 when racial tensions were really high on campus. So, a group of Black students wanted to create a place where Black students could go and feel safe and escape all the craziness that was around them." By stating that Black students needed a place to "feel safe and escape all the craziness" elsewhere on campus, Claire— like many others—positioned Kuumba as part of the story of Black students overcoming struggles at Harvard and, at its core, as a protective space amid a hostile environment. Kuumbabes were well versed in the organization's history, but what did that mean for the present?

The connection to the larger struggles of Black people, beyond Harvard's gates, was evident in nearly every performance, but nowhere as dramatic as in the program for the group's 2009 Christmas concert. The program began, like nearly every concert program, with a greeting letter written by the Kuumba librarian, an elected board position focused on preserving the history of the organization (which, I would learn later, was informally reserved for Black members).[9] The librarian started by juxtaposing times of despair with times of hope. "In a time of darkness, we are accustomed to hearing the wail of despair. We are carefully attuned to our struggle and the helplessness we feel. Yet, sometimes the hope outweighs the sorrow, and the gift outweighs the circumstance." She went on to situate the evening's concert theme, "Why This Jubilee," within the broader narrative of struggle and triumph, writing, "Tonight we share in the jubilation growing from [. . .] enslaved laborers finding comfort in a freeing gospel, modern tribulations interrupted by a swell of inner peace. [. . .] Whatever your creed or background, we encourage you to rejoice with us in the common spirit of triumph." The "jubilee" Kuumba encouraged—celebration, revelry, rejoicing—was subtly positioned as part of a larger story of Black people's triumph, perhaps in an overly romanticized way, and finding freedom from a history of oppression, beginning with "enslaved laborers."[10] Part of the point of the librarian's greeting letter was to connect past struggles to present and future liberation by acknowledging the age-old realities of the legacy of oppression—of which slavery is a prime example—and subsequent triumph.

While slavery is a prominent example of the legacy of oppression of Black people in the United States, did the reference seem arbitrary or impolitic to some who were attending the performance? Harvard only began to explore the university's connections to that "peculiar institution" a few years ago.[11] However, to Kuumbabes, the response of non-Black people to this framing was immaterial; the organization was invested in defining and enacting Blackness in a way that felt authentic to them, and not in a way that was a performance for a non-Black audience, described in more depth in chapter 3. For this chapter's purposes of considering how Kuumba defined what Black meant, the focus on the narrative of struggle and perseverance reflected longstanding traditions in the Black community in the United States; equating Blackness both with struggle and with triumph was not new.[12] But that equation had a particular, and multifaceted, purpose for Kuumba.

The emphasis on struggle and triumph provided students with a way to come to terms with their own struggles at Harvard—particularly for those who hadn't faced such challenges before. This was especially true for some Black Kuumbabes who encountered difficulties in navigating race among their peers in ways they hadn't had to deal with prior to college, struggling to find belonging both among the majority white students and fellow Black students. Sandra Smith and Mignon Moore's study on sense of belonging among Black students at a predominantly white university confirms the trend that Black students who attend predominantly white universities increasingly come from home communities that are also predominantly white and middle- and upper-middle class.[13] When they arrive on campus, they report feeling less closeness to other Black students, but then also face limited opportunities to interact with students of non-Black backgrounds. This may also be true of students who come from predominantly Black, lower-income communities, but attended elite, predominantly white prep schools prior to Harvard, a group sociologist Anthony Jack refers to as the "privileged poor."[14] Consequently, inculcating in Black students a shared racial history of struggle and triumph also became a way to unify Kuumbabes who joined the organization with vastly different life stories.

Further, it is important to note the organization emphasized triumph through struggle—instead of remaining fixated on the ongoing condition of Black oppression and pain, as white students have been shown to do when defining Blackness,[15] which served as a point of racial pride for the group. Overcoming struggle was also often described as the result of a cooperative effort, emphasizing the need to work together as a collective. This implied that despite different lived experiences with struggle and strife, as Black diasporic people, they could all claim part of this legacy and work together to address it. Before that could happen, students had to come to share this view, which happened through a process of teaching and learning within the choir.

Learning about the Struggles

Being a Black space to Kuumbabes meant performing decidedly Black forms of creative expression—those originating in Black communities and those choreographed, arranged, created, or authored by Black auteurs, like "Hlohonolofatsa," from the Soweto Gospel Choir. Concerts regularly included a range of traditional and contemporary gospel, spirituals, folk; selections from various countries, ethnic groups, and tribes across the African continent; and on occasion, popular contemporary songs like John Legend's "If You're Out There."[16] Learning about the history and origin of those works was connected to the larger history of Black people.

Angie Martin, a Black senior who had been in Kuumba since freshman year, brought up the music in describing what made Kuumba a "Black space." She explained, "One, just in the fact that we do celebrate Black music, Black spirituality, Black creativity, and like, that's what it is. . . . There's no changing that. . . . [Kuumba] always sings spirituals and African songs and gospel music, [which] is extremely important." Letting go for a moment of the potentially problematic usage of "African" as an adjective, a discursive move many Kuumbabes made in interviews, what Angie offered went beyond the basic provenance of works performed by Kuumba.[17] Angie remarked that a key component of how the music contributed to what it meant for Kuumba to be a Black organization came in "discussing it," which incorporated learning into the rehearsal process. According to Angie, through discussion—"What's this spiritual mean, that they were trying to cross over Jordan [River]? Let's talk about this. . . . So where are we coming from? Why do you sing it this way? Why are we putting this passion here? What were they feeling? Why's the song even important?"—the choir came to learn and share a view on what being Black meant, one arguably firmly grounded in the narrative of struggle and collective triumph.[18]

The idea that the music contributed to what it meant for Kuumba to be a Black space based both on origin and how Sheldon taught about the works—connecting them to overcoming challenge—is something Ebony Miller, a Black sophomore, also picked up on. When I asked Ebony to say more about how the choir was, as she said, "grounded" in Black issues, like Angie she explained that the music and history of the music provided the foundation. She gave an example of how the music and history moved from the realm of the abstract to the experiential: "So we'll sing a song about struggling, or 'Been in the Storm So Long' is one of the songs that we're singing right now. . . . Once we're starting to learn this song, but we're not really singing it with any feeling or anything, and Sheldon will just stop us and he'll be like, 'Do you guys know what this song is about?'" Sheldon, whom Ebony lauded as being "very good with incorporating everyone into the Black rootedness" of the music, would then explain the history of the piece they were singing.[19] Takiya Moore, another African American sophomore, described moments like these when Sheldon "reiterates the teaching of what we're trying to do and what our mission is, and why we're singing that song," as "when the magic happens," referring to the deeper connections these lessons allow students to make with the music and the context of these songs within Black history.

Sheldon's instruction in the music provided deliberate education in Black history while, again, normalizing the idea of struggle. In the case of "Been in the Storm So Long," Sheldon explained to students how the song's central theme of being in the storm was a metaphor for Black people's struggles. According to Ebony, "That also helps to identify the people in the choir that don't quite know things of struggle. And then [Sheldon will] open it up, like, 'Even if you haven't experienced that kind of struggle . . . we've all experienced hard times in life, and so to channel that when you're singing it.'" It was unclear if Ebony was talking about her white choir mates, or perhaps the wealthy and upper-middle-class Black members, some of whom were Harvard legacies (and Kuumba legacies) when describing "people . . . that don't quite know things of struggle."

Sheldon meant for all members to share this common understanding of Black struggle and the need for community, telling me once in a tongue-in-cheek way, "Everyone is here to learn. Even the Black people who come, a lot of them have no knowledge of any of this stuff. So it's not like they come with a genetic understanding." Student members reiterated this idea, with sophomore Bryanna Norman explaining, "It's . . . a misconception that if you're Black in America, you know all about African American culture." This may have had particular resonance with Black students at one of the globe's most elite educational institutions, who may have felt compelled to dissociate from Black culture and history for the sake and in the process of becoming elite.[20] Consequently, Sheldon used every opportunity, when introducing a song or when prodding the choir to deliver a more heartfelt performance, to make this connection.

I regularly witnessed Sheldon stop rehearsals to instruct on the origins of a song when he wanted students to connect with the song's themes of perseverance and the power of working in community to overcome challenges. He also did this outside of rehearsals, at concerts, and via the email listserv groups. In one instance, when the choir was rehearsing Lebo M's "One by One"—which most students knew because of Disney's *The Lion King*—Sheldon followed up with a video clip by email.[21] He wrote, with his characteristic mix of humor and gravitas, "please. Even if you can't watch the video, the music will lift your heart. A different take for new perspective. More than Animals." The clip was an animated video, produced by Disney, but a world apart from *The Lion King*. Rather than featuring jungle animals, the video started out showing Black children in what was presumably meant to be a South African township. The scene was gray and bleak. Children looked out of windows of dilapidated buildings onto pollution and barbed wire. Then, a colorful feather floated into the hands of one little boy who began to mobilize the other township children. The video ended with the children gathered in a wheat-filled field flying kites under a golden sun, encapsulating the song's message that coming together, one by one, as a community "we [Black people] will win."[22]

While, using a video made by Disney raises doubts about its authenticity or the value in what it reveals about Black peoples' struggles, and though the video doesn't make clear what it's actually referring to—Is it about apartheid? Is it about life's continued inequality today, long after apartheid has ended?—Sheldon drew on the video as a quick visual metaphor to reinforce the ongoing lesson in Kuumba about the need to work together to overcome struggles rooted in history. This somewhat lighthearted Disney version of Black struggle and triumph was part of a much larger and ongoing lesson in Kuumba that further discussion would elaborate on with examples grounded in history.

Indeed, senior Jamison Mthembu, who had grown up in communities around the world, including various parts of Africa and the United States, used "One by One" as an example for how the choir learned about what it meant to be Black and to learn about "[his] history" via the music. From rehearsals, Jamison had clearly taken away a deeper lesson than provided in the Disney video, saying, "'One by One' . . . was sung by young African men in the mines, where they were forced to work as kind of indentured slaves. And so, they're talking about the fact that they acknowledge that now is a period of struggle, but apartheid will not break them or will not take away the humanity that they feel within themselves. They might be living under inhumane conditions, but their humanity is not something that anybody else can take away from them." Thus the cartoon example offered some levity in the face of a harrowing narrative, which I also sensed through Sheldon's regular use of humor when talking about serious issues of racism and discrimination—including his personal experiences being stopped by the police. He deemed it necessary to invest students in this view of what being Black meant, while also keeping them optimistic about the role they might play, that is, so they wouldn't burn out or become embittered.[23]

Lessons such as these, providing implicit and explicit teachings about struggle in the Black community, addressed one of Sheldon's enduring concerns. "There are certain ideas that were central to the Black community that no one was really teaching, because your reality taught you every day. So once that reality, or, rather, the surface of what that reality looked like, shifted, in order to maintain that knowledge, you had to teach it." It was unclear precisely what the "shift" was that Sheldon was referring to. Given his own experience growing up in an affluent Long Island, New York suburb, I understood him to be talking about how expanded opportunities for Black Americans since the Civil Rights Movement had lulled some into ignoring or being oblivious to deeper, systemic struggles that persisted—this was before the emboldening of white supremacist activity spurred on by the election of Donald Trump to the U.S. presidency and the most recent wave of Black Lives Matter protests. Therefore, Kuumba became a space for teaching and for learning. According to Sheldon, "The whole point of Kuumba is that we continue to learn . . . and not just learn for our own sake, but learning so that we can teach other people." The interweaving of song and ritual offered experiential learning to members of all racial backgrounds about Black history and struggle—an experience that Sheldon found particularly important for the Black students.

In this manner, Kuumbabes were apprenticed in a shared understanding of what Black meant and what it consequently meant for Kuumba to be a Black space. Through discussions—perhaps better referred to as interactive lectures, usually by Sheldon—about the history of the songs and the genres, students came to share the perspective that being Black meant being part of a legacy of strife and collective victory.[24] This definition also focused members on action—being Black meant struggl*ing* and overcom*ing,* and implied the need to work together collectively in the service of the community. This was the basis of the definition of Blackness that allowed the group to claim being and remain a Black space even while having a multiracial membership. Further, while such a definition of Blackness might suggest or produce a certain kind of hierarchy wherein those who could claim experiences of strife would be considered to be more authentically Black, my research suggests this definition actually served as a method of equalization. Even those who had not directly experienced certain struggles presumed to be common in Black communities in the United States and across the diaspora could—and in Kuumba, were expected to—take part in eradicating injustices.

Beyond I'm Black, You're Black

For Kuumba members, cultivating a shared definition of Blackness and embracing the view that this definition was something that needed to be taught and learned—regardless of background—was essential for a couple of reasons. First, on an organizational level, it spoke back to criticisms from other Black students and organizations on campus—a criticism shared by at least one Kuumbabe I interviewed—that the organization wasn't "Black enough" given the numbers of non-Black members. Though the numbers were always in flux, the choir was around 18 percent white, 6 percent Asian American, and 3 percent Latinx at the time of this research. Second, on an individual level, Kuumba's definition of what it meant to be Black challenged deficit perspectives of Black people in the United States that students encountered in some Harvard classes—and that were (and still are) communicated widely through societal messages, such as media coverage of Black-perpetrated crime. Kuumba's focus, then, on defining what Black meant was partly about establishing authenticity, or legitimacy as a *true* Black space.

Grace Carter, a Black "super senior"—an undergraduate who spent more than eight consecutive semesters working on undergraduate degree completion—had heard reproachful comments against Kuumba's racial authenticity.[25] She told me, "Kuumba started out all Black, and it's gotten more diverse. And I feel like sometimes, actually Kuumba's been criticized for that by some other Black organizations as not really being a Black organization anymore." Interestingly, Grace chose to take a positive tack in framing the demographics as "more diverse," as opposed to, say, "less Black." Like Daphne and Claire, Grace rooted the group's authenticity in its mission and explained, "I always thought that was ridiculous, because if you have all these people who are not Black supporting this organization that's all about Black culture, I don't see how that's a bad thing."

Within Kuumba, the fact that non-Black people wanted to join was usually characterized as a testament to the strengths of the organizational culture and Black culture.[26] Grace explained, "I think anyone can celebrate this culture, and if other people want to do that, that's a wonderful thing, and I feel like that's part of the purpose." She went on, "If Black people on campus in 1970 didn't feel like they had a space to celebrate their culture, they didn't feel like they were part of the university, and now we have people who are not Black who want to be a part of celebrating their culture, that would only make them more comfortable here, I think." Grace contextualized Kuumba's demographic shifts within the group's history of struggle to find a place of their own at Harvard by saying non-Black members showed that mission being fulfilled.

Grace's comments hinted at the long and deep history among Black Americans of deeming practices, people, and spaces as racially authentic (as "truly Black," or "Black enough") or not. This issue has been depicted widely in pop culture, including in Spike Lee's iconic film *School Daze*. In *School Daze*, while students at a fictional historically Black college spar over political views, their fights encompass a seemingly endless list of other tensions, from what may be considered acceptable forms of Black self-expression—Does an Afro mean Black power? Does hair-straightening equate to wanting to be white?—to issues related to skin color and to socioeconomic status. A more recent spate of books also illuminates this issue, including journalist Elaine Welteroth's aptly titled memoir, *More Than Enough*, and satirical works such as Harvard alumnus Baratunde Thurston's *How to be Black*.[27] The latter pokes fun at the idea that there is one monolithic, static, authentic way to be Black by offering tips to Black and non-Black people alike on, well, how to "be" Black. In some ways, these books are challenges to "the popular concept of blackness: hip-hop, crime and prison, fatherless homes, high blood pressure, school dropouts, drugs, athleticism, musical talent, *The Wire*, affirmative action, poverty, diabetes, the Civil Rights Movement, and, recently, the U.S. presidency."[28] All of these works attempt to offer a reframing of the discourses around what can be considered valid expressions of Blackness, yet that these books even exist serves to highlight the fact that there are widely accepted—or at least well-known—views on Black authenticity. In the case of Thurston's autobiographical text, it also highlights the particular issues Black students at elite educational institutions face in contending with the deeply entrenched, though thoroughly debunked, "acting white" myth, which connects Black students' academic "underperform[ance]" with cultural resistance to "acting white."[29] To some extent, the "acting white" theory implicates any Black person who has achieved normative educational success, as have all Harvard students.

Beyond popular culture, attempts to regulate Black authenticity show up in the schoolyard and in the academy. For instance, there is a grade-school taunt, "Oreo," to denote Black people who are said to be "Black on the outside and white on the inside."[30] Similarly, anthropologist Signithia Fordham, in her 2010 article "Passin' for Black: Race, Identity, and Bone Memory in Postracial America," listed those who were "guilty" of *passin' for Black*—embracing a socially constructed identity as if it were inherent in the body or based on genetic inheritance—despite the lightness or darkness of their skin."[31] She also listed those who were "innocent of this masquerade," saying they were "not culturally Black, even though they do not differ in apparent ancestry from those who identify themselves as culturally Black."[32] The "guilty" list of those who could be considered culturally Black included the likes of the Obamas, Cornel West, Lani Guinier, Fannie Lou Hamer, and Halle Berry, whereas the "not guilty" list included Clarence Thomas, Ward Connelly, and John McWhorter, among others. While Fordham presented a complex argument about what passin' for Black meant, those listed as not guilty had elsewhere been accused of not prioritizing the interests of fellow Black people and of being "uncle Toms," an accusation that normatively successful Black students, such as those who made it to Harvard, felt implicated by, as many Kuumbabes shared with me.[33]

Around a decade before my research, Kuumba found itself on a list similar to Fordham's "not guilty" list. In the *Black Guide to Life at Harvard*, a comedic set of essays, Kuumba was named as one of the "Top 10 Organizations that Need More Black People (Actually, this isn't funny. It's kind of serious)."[34] Of Kuumba specifically, the *Black Guide* said, "with a name like Kuumba, one would think it would be deep with Black people, but one would be surprised."[35] Black Kuumba members were keenly aware of this potential criticism and were quick to explain why Kuumba was indeed a Black organization, often framing its authenticity in terms of the group's mission, history, and music. As one student explained, "Although people of all different backgrounds can join Kuumba, like that's not the purpose of Kuumba. First and foremost, it is a place for Black students and it was founded by Black students for that purpose and to celebrate *Black* creativity and spirituality. So, it is a *Black* organization." Several Kuumbabes went as far as to argue that Kuumba's focus on actualizing the group's mission—to celebrate Black creativity and spirituality and serve as a safe space for Black students—made Kuumba a Black space and *more*, suggesting that Kuumba was more authentic (or more *than* authentic?) as a Black organization. Takiya Moore exemplified this view.

Takiya, like some—but notably not all—Black Kuumbabes participated in other Black student organizations on campus. When I asked her how her involvement in those other organizations compared with that of Kuumba, she let out a sigh. She began, "I don't know if it really does compare, because the means at which the members of those other organizations are connected, and the means at which Kuumba members are connected towards each other, are quite different." Takiya went on, "I feel like, because with some other Black organizations, it's more of a thing of, 'I'm Black, you're Black. So then, that's why we need to like do this together.' Which, of course that should be. I mean, that's the initial reasoning of joining. But then it doesn't really go past that." Kuumba went "past" that, "that" being what Takiya implied as the obligation of Black students getting together simply due to their shared race. Kuumba went beyond this through cultivating a shared sense of purpose and peoplehood, through learning about the mission, and through the space the music provided to bring that mission to life. As Takiya explained,

> With Kuumba, I feel like it's, "Okay, I'm Black, you're Black." But then also, like because of that, and because of the mission that we're trying to do, there are certain things that we need to do in order to go forth . . . like working together as a unit and like supporting each other . . . whereas in other organizations, like that's not really established or focused upon. . . . It's like the Black community on Harvard's campus is generally strong. . . . But with certain groups, there's not like, "This is part of our group's mission to be united." Whereas with Kuumba, that's the necessity.

Takiya was excited to be in a group with a mission and goal beyond simply being with Black kinfolk (or skinfolk), which has been a critique of shallow forms of identity politics.[36] Surface-level approaches to organizing often disregard differences within what are positioned as homogenous groups in the same way that Black students are regularly regarded in predominantly white institutions.[37] In Kuumba, students weren't coming together just because of some assumed likeness of identity, but because of what they wanted to work together to do as people with a shared diasporic history. This brought together Black students from various backgrounds who found Kuumba's collective action–oriented, inclusive, self-determined view on Blackness to combat negative experiences they encountered elsewhere on campus, on one hand, or, on the other, to provide a space where they felt free to explore deeper connections with their own Black identities in ways not available elsewhere on campus.

We Have a Voice

Where the Black space of Kuumba and the accompanying lessons on what being Black meant might have given some white Kuumbabes a jolt of discomfort juxtaposed with the whiteness of Harvard at large, for just that same reason Kuumba was often described as providing a sense of comfort to Black members. Bryanna Norman grew up in a lower-middle-class neighborhood in the South. Her round face and high-pitched soprano voice made her appear younger than her age. She described how she regularly felt "a bit alienated" in classroom discussions. Though she was majoring in math, Bryanna had taken African American studies classes, which she said emphatically addressed issues that "affect my family." What was abstract intellectual content or obligatory course material to some, in other words, was deeply personal to her. She contrasted her first-person perspective with the more detached stance of her peers. Her voice became more impassioned, picking up speed, as she described classroom conversations she had participated in about the plight of African Americans. "For example, the issue that there are a lot of Black men who are incarcerated, like, I see that a lot in my family. Drug problems, welfare problems, all these types of things like we talk about in abstract [in class], I see, like, the idea of poverty. These affect people that are close to me." For Kuumbabes like Bryanna, the lessons Kuumba provided on what it meant to be Black provided a necessary counter to these deficit perspectives she encountered elsewhere. In Kuumba, Black meant struggle, but it didn't stop there; it also meant perseverance and triumph.

More than one hundred years after W.E.B. Du Bois asked his famous question—"How does it feel to be a problem?"[38] Bryanna demonstrated that this question still plagued Black people, even those who had made it to Harvard, that same institution that had granted Du Bois a PhD in 1895. Speaking to fictional classmates, and perhaps professors, Bryanna said, "You're talking about these issues but you're not attaching names to those people. . . . It's kind of like we're talking about, 'Oh, this is a problem,' and you want to fix it. And like, at some degree, I don't want to be identified as a problem, because I worked really hard to get here." The confluence of race and class impacted Bryanna's campus experiences. "I don't come from a rich family at all, and I came to this school which is kind of prestigious . . . and like, some people who talk about these issues have no idea what they're talking about in terms of experiencing it." In fact, Black Americans, even those in the middle class, are likelier to be personally affected by incarceration and family histories of poverty than their white peers of the same socioeconomic background.[39] Danielle Allen's *Cuz: The Life and Times of Michael A.* sheds light on this phenomenon.[40] Allen, a Black tenured Harvard professor who holds one of the institution's highest ranks as University Professor, recounts the story of her cousin, Michael, who was incarcerated for eleven years after being tried as an adult for an attempted carjacking at age fifteen, only to die at the hands of his lover after being released.

Bryanna noting that she "worked really hard to get here," revealed how powerful the ideology of meritocracy was at Harvard, and how alienating it could be for Black students who were at risk of being seen as "problems," or part of a group that was seen as a "problem," by classmates who studied social ills in minority communities.[41] Bryanna's concerns were founded. Around the time of this research, the campus conversation around affirmative action, leading to a lawsuit that accused Harvard of discriminating against Asian Americans in the admissions process, was gaining traction, following the U.S. Supreme Court hearing on Fisher I.[42] This caused some Harvard students like Sarah Siskind to publicly decry race-based affirmative action. Siskind, who admitted to being a Harvard legacy and thus a beneficiary of a type of affirmative action herself, wrote a widely read and incendiary op-ed for the campus paper, *The Crimson*, that stirred discussion— and emotion—across campus, which several Kuumbabes told me they heard as saying that they and their Black peers weren't worthy of their spot at a preeminent Ivy League institution. Having a community like Kuumba that was reflective of, in Bryanna's words, "how I grew up," that normalized her lower-middle-class Black upbringing, was essential for her. Kuumba became a shelter of sorts where she and others felt they could be valued for all the strengths and talents they brought to Harvard. Kuumba was "the one institution on campus where I can clearly say, we're celebrating Black [culture], and like I can clearly connect it to . . . how I grew up and how I see things," according to Bryanna. There were no caricatured representations to overcome in Kuumba.

While all Black Kuumbabes I spoke with mentioned feeling pressure to defy or challenge limited or stereotypical views of Black students on Harvard's campus, students from lower-middle- and working-class backgrounds—those not shielded by class privilege, like Bryanna—seemed especially attuned to the negative stereotypes that might characterize them.[43] Angie Martin came from a background similar to Bryanna's, though Angie was from the Northeast. She echoed this need for a space that "reflect[s] the Black community," that is, a place that felt authentically Black, where Black students defined for themselves what "Black" meant, where the multiplicity and nuances of their experiences were honored, and where their customs and norms were enacted—and not as a spectacle. Angie characterized such a space as "where people understand what it is you go through when you're going to certain classes, or what it is you go through when you go home." This addressed the issue raised by Bryanna of sitting through classes that seemed to stereotype Black communities from a deficit perspective. Angie wanted a Black space where she could go and talk about her experiences on campus and also make connections to her world beyond Harvard. Angie recognized that a community like the one Kuumba provided was not important just for offering protection to Black students in the face of stereotypes on campus, but in that as a Black organization, it released students from expectations on campus that they are "representing all the Black community."[44] Of Kuumba, she said, "You feel at home, like where you don't feel you're representing all the Black community at all times, like you can actually chill and joke about things within the Black community, and not feel as though you're embarrassing us."[45]

I regularly saw this joking dynamic at play in the characteristically Black style of humor Sheldon and choir members would engage in at rehearsals. I knew this type of jibing and joking well from being on the receiving end of my cousins' and siblings' teasing. In Kuumba, who was and was not on rhythm was a popular theme of such jokes when the choir would incorporate foot or hand motions into songs. Sheldon was known for saying, "Rhythm doesn't correspond with melanin levels." As Black people were stereotyped as having natural rhythm and being good dancers, such joking played on and challenged stereotypes. It offered alternative conceptions of what it meant to be authentically Black on a campus where students felt constricted by racist stereotypes. Further, such joking made race explicit, something that could be talked about directly, and laughed about, within the wider Harvard world in which race was no less present, but often acted upon in tacit ways. For instance, both Angie and Bryanna felt that Black students were under constant, though unstated, surveillance. As Angie saw it, her Harvard classmates were watching her as a "representative" of all Black people, given that her individual actions ran the risk of "embarrassing *us*," meaning Black people at Harvard—and, it could be extrapolated, beyond Harvard, if interaction with her was her peers' only interaction with Black people. Though Bryanna and Angie might appear dismissive of their classmates' limited perspectives, the feeling that others were watching them created a certain amount of pressure, compounding the pressure they already felt as pervasive at Harvard.

Angie was concerned that without Black student organizations like Kuumba, students could "lose their identity within this huge, diverse space" of the University. She connected this back to Kuumba's teaching and learning about what it meant to be Black by saying that Black organizations could help students maintain and develop their sense of identity through helping them with "understanding where it is that their ancestors came from." Research supports Angie's concerns. For instance, sociologist Carson Byrd found that elite college students of all races "withdraw their connections to racial and ethnic groups to remove any deterministic logic of why they, as individuals, are in the positions they are currently in or could possibly find themselves in later in life."[46] In this way, Kuumba's focus on the collective struggle and perseverance of Black people that Angie hints at directly confronts this individualistic view that Byrd found. Kuumba made a space for Black students to explore what being Black meant on their own terms.

Similarly, in critical scholar Rubén Gaztambide-Fernández's study of students at an elite boarding school, he found that some Black students perceived the need to alter their behavior to fit in on campus.[47] Gaztambide-Fernández noted that there was a paradoxical dynamic at play where students of color believed they were admitted to the school to contribute to diversity, but then felt they must present themselves in a way that conformed to the expectations of the school's culture.[48] While their white peers thought they were having an "authentic" experience with a person of another race, students to some extent were putting on a deliberate performance to fulfill their peers' expectations.[49]

Though these social expectations of students from underrepresented backgrounds usually went unspoken, Angie and Bryanna felt that their ways of expressing their Black identities were undervalued on campus outside of Kuumba. And, to fit into that structure, they were expected to compromise their forms of self-expression.[50] This was captured in Angie's reflection on the marginalized status some students felt on campus:

> Because [Harvard's] so non-Black [laughs] that people are so—it isn't even representative of, you know, the U.S. in general. . . . When you're even more of a minority, you need to find that space. You need to have that space, because, well, it reminds people that you're actually here, you're on campus. It's not like, that you see one or two [Black students] every once in a while, and no, it's like, we're here, we're strong. We have a voice.[51]

In Angie's view, it was through the music that Kuumba was able to provide such a space for students and was able to challenge other Harvard students' potentially stereotyped views of their Black classmates. However, while Kuumba sounded like it had a singular voice when the choir sang, this collective voice was comprised of many different Black voices that the organization sought to unify.

Black People Who Are (Not) Used to Being Around Black People

Angie's and Bryanna's experiences of feeling like outsiders as Black students on Harvard's predominantly white campus was a common one, but other Black Kuumbabes who sensed that they had not had the "typical" Black American experience prior to Harvard described feeling like outsiders even among Black students. That sense of alienation or distance from the Black community at Harvard was typically expressed by African American and multiracial students who were not raised around other Black youth. For these students, Kuumba, with its dynamic and expansive view on what Black meant, was an organization in which they felt their "non-traditional" experiences growing up would be validated as authentic and where they could develop a strong(er) sense of Black identity.

Freshman Jason Thomas was one who struggled to find a niche among fellow Black peers, which he attributed to the diversity of backgrounds from which students were coming. "Well for Black students, first of all, we're all coming from different places. We were all raised in different ways, from different, sort of, social environments, cultural environments," began Jason. While students were coming from different backgrounds of social class, geographic region, and so forth, the issue for Jason was that prior to Harvard, the majority of his friends were not Black.

Raised by a single mother who emigrated from the Caribbean, Jason tested into an elite public exam school in the northeastern city where he grew up. In his home community and at his exclusive exam school, Jason was not used to socializing primarily with other Black peers; instead he described himself as having "been surrounded by people from many different cultures, not just Black people." At Harvard he felt the expectation that Black students should have a natural affinity with other Black students on campus, saying, "I think there are Black people here who are used to being around Black people, and are so-called 'culturally Black,' quote-unquote, that are just a lot more comfortable around Black students that they have more in common with." Jason's use of the phrasing "'culturally Black,' quote-unquote" showed his own tenuous feeling of belonging in this category, and perhaps a tension with how people saw him—as phenotypically Black, given his deep brown complexion and tightly coiled, ebony hair—and how he saw himself. By culturally Black, Jason was likely imagining— and reifying—the types of home and family experiences described by Angie and Bryanna that became caricatured in dominant society. To be considered a "real Black person," he implied, one must feel "comfortable" in the company of and have had extensive precollege relationships with Black people outside of one's relatives. Anyone who deviated from this norm was suspect as authentically Black.

Though Jason understood the campus expectations—and arguably the expectations of American society at large—of being "culturally Black," he said that this might not be the case for everyone. Jason explained, "Some people, they are more comfortable around people from other cultures. But it's weird when you're Black and that's not your type of situation, where you're not really comfortable around just one, like, group of people, culturally." Jason may have felt the subject too taboo and difficult, and switched—consciously or unconsciously— from talking specifically ("you're Black") to using vague terminology ("one, like, group of people"). People like himself, who were not raised in predominantly Black settings and lacked fluency in what might be considered authentic Black cultural vernacular, felt "weird," according to Jason.

Jason encountered a twin set of challenges, both wanting to form more significant relationships with Black peers, and seeing the need to do so, to some extent, because of the sense that he was being excluded from other groups. It was only at Harvard that Jason came to feel "categorized" as Black and learned "that it's really important to be around people with whom you have a cultural similarity." This was a lesson hard-learned for Jason, who explained further, taking his time, his low bass voice reverberating in my tiny office. It was May and well past the time freshmen students had chosen their sophomore year roommates. But, as Jason slowly revealed, racial divisions, including divisions among Black students, had impacted his room selection experience for his upcoming year. As with all Harvard freshmen, his first-year roommates were assigned, and the composition of the group revealed the Freshman Dean's Office's deliberate, though somewhat tacit, diversity agenda. "There are two white roommates. I have two Asian roommates. And I'm the Black roommate, and I have one other Black roommate." Jason expressed some ambivalence about this arrangement. "It kind of seems like some sort of social experiment." This "experiment" assumed an essential difference based on students' racial backgrounds and grouped them as such to maximize their opportunities to interact with peers from different backgrounds, in a move that could be alienating to students of color all the same.[52]

Jason went on to describe the dynamic he observed in how his motley group of roommates had made friends. He said, "It's really interesting to see the kind of people we attract. And some of us don't really have to try at all to attract people. They just kind of come." He implied that the white and Asian students were the ones who had no difficulties in making friends, saying, "For Black people, it's different, because, I don't want to say that we're not trusting of each other, but you kind of have to make more of an effort to get together. . . . It's not as, you know, welcoming and warm." Jason's experience of alienation occurred at two levels. On the one hand, Jason felt that his white and Asian peers effortlessly "attract[ed]" friends. Black students, on the other hand, not only did not attract friends from other racial groups, but had a tougher time making friends with other Black students. Jason told me about how he had hoped to continue living with his freshman-year roommates, but they all made plans to continue living with each other that did not include him. Though Jason ultimately found roommates, his body language, as he slumped in his chair, and his speech, measured and reticent, conveyed his hurt. The people he thought were his friends essentially left him to room with others. The decision of Jason's roommates may have had nothing to do with race—and perhaps it is even likely that it wasn't consciously about race—but Jason couldn't shake this notion that their choice to ditch him was linked to his larger sense of alienation from other Black people.[53]

This experience led Jason to conclude that Kuumba "really need[s] to be responsible for kind of helping to bridge the gap between the different kinds of Blacks that exist in the [Harvard] space." Finding it a challenge to make friends with non-Black peers, and feeling like he didn't quite fit in on campus because of his race, Jason looked to his Black peers for support. Yet, he felt uncertain in approaching them, too, worried that he might not appear "culturally Black." In

Kuumba, given the focus on teaching and learning and coming to a shared view on Blackness grounded in the organization's mission, Jason didn't feel marginalized because he had an "atypical" Black experience growing up. Though Jason would be considered a "privileged poor" student, drawing on Jack's categorization, having attended an elite high school, and though privileged poor students tended to be more adept at navigating the Harvard context, Jason demonstrated how sometimes even having a prep-school background was not enough to provide Black students with the skills and level of comfort on campus needed to thrive.

While Jason shared one of the most heartrending stories highlighting the feeling of being an outsider as a Black student at Harvard, he was not alone. Claire Senai, who identified as "mixed" and could probably be easily mistaken for Middle Eastern, was another student who spoke about this. Though she came to the same conclusion as Jason about the importance of Kuumba in providing a space for Black students of different backgrounds to form community and explore their identity, she started from a very different place. Raised in a "white town" on the West Coast by her white mother, Claire attended a "white high school." Claire's father immigrated to the United States from East Africa as a teenager, but she didn't grow up as part of any particular Black community, whether East African or African American. Claire didn't describe being excluded from relationships with white peers, as have other biracial students at predominantly white campuses.[54] Rather it was that she didn't feel quite included in other Black groups and didn't participate in any "other *Black* organization," she said emphasizing "Black." Thus, Kuumba was Claire's "Black thing, I guess . . . that I do on campus," she said, laughing. Her tone was oddly dismissive, exposing her insecurity about identifying as Black. She paused, and then confessed, "That's not, I guess, a great way to say that."

Being "mixed" myself, I empathized with Claire and asked her to tell me more about what it meant for her to be a member of a "Black student organization." She revealed that Kuumba's expansive definition of what being Black meant, grounded in the mission, made her feel secure in exploring her identity within the organization. Claire explained, "Well, for me it's a big deal, because I'm mixed." It was specifically a sense that other Black student organizations would not be fully accepting of her background that steered her away from joining. "At the beginning of freshman year, I think everyone considers every group." Claire and I both knowingly laughed about Harvard students' propensity for overcommitting to extracurricular activities. She continued, "I was like, 'Mmm, do I want to be in these things?' Then I was like, 'No, not really.' I think that just comes from the fact that, like I said, I was raised in a white place." Claire again laughed, recalling her perception that at Harvard "a lot of people here seem to be really sure about their identities even if, like, I don't know if they really are."

Claire demonstrated how the institutional context in particular influenced students' struggles to figure out who they were and wanted to be as adults.[55] The environment was such that even when students hadn't quite figured it out, they believed they should present the appearance that they had.[56] For Claire and students like her, who were doubly struggling with where they fit in socially given their racial identity as either mixed race or Black, and who grew up around non-Black peers, the potential for alienation and isolation was compounded. For example, having not joined other Black organizations her freshman year, Claire initially felt "a little left out, like I should have joined one of those things, because, I think," the pitch of her voice increased to sound more like a question than an affirmative statement, "most Black people on campus are part of like BSA [the Black Students Association] or . . . I feel, I mean, I guess, most of, most Black students I know are in BSA, BMF [Black Men's Forum], ABHW [Association of Black Harvard Women; pronounced ahb-wah], or whatever." Claire was referring to the largest Black student organizations aside from Kuumba.

Though she continued to mull over her decision not to join other Black student organizations, Claire found that Kuumba fulfilled her need to "figure out" what being Black meant to her, positioning the organization as something one could use to build identity, both as an external signal to others and to negotiate internal questions. She said, "Being part of Kuumba has . . . made me more connected to the Black community here. And, that's made me more, um, I guess—" After pausing briefly, she continued, "—able to figure out . . . what being Black means for me." According to Claire, she could explore her Black identity in Kuumba specifically because of the organization's diversity and openness to members of all backgrounds. She said, "I know that it was started to be a safe space for Black students. I think that now it's become a safe space for anyone who wants to be in it. So, that's a really big thing for me." In a way, then, the racial diversity of the group signaled to some Black students that this was a different kind of Black student organization, one they could join without fear of revealing themselves as racially inauthentic. Nonetheless, it is possible and perhaps even likely, given Kuumba's history, that the organization felt welcoming to Black students from diverse backgrounds before it became so racially diverse.

Both Jason and Claire proclaimed Kuumba a safe space. This was part of the organization's mission statement but was interpreted by these students to mean a place where they could be accepted even if they did not have what they considered to be a conventional or expected Black experience growing up. Kuumba was safe because it was a place where they felt their perceived differences would not be judged, as Claire, Jason, and other Kuumbabes told me. Further, it was a safe space because it was a site where they could also learn or "figure out" how they fit into the broader Black community, both presently and historically.[57] Consequently, the deliberateness with which Kuumba taught about Blackness—in particular as part of the legacy of struggle and triumph—contributed to students' developing sense of authenticity and was a result of the fact that they came to the organization from so many varied backgrounds.

———

The Black space fostered by Kuumba was about celebrating Black culture, not just about being Black. It was about being part of a history of collective struggle and perseverance, and jointly learning what that *meant*. What it meant to be Black was not only about who someone was, but also what that meant for what they should do—*being* and *doing*.

Focusing on actions instead of labels challenged the way Harvard itself talked about the value of diversity, as well as the ways race was used to exclude on campus and beyond, wherein who someone was—or what an organization was, for that matter—was often based on limited perceptions about types and categories of people. Labels could be reductive and actions could speak loudly. What you did, beyond who you were, mattered in Kuumba. Takiya framed this from a stance of superiority—this was what made Kuumba different, and, she suggested, better than other organizations.

Hence, non-Black members did not undo Kuumba's position as a Black student organization, nor its mission and purpose. Claire proclaimed, "You can still have an organization that's meant to celebrate a certain type of culture but have other people, people from other cultures participate." Because of the mission that focused on a particular action, "to celebrate," the members maintained that Kuumba was authentic regardless of membership. What made Kuumba a Black organization was that it continued to honor its history, enact its mission statement, and celebrate the Black music at its roots, all of which were grounded in a narrative of the struggle for justice.

While this conceptualization of what it meant to be Black and to be a Black organization served as a point of pride and unity for group members, it also reflected the shifting views on the place of Black students on campus, and the organization's tenuous position among the Black community as an organization that welcomed non-Black members. When Kuumba was founded, the group was an affirmation of Blackness, a declaration that it was good to be Black in the midst of a culture where these students felt castigated and suppressed, a culture where their Blackness was deemed a problem, where they were *too Black*—or maybe not white enough, rendered both hyper-visible in their difference and invisible in terms of being included as equals on campus. Now, over forty years later, the group had endured, but was facing a nearly opposite problem—it was *not Black enough*, according to some.[58] The group was now embraced by the administration—by the same institutional forces that the group's founding members were fighting against in 1970. The group was now a beloved symbol of diversity. But the problem was that among the (now much larger) Black student population of the school, and in particular among the abundance of Black organizations that now proliferated on campus, Kuumba was seen as insufficiently Black.

The tension between feeling too Black, both as hyper-visible and invisible, and not Black enough wasn't something just the organization grappled with. Individual members of Kuumba experienced this tension on campus. Both Angie and Bryanna felt simultaneously hyper-visible and invisible in their classes, where Black communities were pathologized and their lived experiences went unacknowledged. Other members, like Jason and Claire, described not feeling like they had had "typical" (authentic) Black experiences growing up and attending school in predominantly white or multiracial communities. Kuumba functioned to create a safe Black space by explicitly defining for all members what Black meant *on their own terms*, actively resisting stereotypical and reductive definitions, and by embracing a definition that could include all members, specifically by focusing on what members *could do* (or should do) to support the Black community in persevering in the face of injustice.

Verse II

STAYING BLACK

"And me, being Black, and what am I entitled to more of that this person is not?"
—Leela Johnson, Senior

Rochelle Perry, a Black Southerner with a copper-hued complexion—who was Kuumba's president during one year of my research—emerged from the congregation of choir members at the front of Harvard's Memorial Church. She looked out at the packed pews. The front rows were bursting with scores of Kuumba alumni, parents and family members, and choir members taking a semester off from performing. Hundreds of friends and classmates, professors and advisors, and fans from the community filled the rest of the nave. No seat was empty; there were never empty seats at the consistently sold-out Kuumba concerts.

Rochelle began her welcome by describing Kuumba's founding in the 1970s during, she punctuated, "more racially turbulent times." A low buzz in the audience grew at the mention of this historical moment. Scattered hands emerged from the audience, seconding her statement, acknowledging her truth. Many others nodded their heads. A few said "Mm-hmm" softly, as if hesitant to interrupt Rochelle. Others exclaimed "Yaaas!" The silent choir on stage was met by a not-so-silent chorus of acknowledgement from the audience. With body and voice, the audience affirmed Rochelle's message: Black students had been able, for more than forty years now as part of Kuumba, to not just survive at Harvard, but to thrive.

Rochelle's no-nonsense voice drew on the audience's energy, like a preacher urged on by her congregation. She rode the buzz of the crowd, both encouraging it and speaking above it. She explained that while the mission of Kuumba was still to create a safe space for Black people, the composition of the choir had changed. "You can tell," she said with a smirk, motioning to the ensemble on stage, whose range of hues ran the gamut from taupe to ebony, copper to cream, and everything in between. Here was a choir that, for their first concert in 1970, did not even permit non-Black students to attend. Look where we are now, Rochelle seemed to be saying, with a mixture of defiance and a hint of displeasure.

Connecting Kuumba's focus on serving the needs and interests of Black students—despite the racially diverse assemblage of choir members—to her experience as a Harvard undergraduate, Rochelle went on. She explained how this year had been good for her because, as a senior having fulfilled other requirements, she had been able to take only "AFAM" (African American Studies, pronounced "af-am") classes. Now, she said humorously that she "actually do[es] the reading" and "no longer skip[s] classes," subtly reinforcing that this was because the AFAM courses presented material that felt relevant and, perhaps, nourishing to her. Being part of a Black space, or multiple Black spaces, was important to Rochelle and she wanted to convey this.

While it was customary, even expected, for each of Kuumba's Christmas and spring concerts to begin with a brief oration of the group's history and mission, I had not before heard and would never after hear any other Kuumba president take on the racial diversity of the choir in quite the same way. Rochelle, who during a different concert opening said when she first joined she thought Kuumba was a "bougie" organization, meaning it suffered from a middle-class pretentiousness or was siddity, was open about calling out what she viewed as problematic race and class dynamics in the group. This time, Rochelle's phrasing and gesturing were deliberate in bringing attention to the presence of the non-Black choir members, her tone both accusatory and protective— the same tone I have at times heard longtime residents of certain neighborhoods use when speaking of gentrification. Had I heard ambivalence when she spoke those words? Was she was alluding to the ideological tug-of-war between being open to non-Black members while circumscribing their participation through organizational norms and practices? This was a distinction many Black Kuumbabes made by differentiating between having a predominantly Black membership in Kuumba—as described in Verse I, the organization had about two-thirds Black members at the time and 18 percent white members— versus a more racially diverse membership. Senior Lauren Washington, drawing on the wording of Kuumba's mission to "celebrate" Black creativity and spirituality, compared this dynamic to "us celebrating ourselves"—that is, Black people celebrating Black people—versus "them celebrating us"—Black people being celebrated by others.

Kuumbabes described Black people participating in the group's mission ("us celebrating ourselves") as fundamentally different from non-Black people participating in this mission ("being celebrated by them"). Both were welcomed and served functions in the group, but "us celebrating ourselves" was prioritized. As we shall see, at times this meant hurt feelings and painful emotions, particularly for the white participants. Yet, group members came to accept, believe, and assert that to be an authentic Black organization and serve as a safe Black space, a majority Black membership and leadership had to be maintained and, in the words of Black freshman Malik Rose, non-Black members had to learn to "respect the space," that is, possibly cede their own interests to the group and to the sovereignty of the Black members. Kuumbabes came to espouse this view because they believed it was the only way to actualize the mission of being a safe space for Black students and to authentically celebrate Black spirituality and creativity.

In Verse I, we saw how the organization defined what it meant to be a Black space, specifically, how they defined "Black," how they taught this definition, and how they used this definition to establish Black authenticity and to be inclusive of Black members from diverse backgrounds. In this chapter, we continue exploring the issue of authenticity and what it means to be a Black space. Here, the focus shifts to how Kuumba ensured the safe Black space they intended to foster would remain a Black space—how they kept the Black space Black, actualized an authentic Black space amid a multiracial membership situated at a predominantly white university, and how Kuumbabes conceived of the role of non-Black students as part of this endeavor. In this context, they believed their ability to maintain a Black space on their own terms could be encroached upon at any time.

Us Celebrating Ourselves

"Would that be going so very far from our mission that we've forgotten ourselves?" Lauren Washington, an African American senior, was wondering aloud about the possibility of Kuumba having a white director. There had been some discussion of a popular white alumnus, Gregori, who rumor had it said he wanted to one day become the director of the organization. When Lauren brought this up, I remembered seeing Gregori perform with Kuumba years before I began this research. I had never met him, but his enthusiasm on stage left an indelible impression. He always seemed to be carried away by the music, really feeling it—emphatically moving in time to the rhythm of whatever song they were singing.

Lauren found the multiracial membership to be "powerful" in "acknowledge[ing] the richness of the Black culture," but there was a limit to how far the group could stray from its essential Blackness. Lauren exuded pure joy, beaming when talking about Kuumba, often unable to suppress a smile. But when talking about the possibility of a white director, her tone changed, and she became more measured in her speech. "I can't see the choir getting behind that very well because that does seem like it's moving away from what we wanted. But in a way, I'm still really undecided about it." In one of the only times I heard a choir member employ such a description of a non-Black person, Lauren described Gregori: "I think it was [names a prominent Black professor at Harvard] that said Gregori is really a Black guy in a white guy's skin." She seemed to be making an exception to the view that only Black bodies could authentically represent Blackness and Black interests.[1]

Yet, Lauren was cautious. "I think us being the leaders of the choir is also very powerful, so Black people determining, as a choir, this is how we're going to celebrate our creativity and spirituality." The Black space, then, was about Black people maintaining authority over Black representation. Lauren continued, "Some people are worried that if the face of Kuumba is a white person, and we're singing Black songs still, then maybe it becomes an issue of—because it's an external representation—how authentic is that representation?" Lauren's concerns about the "face" of the organization sounded like concerns about blackface and harmful misrepresentation. She allowed that this might not be the intention of non-Back members, "even though Gregori, or whoever the person may be, can understand Blackness and the experience and the creativity and the music, there's something different when not being a member of that community that changes the perception of the representation."

There was the subtle acknowledgment that while someone like a particular white alumnus or member might understand the aims of Kuumba, at issue was also the *"perception* of the representation." Kuumbabes were concerned both with how the public would perceive a white person as the "face of the choir," as well as the ramifications for the group's mission and purpose. Lauren articulated one troubling implication most succinctly: "Then it's not us celebrating ourselves. It's them celebrating us, which is just different. It's not necessarily worse, it's just different and people may not necessarily be ready for or in favor of a change in that manner." Lauren's concern was not whether a white person was capable of leading the choir and making choices about music that were rooted in the Black experience, and presumably related to the historical struggles and triumphs of Black people. Rather, Lauren's concern was about the differences she imagined to be inherent in a Black group "celebrating" itself versus *being celebrated by* those outside of the group. Though in this conversation, Lauren and I were talking about the leadership of the organization, this issue extended to membership and generally to how the organization was run.

Being celebrated *by* was counter to Kuumba's liberatory message of perseverance through struggle within the Black community. Kuumba was an organization that did for itself, that figured out what concerns were important within the Black community at Harvard and addressed them. Being celebrated by, conversely, conjured images of well-meaning social workers coming into a community and implementing initiatives doomed to fail because they did not understand, maybe did not respect, the people in those communities. This reminded me somewhat of the historical image of (white) Lady Bountiful, known for spreading her charity and benevolence to those in need, though reinforcing patriarchy and white supremacy in the process.[2] Being celebrated by hinted at paternalism and appropriation. Indeed, from blackface minstrels such as George Washington Dixon to Elvis to Vanilla Ice, American history is littered with examples of the cultural appropriation of Black-identified art forms and culture by non-Black people and, at times, the lampooning of those art forms and the culture.

At the root of Kuumba's concerns were what performance artist and scholar E. Patrick Johnson has described as two primary threats of cultural appropriation, particularly in terms of white appropriation of Blackness: cultural usurpation and the commodification of Blackness. Of cultural usurpation, Johnson has written, "In many instances, whites exoticize and/or fetishize blackness [. . .] Thus, when white-identified subjects perform 'black' signifiers—normative or otherwise—the effect is always already entangled in the discourse of otherness; the historical weight of white skin privilege necessarily engenders a tense relationship with its Others."[3] This was what Leela Johnson, a senior who was of East African and Caribbean descent, meant when she said, "*White people get everything* in terms of like, exploring cultures" (emphasis added), describing a formerly Black student organization—discussed below under the pseudonym Harvard Isicathulo—that had been "gentrified," in her words. White was dominant and everything else was Other. Diversity initiatives on university campuses were no doubt well-meaning, but from this perspective, they were less an attempt to alter the biases of white students and more a means to provide a smorgasbord of experiences for white students to try on Otherness.[4]

At stake in the debate over the role of non-Black members was the issue of presenting a caricatured view of Black creativity and spirituality versus a genuine one in which group members could take pride. Words like "blackface" and "gentrification" came up as Black members talked about the negative turn Kuumba could take if the organization was no longer majority Black or had non-Black leaders in key roles. Sophomore Bryanna Norman explained, "This needs to be a majority Black choir, because it sends the wrong message, first of all, when you're not all Black, well, a majority Black, and you're trying to celebrate Black spirituality. . . . It's kind of like . . . blackface. You're white, but you're dressing up as Black." Several Kuumbabes told me that they "feared" the possibility of losing the Black space in such a way. However, that fear seemed like an abstraction—a hypothetical possibility, and something to be wary of and fight against, but not an actual, looming threat. Indeed, the group as a whole, and the various members individually, regularly discussed and reflected upon these possibilities—which became a way that all members came to espouse this same view about the need for a Black majority choir—and thus they felt secure in the present structuring of the group that these "fears" wouldn't come to fruition. This was something that was informally taught, though; not all Kuumbabes joined the organization sharing this view, including Leela.

When I asked her whether there was anything she struggled with in Kuumba, Leela explained, "I'd spend a lot of time questioning, like what do I really believe in terms of who's entitled to what, and what is this space for, and where do white people and non-Blacks exist in Kuumba?" She herself had gone from thinking—as had students she had seen in new first-year classes—"'Oh, my white friend here is just as entitled to this space as my Black friend,'" to questioning, "And me, being Black, and what am I entitled to more of that this person is not?" Leela ultimately determined that a safe space for Black students was necessary, but "I ended up just feeling like, as long as people are celebrating Black culture spe-cifically, and not trying to make this like some other multicultural showcase, then I think that it's all good at that point." By "some other multicultural show-case," I sensed Leela decrying Harvard's institutional approach—readily embraced by the general student body—of "integration and celebration," an approach exemplified by large cultural performances and food festivals that typically lacked any substantive analysis of or engagement with issues of power and oppression related to those differences.[5] As we saw in Verse I, such a view that lacked ground-ing in, for instance, the historical struggle of Black students on campus, and did not recognize the anti-Black context, was antithetical to the type of safe Black space Kuumba intended to foster. So, resisting the "multicultural showcase"—implicitly resisting the "white space" on campus—by focusing specifically on the Black-oriented mission of the group became the foundation of keeping Kuumba's Black space Black and was a view members such as Leela came to embrace through participation in Kuumba.[6]

To teach this lesson of the dangers of cultural usurpation of the space—"them celebrating us"—Kuumbabes passed along the story of Harvard Isicathulo. Much like morality tales are passed along from generation to generation in any com-munity, Kuumbabes shared this story year after year as a warning to be heeded. I surmised that the story, about a group on campus that performed the Isicathulo style of dance that originated in South Africa, came up as Kuumbabes discussed what it meant for Kuumba to be a safe space for Black students in structured and unstructured conversations. Though I had only seen Harvard Isicathulo perform twice in my half-decade at the college, the legend of the group lived on as a cau-tionary tale of what could happen if a Black organization started ceding to the needs of non-Black members.

Isicathulo was a political art form, by differing accounts either originating around World War I with Zulu students in rural missions who were not permit-ted to perform traditional dances or by Black miners during Apartheid as a substitution for drumming, which was prohibited by authorities.[7] In the case of the miners, they used what they had available to them, such as tin cans and Wellington boots. In both situations, white colonial forces restricted Black expression.

The story goes that Havard Isicathulo began as a Black student organization with a majority of Black members. At some point, the non-Black members began to outnumber the Black members and, Kuumbabes implied, made decisions about the group's direction that were not aligned with the needs and interests of the Black members. This ultimately resulted in the group having few if any Black members; many students in Kuumba said they did not know it was supposed to be a Black student organization in the first place. I also did not know the group had started out with the intention to be a Black student organization when I saw them perform. They presented a dance that looked very much like stepping to me, which is popular among African American youths, but I did not recall seeing any Black members in the group.

In any event, the image of Harvard Isicathulo remained one about what was to be avoided at all costs. And, in what may have been meant as a reclaiming of the Isicathulo style of dance, two Kuumbabes with South African heritage performed an impromptu Isicathulo dance at one of the Kuumba concerts I attended during my fieldwork. Wearing borrowed rainboots as a stand-in for proper wellies, the two young men took the stage in between two musical numbers, stepping, stomping, and clapping rhythmically in coordination. The performance prompted a comment from the professional director, Sheldon, via one of the group email lists after the concert. In recounting what made the concert great—or, revealing Sheldon's humor, why it was a concert that "DIDN'T suck"—he wrote, "Isicathulo cameo—'nuff said. [. . .] You all should be proud." I couldn't help but wonder if these men intended the performance as an assertion, a reclaiming, of authentic Isicathulo.

Not naming Harvard Isicathulo specifically, senior Angie Martin gave a related example, distinguishing Kuumba as a Black, as opposed to multicultural, organization. "We don't refer to ourselves as a multicultural organization. We're a Black organization. We celebrate Black spirituality and creativity. We don't want a situation like in some other organizations where it started off Black and now it's not. It's other people trying to do Black music, other people trying to celebrate that tradition. . . . If anyone's celebrating it, it should be people who are Black." Through this story, Kuumbabes came to terms with what may have been a moral quandary for some, such as Leela. Considering the need to place parameters on non-Black members' participation in order to protect the Black space, she questioned, "What do I really believe in terms of who's entitled to what, and what is this space for, and where do white people and non-Blacks exist in Kuumba?"

AN AUTHENTIC SOURCE

"I feel like the majority of Kuumba should be Black, because, while . . . anyone could celebrate Black spirituality—which is why I'm so proud that Kuumba has members that are not Black who want to celebrate it—you still need . . . an authentic source." Bryanna Norman, who told me she had thought a lot about the need to have a majority Black membership in Kuumba, spoke very matter-of-factly about the racial composition of the choir. She went on, "While I think there's a need, or there's accomplishment, in that we have members of Kuumba who are not Black, I feel like the majority of Kuumba needs to be Black, that leadership for the most part needs to be Black, because we need that authenticity." Bryanna was getting at a key component of Kuumba's approach to maintaining a safe Black space at Harvard: while the mission, history, and music were essential features, similarly important was having a sizable portion of Black members— who uniquely "understood" the *embodied* experience of Blackness—which could, in turn, it was reasoned, attract more Black students to join.

Bryanna who showed up for our one-on-one interview with her midnight-black locks blown straight, framing her deep cocoa face, a change from the braids she wore most of the year, described her feeling that Black members were more than just "celebrating" Black spirituality and creativity. She said, "You need someone to bring those experiences. Like those readings, you need someone who actually *feels* those things to say them, like, not just 'I'm celebrating it,' but 'I experience it.'" When she referred to "readings," Bryanna was referencing the poems, short stories, and brief dramatic interpretations that were performed as interludes between musical numbers at Kuumba concerts. During one of the group's spring concerts, one of the readings was Maya Angelou's "Still I Rise."[8] The final stanza of the poem, which is essentially about Black peoples' ability to endure and persevere in the face of great hardship and racism, includes the lines: "Leaving behind nights of terror and fear// [. . .] //I am the dream and the hope of the slave." To Bryanna—and, I'm guessing, most other Kuumbabes—it would have been an affront to the group's mission, not to mention the historical legacy of Blackness, to have a non-Black person recite these words that were written from a Black person's perspective and imbued with historical meaning and context about racial oppression. What would it mean—and would it constitute minstrelsy—Kuumbabes questioned, if a white person, for instance, stood on stage in front of the predominantly Black choir and spoke of being the "dream and hope of the slave," as "Still I Rise" concludes? Again, both explicitly and implicitly, the group saw a difference between being able to celebrate Black creativity and spirituality—which anyone could do—and experiencing it—which only those who lived in a Black body could do. Bryanna said that this authenticity of lived experience allowed Black choir members to bring an added depth to performances. "You need a sense of authenticity to bring that sort of Black spirituality." Herein lay a central dilemma for Kuumba about maintaining the Black space: if only "authentic" (i.e., Black) people could offer this "Black spirituality," did this contradict the multiracial membership?

Angie Martin and most Kuumbabes I spoke with resolved that the Black space didn't need to be exclusively Black to be authentic, but it did need to have a majority Black membership. Angie offered, "I don't think it could be called . . . a Black organization if Blacks were the minority in the choir. So, I think that's again where the recruiting comes in, where we're actively recruiting Blacks, and still welcoming everyone else." Thus, recruitment of new Black members was one practice the group engaged in to keep the Black space Black. Many Black members, and Sheldon, explained to me that at the student activities fair each fall, Kuumba focused on actively targeting Black students. If Kuumbabes who were volunteering at the fair saw students they perceived to be Black freshmen, they proactively attempted to get them interested in coming to rehearsal. While first-year students of all racial backgrounds were welcomed if they showed up at rehearsal, Kuumbabes would, for the most part, not attempt to recruit non-Black freshmen at the fair.

While Black Kuumbabes were unapologetic about this practice, arguing it was necessary to maintaining a majority Black membership, which was, in turn, necessary for maintaining the safe Black space, Leela called the practice of only actively recruiting Black members "controversial." Leela was a practiced singer, which was clear by the melodiousness in her voice. Looking both cool with her hair in twists and in her casual dress—sweater and Harvard sweatpants—and studious in her gold wire framed glasses, she explained, "One of the members who has been in Kuumba for over four years was saying that he was hurt by the fact that when he walked by—he's white—nobody was like, 'Oh, you should join Kuumba,' at the freshman activities fair." Leela described how another Kuumbabe responded to this reaction. "Someone else was like, 'Well why should they? You're not Black.'" When Leela heard this exchange, at first she thought, "Whoa, that's crazy!" Leela saw the importance of recruiting Black students to Kuumba but was also hesitant about this strategy. In thinking about whether non-Black students should be recruited, she said, "That was an interesting question, and I don't know. I honestly feel like there should be a stronger focus on recruiting Black people, because it's so hard to get Black people to do things here, since there are so many different groups, and there's only like a limited number of Black people. I knew that, because people were trying to get me to do all kinds of things. I'm like, 'I can only do one thing.'" Leela's comment treated Blackness like a commodity and recognized how others did the same: Black bodies were needed to populate the choir and maintain its racial authenticity just as they were sought for participation in other organizations.[9] In this way, within the larger context of the predominantly white institution, the dehumanizing view of Black bodies as numbers persisted to be an issue in the Black space. At the same time, research has documented the need to focus in part on these numbers in order to cultivate an atmosphere where Black students can experience a sense of belonging.[10]

This created a bind in which to maintain the safe Black space, an authentically Black space, Black members were needed, yet there was a sense that there was a scarcity of Black students on campus. Given this dynamic, Kuumbabes focused on the proportion of the choir that Black members comprised. Jamison Mthembu, a senior who had held a variety of board leadership positions, told me that he had read a paper that applied a statistical model that predicted the decline of Black members with an increase in white members in Kuumba—in a sort of reversal of the "white flight" phenomenon in which white residents move out of neighborhoods as Black people move in. He explained, "It's called a Schelling Segregation Model, which is used to model white flight around the United States. And so, this model was kind of applied to Kuumba, because at some point, when white members did start to join Kuumba, the level of Black members spiked way down to like 30 percent Black, at some point, during our . . . years here." Jamison, who elsewhere said he appreciated the racial diversity of Kuumba, shared this information in a straightforward way that didn't take a stance on exactly what the "right" racial balance should be. In fact, no Kuumbabe I spoke with ever put an exact number or percentage on what they thought that balance should be or what would be ideal. After years of working with students, this type of intellectualization struck me as very "Harvard," in some ways removing the affect from negotiating Black identity.[11]

Though Jamison didn't have the statistics available and wasn't sure of his estimates, he described what he knew of the history of the model and the racial balance conversations: "So all through the Seventies, it was Black, and then in the Eighties, there were non-Black members who joined. And then that's when debates about what does it mean to be an authentic Black space if there are going to be non-Black members joining the space, and how do we deal with that?" Jamison continued, "I guess the discussion turned ugly, and a lot of Black members left. And so, the level of Black members in Kuumba at the time was pretty, pretty low. And then it spiked up again, and then it went down again and spiked up again. So, it goes through cycles." While Jamison's account lacked certainty, and no Kuumba members or alums seemed able to provide me with more details, this account of ups and downs was the story all shared. Even if it lacked accuracy, this account formed an important part of Kuumba's rationale for focusing on recruiting Black members—they attracted more Black members and, in turn, the safe Black space remained Black.

With the balance always in flux, Jamison saw a need for "education"—for all members—on what Kuumba meant. Speaking of his own initial reaction to seeing Kuumba perform, he said, "When I saw Kuumba onstage, I didn't think of it as a Black organization. I just thought of it as a performing arts group that was singing Black music or celebrating Black creativity, right?" Jamison hinted at the ambiguity around what Kuumba was, given, for instance, that the organization didn't have "Black" in its name and that concertgoers clearly saw a racially mixed group. Therefore, it became even more important to bolster the presence of Black student members, to demonstrate and maintain the group's authenticity.

Further, Kuumba did not exist in a vacuum of time or place. Some of the discussion about the need to be authentic was animated by other Black Harvard students' perceptions of the group, as well as in terms of Kuumba's relationships with other Black student organizations. Jolaade Abedayo, a junior from the Northeast, commented on how the Black community at Harvard held negative perceptions of Kuumba because of the racial composition of the group. I was surprised at Jolaade's openness in sharing this critique of Kuumba, given that she told me prior to the interview that she didn't really enjoy talking with people or being the center of attention, which I took as evidence of being insecure, painfully shy, or both. Yet it didn't take any prodding to get her to share a story about her class cohort from first year: "When I first joined Kuumba, like a lot of the [freshmen from my class year], like, the Black community would all come to Kuumba. And then slowly, as always happens, they stopped coming." She asked some of her classmates who stopped attending rehearsals why they had chosen to leave. "One of the people I asked—'Why don't you come to Kuumba?'—and he was like, 'Because Kuumba is a Black organization, but they have so many white people.'"

The missing voices of these Black students who chose to stop participating in Kuumba form a lacuna in this story. Therefore, this re-enacted exchange left me with many unanswered questions. For instance, what were these Black students who had chosen not to participate in Kuumba because of the white members concerned about? In what ways did they imagine it mattered that there were white members of the Black organization? And, what were the implications for fostering multiracial safe spaces? It also raised the question of what it was about Kuumba that would attract and retain white members, in contrast to other Black student organizations. After all, Harvard rules since 1985 would have prohibited any group from denying membership based on race.[12] To this last point, I had a sense that it was the performance aspect of Kuumba, which provided just the kind of multicultural experience prized by elites, that contributed to this.[13]

Explaining further, during her junior year, Jolaade said the impression of the group was that "Kuumba has gotten more Black. . . . I mean . . . a majority of them [Kuumbabes] were always Black. I guess it was just way more that it . . . mitigates the appearance of white people." Here, she revealed how powerful our visual perceptions can be: just *seeing* a bunch of white people could diminish the way people thought about the group. Jolaade subsequently touched on the issue of racial "balance." When I asked her if it mattered what the balance was, she said, "I think it matters to the Black community. . . . At a certain time, the Black community was against Kuumba . . . like, the fact that . . . white people outweighed the amount of Black people." In addition to the racial balance mattering to the Black community, Jolaade noted that "it does matter to an organization, because I feel like if you say you're a Black organization, but your membership doesn't reflect that, it takes away from the message." Echoing the idea introduced by Bryanna, Jolaade felt that Kuumba needed Black members in order to not take away "from the message." Angie corroborated this view: "It's not that we exclude non-Blacks. It's that we still want to have a large Black presence in our choir, so we can . . . go after, you know, African American freshmen to make sure they come out to the choir." This suggested that the real issue wasn't actually the numbers (just having a majority of the members be Black wasn't enough), but rather that it was something more subtle—perhaps related to the idea of "us celebrating ourselves"—that the presence of too many white people (even if they were not the majority) could change perceptions of the group as a whole.

Overall, there was the implication that the organization would not have had to work as hard to ensure and publicize its Black racial authenticity if the group were exclusively comprised of self-identifying Black members. And it may have been the group's authenticity that drew Black and non-Black members alike to the organization. Further, both Black and non-Black students struggled with what at times seemed like exclusionary practices in the name of racial authenticity, which came up in discussions about who could serve as the Kuumba president.

The Face of the Organization

In addition to maintaining a majority Black membership, Kuumbabes were particularly concerned with having a majority Black board, and specifically having Black students in key board leadership positions—namely the positions of president and vice president, and to a lesser extent, librarian. The importance of having a Black president came up frequently in my interviews. Leela said, "It's not like the whole choir has to be Black, but just that people can look at it and say, 'Oh, okay, this is Black.' So [non-Black students] understand that when they come onto [the] board and when they're applying . . . people have been nominated for president who weren't Black, and they've declined respectfully." I had seen this myself at the beginning of my time with Kuumba. Though board positions had been decided the previous spring, the vice president had to step down over the summer and I was privy to the new nomination and election process.

A student was first nominated by other members, and then had to accept or decline before moving forward in the process, which spanned a couple of rehearsals and included a speech and a position paper about why he or she was qualified for that particular board position. During the nomination process I witnessed, several students of various racial backgrounds were nominated and declined. Therefore, I did not make much of one white, Jewish student's decision to decline the nomination. She had appeared to be a very active member of the organization, so I thought she probably could have done a good job as vice president. At the time of this nomination process early in my research, I was unaware that part of her decision was likely informed by this group norm. I only came to learn about this unwritten practice through my interviews. That is, though several Kuumbabes referenced conversations about Black leadership, and though Sheldon recalled an explicit conversation with the choir during one rehearsal regarding this expectation, no such conversations took place in my presence. Hence, there were parameters, albeit informal, on members' participation based on race, and the conversation over who should be president in Kuumba became a means for ensuring that the organization would remain one that could be called authentically Black.

Freshman Jason Thomas put it quite plainly. "We can't have people who aren't Black representing a Black organization." Jason made a similar distinction to the one Bryanna made about the difference between "celebrating" and "representing" when I asked him about the role of non-Black members. He explained, "Well, their relationship with the choir is a bit different. . . . Their role, I think, is to help us celebrate Black achievement, Black strength, Black spirituality. But because they're not in fact Black, they can't be the face of the organization. . . . It's not rooted in . . . having people from outside the African diaspora to represent the strength and the message of what's in the African diaspora."

I asked Jason to help me better understand the distinction he was making between celebrating the culture and then representing the group. He offered, "Mainly when I say that, I mean being on [the] board, like being president, for instance. It's kind of hard to just praise something that you're not." Jason was making a nuanced point here in saying, "It's kind of hard to just praise something that you're not," suggesting that even if non-Black members had the best intentions, they simply wouldn't be able to "praise" "Black achievement, Black strength, Black spirituality" in the same way. This was a view grounded in Kuumba's focus on self-sufficiency and group uplift within the Black community.

Beyond the doubts he personally expressed about having a non-Black member be the "face" of Kuumba, Jason, balancing issues of internal authenticity and external perceptions like most of my Black interviewees, noted that Kuumba alumni and others outside of the current membership also influenced his view. "I guess people, alums, non-alums, might think we're being a bit inauthentic if we have people who aren't obviously Black representing the group. So, I think that that's also another thing that we pay attention to." But by "obviously Black," was Jason suggesting the president must be phenotypically Black? Must be a certain complexion shade? I know from alumni that a few years back, the president was a woman who identified as half-Black and half-Jewish. Was she "obviously Black"? Did Jason mean "culturally Black"? In my conversations with current members, Kuumbabes from the United States and countries in Africa and the Caribbean, as well as biracial students, were all considered equally, authentically Black. Only the biracial students themselves sometimes questioned how their experiences with white parents impacted their racial identity both within the organization and without.

Jason agreed with the limits of participation in place for non-Black members and said, "I think our non-Black members understand that, too. . . . They don't love [Kuumba] any less because of that."

Sheldon shared a very different story. He decried the current situation, saying that we were living in the "age of PC, which stands for Punk Conversations," where people "are less likely to say what needs to be said." He recalled one rehearsal where he took up the otherwise "unspoken rule that a white person can't be president of Kuumba." He addressed the group by saying that this unspoken rule existed, "so let's speak it. A white person can't be president of Kuumba. Let's talk about why." At the end of the conversation, he remembered seeing one white woman "who was just crying." He wanted to reach out to her to engage the conversation further but sensed that she wasn't "feeling that we could talk at the moment." Similarly, the white senior that Leela described as being upset at not being actively recruited by Kuumba might also disagree with Jason's assessment. Yet, all the non-Black students I interviewed espoused the view that only Black members should hold key board positions. Echoing Jason, these students said this was necessary for Kuumba's authenticity as a Black organization. Perhaps the students who were deeply upset by these practices didn't participate in interviews. Maybe they stopped participating in Kuumba altogether. Or maybe contradicting these firmly held beliefs and practices was too taboo for anyone to say out loud on the record.

Daphne was one student who spoke with me about being nominated for a Kuumba board position—librarian—and declining because she wasn't Black. Daphne, whose parents immigrated to the United States from Korea before she was born, noted that her decision to decline the nomination was not a matter of not feeling honored or not wanting to take on the responsibility. "It's something that I would gladly have taken on, that I would like to do, like run for." However, Daphne understood and agreed with the expectation that a Black student should have the role. She explained, "Kuumba at its heart is still a Black organization. And . . . Sheldon was like, we should probably never have a non-Black president. I agree. It's still about being Black at Harvard." For Daphne, not being Black herself meant she could not possibly fulfill the role in the way that was needed by the group. "As much as I would like to contribute to it, that's something I would never take on, just because I don't think I will ever fully understand what it means to be Black." Of her decision to withdraw, Daphne said, "I think it was the right choice. . . . I think I may have done an okay job as librarian, but I think somebody else could have done it better." Daphne provided a reason for why someone else—a Black someone else—could have done it better: "There are some things that I won't even think about, just because I haven't experienced being actually Black. And being the librarian is all about the history of Kuumba and the struggle that's come along with instituting this organization." And, indeed, a Black student ultimately took on the role.

While Daphne's decision to withdraw from the librarian race could be interpreted as an indicator of second-class status in Kuumba, non-Black members
did not describe it this way. To these students, stepping back from certain roles
in the group was a way for them to contribute to supporting the group's mission. All members were charged with fulfilling the mission, but the ways in which
they did so varied based not only on race but also proclivity and skill. In Daphne's case, she settled on other ways to contribute to the group by taking on a different leadership role, as an assistant director.[14] She said, "I feel like assistant
directing is a good way for me to pitch in, because I love music. I feel like it's a
way in which I could contribute . . . without taking over, or without making
people uncomfortable that, you know, it's not somewhere where I should be. It's
not my jurisdiction." In the face of encroaching on the safe Black space by taking on the position of librarian, Daphne found retreat in the music; the music
was a place that could be within her "jurisdiction." Since music was central to
Kuumba and students described music as being very much a part of what made
it a Black organization, Daphne's framing presented an interesting paradox.
Music was deployed by students in various ways to mark Kuumba as a Black
organization, as described in Verse I. Yet it was also frequently viewed as a shared
domain among students of different backgrounds. Daphne, for instance, had had
formal classical cello training growing up. Paul Dixon, a white freshman,
had bass training and positioned himself similarly. He ended up taking on a
board position related to communicating with affiliated musicians.[15]

In framing her decision to withdraw from the librarian race, Daphne also
noted not wanting to "take over." The idea that non-Black interests might "take
over" or acculturate the Black cultural emphasis within Kuumba was one of the
biggest threats members perceived in welcoming non-Black members to participate. As shown here, this wasn't just a worry by Black members, it was a worry
shared by all members; even though Kuumba's mission, and its unwritten stan-
dards, were so strong and widely shared, Black and non-Black members did not
take for granted that all would come to the organization ready to participate in
ways that would protect the Black space. Given this concern, and that it seemed
so well-known among members that non-Black members should not take on certain leadership roles, I was curious about how non-Black members wound up
being nominated in the first place.

I asked Leela about this. She believed the freshmen members were likely
responsible. "They see people, they're like, 'Oh, this person's great. I love her.'
And they'll sign them up. And so I know when I see the names [of board nomi-
nees] and they're all over the place, I'm like oh, that's the freshmen. And they
really love all these different people." Leela may have been speaking from her
own experience. "I think maybe end of my freshman year, maybe sophomore
year, I was hearing a lot of like, 'the president has to be Black.' And at first, I was
like, 'Whoa, wait, that sounds messed up.' And then they delve into it, and you

start to understand more." When she said, "they delve into it," Leela meant that upperclassmen and current board members, as well as Sheldon himself, presented the case for why Black members should have certain leadership positions. She explained further, "So I don't know if this happens to everyone, but for me, I came from, like, my Pacific Northwest 'We should all be friends, and let everyone do what they want to do' [background] to . . . feeling like this organization is fighting for something. . . . While it's not ideal to have to, not deny, but push someone away from a role, it's still sort of necessary." Leela revealed that Kuumbabes felt they were in a fight for authenticity and representation and that the cost of "pushing [non-Black members] away" from certain roles was worth the discomfort or temporary disappointment it may have caused. This was not a misplaced concern, given that elsewhere, research has shown how white families have rerouted educational resources from communities of color to their own children, described as "opportunity hoarding" or "accumulation by dispossession."[16]

Leela's own experience also demonstrates the learning curve for at least some new members, and the way that seemingly all of the group came to espouse the same vision of racial authenticity. Students—especially Black students who had come from primarily non-Black communities and schools, like Leela—might arrive at Harvard and Kuumba thinking that it "sounds messed up" to say that the president of a Black student organization had to be Black. But, through listening to testimonials of other Black students, they came to change or reexamine their views. For Leela, the turning point came through relationships with other Kuumbabes who had had different experiences of being Black:

> Meeting with people like Rochelle, who came from the South, she's had to go through a lot more because of her race than I have. And so becoming aware of that made me understand why it's important for Kuumba to still, in this day and age, be catering to the Black population, and part of that means being at least a majority Black institution, or making sure that the majority of the leaders are Black, or at least the president.

In this single example, Leela captured a sentiment that pervaded my interviews about what it meant for Kuumba to be an "authentic" Black organization, why it needed to be so, and some of the means by which that was ensured.

———

Kuumba in the early 2010s—as today—existed at a time when Harvard would not permit any officially recognized student organization to "discriminate" (restrict membership) based on race.[17] Therefore, in a way, Kuumba had to permit white and other non-Black students to participate in the Black space. And, as I've shown here, nearly all Black Kuumbabes welcomed members of all backgrounds.

At the same time, the organization remained vigilant that the Black space, as such, remained Black, so that it could also remain safe and shield students from the potential "outsider status" they might experience in the white space of the university. This was achieved through centering the priorities and leadership of Kuumbabes and required non-Black members to forego some of the privileges they might experience elsewhere on campus and all members to take up the view that this was necessary. This was what Malik Rose meant when he commented on the group's racial diversity by saying, "I think it's great. But I mean, I think it's still important to know that this is still a Black organization, and this is a Black space." As if speaking to the non-Black members, he said, "And by you coming into the space, then you need to respect it." By "respect" Malik meant a number of things, including a willingness to support the organization's efforts to maintain Black racial authenticity, including not attempting to take on leadership positions reserved for Black students. This was something the non-Black members had to embrace if they wanted to be part of Kuumba.

In many ways then, maintaining the safe Black space was about resisting the white space, which is essential in conceiving of "safe space" in the Ivory Tower. Sociologist Elijah Anderson describes "the white space" as settings, including educational institutions, "in which black people are typically absent, not expected, or marginalized when present."[18] The point of marginalization is important. Anderson notes that the "moral authority" of Black people is undermined in the white space, and thus,

> When present there [in the white space], the black person typically has limited standing relative to his white counterparts and is made aware of this situation by the way others treat him. [. . .] In the white space, small issues can become fraught with racial meaning or small behaviors can subtly teach or remind the black person of her outsider status. [. . .] [B]eing white is a fundamental requirement for acceptance and a sense of belonging in the white space.[19]

Belonging in the Black space for Black Kuumbabes was key. Angie summed it up, "We aren't here to be more welcoming to non-Blacks. This is a Black space. You [non-Black members] need to come in, recognize that, and appreciate that . . . you can take part in that space . . . Being more welcoming to non-Blacks isn't going to become one of our priorities, because that's not what the choir is about. Like, we're not meant to change to accommodate non-Blacks." Therefore, Kuumba was an organization defined by acceptance and anti-exclusion at the same time that it maintained parameters around forms of participation for members of different backgrounds—keeping the Black space Black not by curtailing who joined, but specifying how they participated—in order to fulfill its mission of serving as a safe space for Black students.

Bridge

NON-BLACK MEMBERS IN THE
BLACK ORGANIZATION

"There are things that just need to be said and realized. You are welcome, but know that you are being welcomed into a Black organization and what that means. . . . We can all struggle together."
—*Sheldon K. X. Reid, Kuumba Director*

Despite the bone-chilling cold of a Cambridge evening in late January, returning Kuumbabes and prospective new members were abuzz as they arrived at the Student Organization Center at Hilles, where Kuumba rehearsed. Everyone called the building "the SOCH," pronounced like the "soc" of "social," which was fitting for a building the university described as "50,000+ square feet of space dedicated to student life at Harvard College."[1] That description was more aspirational than a reality at the time, though, as the SOCH always felt deserted until I got to the Kuumba rehearsal in the "Penthouse," a cavernous, no-frills multipurpose room on the top floor. On this evening, the Penthouse was brimming with returning and aspiring Kuumbabes. To add to the sense of excitement, recordings from past performances were being blared on a makeshift speaker system.

I looked around before deciding where to take my seat. The space sacrificed aesthetics for utility. It was simply constructed, with blond wood walls on two sides and floor-to-ceiling windows on another. Pea green wall-to-wall carpet covered the floor, and metal chairs in shades of institutional orange, brown, and blue were stacked on dollies at the back of the room. There were also nearly a hundred other chairs, arranged in three sections. At the front of the room sat a baby grand piano where Sheldon, in his uniform of jeans, sneakers, and a crimson T-shirt that popped against his deep brown complexion, was perched, ready to begin directing the choir.

I settled on what had become my usual spot at the back of the alto section sitting behind Rochelle Perry. We exchanged stories about winter break before

turning our attention to a potential new member seated next to me, one of many
unfamiliar faces in the crowd. The woman, who appeared to be white, explained
that she was a student at a nearby art school. There were always a few Kuumbabes
from other local colleges, and at least one older community member, during my
time researching the organization. When Rochelle and I asked this recruit about
her interest in Kuumba, she explained she had family friends who were involved
and she was just now able to work out her schedule to attend. We quickly wrapped
up chatting; it was time for the formal part of the rehearsal to begin.

Instead of starting by practicing a song as was typical at the twice-weekly
rehearsals, two alumni, both Black men, were invited to speak. First was Ken
Reeves, a staunchly-built man who must have been in his sixties. Reeves was a
founding member of Kuumba as well as the former mayor of Cambridge, and
the first openly gay Black man to be a U.S. mayor. Clearly a skilled orator, with
each utterance sounding deliberately chosen and delivered, Reeves commented
on the changing racial composition of the group, setting the scene to ensure
Kuumbabes—and potential new members—understood the tradition they were
a part of. He described how, in the aftermath of the student protests during
the late 1960s and early 1970s, the Black population on campus went from
"very few . . . including some African princes," to "in excess of one hundred."
Thus, Kuumba started during an exciting and turbulent time for Black students in terms of developing community among one another. "When we started,"
Reeves said, "we were all *Black*," overtly stressing the word "Black." But he concluded by noting that the group now included "Asian and Caucasian" members
and, speaking to all, he said, "You have joined here a family that will be with you
for always."

I was curious, did Kuumba always have an alum speak at the very first introductory meeting? Was having an alum speak and frame the founding of the
organization in this way a means of ensuring that everyone understood the mission and history? Was it set up to discourage non-Black people who would not
respect the Black space (see chapter 3)? Reeves was saying both that Kuumba
was a Black space and that everyone, regardless of race, could be part of the
"family." But what did non-Black members and potential members, like the
woman seated next to me, hear? How did they make sense of their participation
in a Black organization?

In this chapter, I share the voices of six of the approximately eighteen total
non-Black students "in the Black choir," to paraphrase Anna Reid, one white student who participated in this research. The group includes Anna, Emily Taylor,
and Paul Dixon, the two white women and one man who participated; and
Daphne Han and Sei Matsuura, who identified as Asian American. I also include
Francisco Diaz, who described himself as, "Black, but my ethnicity is Puerto
Rican." This, he said, could cause confusion, and "gets difficult," leading him at
other times to say, "I'm Puerto Rican, not Black." He often settled on, "I just say

I'm brown, whatever, because it confuses people less."[2] Together, these students show how the whiteness of the elite university context—in part through the implicit framing of diversity as being something to learn from—made available, and predicated belonging on, certain ways of being that were raced and gendered. This subsequently impacted students' choices for joining and remaining in Kuumba and how they navigated their role as non-Black members in the organization.

MUSIC AND FAMILY

To a person, the students I interviewed named the musical aspect of Kuumba as being what first attracted them. Emily said, "I love singing," and Sei said pretty much the same: "I guess I really wanted a place where I could sing." More typically, these students had heard Kuumba perform and "fell in love," as Anna put it. Or, as Paul explained, "My first exposure to Kuumba was at the freshman convocation this past late August or early September. . . . We were sitting in Harvard Yard, and I was kind of bored. It was so, so hot, and out of nowhere, just Kuumba came up, and they sang. I'll never forget. And just after that . . . I was caught like a fish on a line, I guess. I said to the person sitting next to me, I want to do that." Daphne, a former cellist, and Paul, a bassist, were the only two who had been musicians prior to Kuumba.

For Anna, Emily, and Paul, that much of Kuumba's repertoire could be recognized as gospel or Christian was also appealing. Unlike Daphne, Sei, and Francisco, the white participants all identified as Christian. (Daphne described her religion as "none," Sei as "Buddhist, exploring my relationship with God," and Francisco as "not sure.") The spiritual aspect of the music was particularly alluring to Anna, who was active in Christian fellowships on campus. Beaming, she exclaimed, "I would go to these Kuumba concerts [before joining] and I just remember I would think like they would get a whole Memorial Church or Sanders Theater up and dancing and clapping about the blood of Jesus. And I was like, what kind [of] people are these who can get a group of Harvard students and faculty rejoicing about God!" Anna noted, though, that Kuumba was not a Christian fellowship or organization—as all Kuumbabes who discussed religion were sure to mention—and that not everyone experienced it as such, which was evidenced in my interviews with students who were Muslim or not religiously observant.

While the music might have initially attracted students to Kuumba, it was, going back to the words of Ken Reeves, being part of the Kuumba version of an idealized "family" that proved an irresistible draw. Students were quick to tell me how Kuumba was a huge time commitment for already overfilled Ivy League schedules. "Sheldon even said that at our winter concert last time. He's like, 'You know what, if you come to one rehearsal, if you come to one concert, like, it doesn't matter if you're part of the choir or not, you become part of the family.' And I think that's really true." Anna swept back her tawny hair as she explained to me what it meant for Kuumba to be a "family" for her. It was a crisp early spring afternoon in New England; Anna's pink sweater offered little contrast to her cream-colored complexion.

Anna, whose brother and non-Kuumba friends gibed her for being a "white girl in the Black choir," explained how she felt like part of the Kuumba family with particular acuteness when she returned after taking four weeks off to work on her senior thesis. Her piercing blue eyes were alert when she said, somewhat in jest, "When I came back, I felt like it was like the prodigal daughter returning and not because like anyone was upset but everyone was like, 'Anna, where have you been? We've missed you! Are you coming back?'" This bolstered Anna's belief that a strength of the choir was in "letting people come as they are and be who they are and just being really affirming of that."

Anna was not the only one who repeated director Sheldon Reid's belief, recited by Sheldon himself at more than one concert, about the seemingly boundless Kuumba family. I heard this same idea from numerous Kuumbabes, including almost all of the non-Black participants. (The only exception was Emily, for whom, based on the consistency with which members drew on this metaphor, this might simply have been an oversight rather than a deliberate omission.) Indeed, the proclamation about expanding the notion of the Kuumba family was repeated often enough on campus that I was aware of the sincerity of this claim even before I began conducting my research. At first, I attempted to sit along the periphery during rehearsals, dutifully watching what the members—the "real" members, in my mind—were doing. When the choir began practicing a new song and the sheet music was handed out, I would respectfully decline, saying, "Oh, I'm not really in the group." More than once, African American senior Lauren Washington refuted my claim, and said with a smile and determination, "Yes, you are!" I would say jokingly—or perhaps not so jokingly—that no one wanted to hear my singing. But Kuumbabes would then remind me, as they did at the very first rehearsal I attended, that this was a non-audition choir. No one was turned away; everyone could belong to this family.

My purpose for including this section on these students being drawn to Kuumba for the music and staying for the familial aspect is to highlight that, in contrast to findings from other research on non-Black participants in Black student organizations, none of these students joined because they were specifically looking to be part of a Black student organization. None of them arrived at college seeking out a Black cultural group in which to participate. However, with the exception of Sei, they all described formative experiences with Black communities or Black-denoted art forms prior to joining. Anna, for instance, was a congregant at a local, predominantly Black church, and Paul had studied the works and history of Black musicians in the United States extensively as he learned to play the bass. Further, echoing the findings presented in chapter 3, many of these participants expressed concern about having non-Black students join and how that would impact Kuumba. Yet, while Daphne and Sei expressed being conflicted about their role as non-Black members, and Anna and Emily questioned whether it was appropriate for them to join Kuumba as white people, Paul did not.

Just Another Thing That Made Me Different

For the three students of color, joining a Black student organization provided an opportunity to distance themselves from racial stereotypes and raced expectations related to the group with which they were identified. Francisco, who was a senior at another highly selective university nearby, discussed this as influencing his decision-making process. This is one reason I include Francisco's voice in this section, even though as a Puerto Rican with a dark tan complexion he usually, but not always, identified as Black. In describing how he wound up participating in Kuumba, he reflected on how he gravitated toward Black student organizations, in part, because he felt detached from "the Hispanic community" on his campus, given his failure to meet assumed cultural expectations.

Francisco always looked urban cool: black, low fade haircut, manicured beard and mustache, "bling" in both ears, and rubber bands on his wrists of the same sort as the "Livestrong" bands popularized by Lance Armstrong, though Francisco's were varying colors including green, black, yellow, and white, and read "Kuumba Singers." He agreed to meet me one morning at a Starbucks near his campus. I strained to hear him over the background noise while he explained how he felt attending his first rehearsal. When he first joined, Francisco wasn't sure how he would be accepted: "When I got there, I was nervous, but the people in Kuumba . . . are all just incredibly outgoing and incredibly nice and friendly."

In contrast, Francisco noted, "I'm Puerto Rican, but I haven't felt very close to the Hispanic community at [my university] in general, the Latino community. . . . Maybe it's because, you know, I step and I sing music from the African diaspora." He was drawn to these Black-identified creative forms, as he explained, having grown up in a big city in the Northeast where he had "Hispanic friends. But I also—I probably had an equal number of Black friends. I guess for me, I was more accepted by the Black community at [my university]." Early on, Francisco had joined both a Black men's group and Latino men's group, "but kind of faded out of [the] Latino men's group after I realized I didn't actually hang out with any of those guys." He determined the Latinx community on his campus was not for him, exaggeratedly saying that students who didn't participate "in every culture show" or serve "on the board of every Hispanic group on campus" were ostracized. He concluded, "I thought that was bullshit. And you know, [I] kind of segregated myself from that group."

As Francisco explained further, he revealed an attenuated relationship to the Latinx community on campus for deeper reasons than simply not participating in cultural shows, for example. He said,

> I think one of the things that kept me on the outskirts was . . . I pretty much understand all Spanish, but I'm very hesitant when it comes to speaking it. So that was just another thing that made me different, I guess. I don't know. I mean, I would consider myself Puerto Rican, and I'm very proud of my Puerto Rican heritage. I eat the food. I've been there countless times. And the only thing, I think, that makes me, that I don't have or whatever, is that fluency. So I'm very, I guess, defensive about it, and when people put it into question, I felt like just cut off by that, and it kind of deterred me from really becoming a part of the Latino community as such. . . . I guess it was mainly that, and the cultural thing was a big one, but I think it was also the language thing.

I could hear the smooth tenor in his voice as he continued, "It's not like I was like, 'Hey, you know, I've been put on the outskirts, I'm trying to get back in.' I feel like if I'm not completely accepted for who I am, then I'm not going to fight to be a part of a group, because it makes no sense. When I saw that happening, I decided that was enough for me."

What Francisco experienced wasn't anomalous. Racial authenticity in some contexts demands knowledge of particular traditions and circumscribed activities, which can lead to a hierarchy of "cultural superiority" (i.e., certain ways of being are esteemed and others are looked down upon).[3] This could be especially true for those who choose to socialize outside of their racial or ethnic group, as Francisco did growing up. Francisco's experience is also reflective of the sanctions imposed within immigrant groups for embracing rather than rejecting what might be considered U.S. Blackness (Blackness associated with descendants of enslaved Africans in the United States).[4] Not meeting expectations of authenticity could lead to feelings of alienation. Alternatively, it could also lead those who didn't "fit in" to conform.

Conforming was exactly what Daphne, who had a similar experience to Francisco's, refused to do. Daphne suggested that her "natural inclination" might be to spend time with other Asian Americans on campus, but that she wanted to avoid stereotypes. She explained, "It's basically my reaction against grouping myself." Daphne had taken this position of disavowing stereotypical expectations since childhood. She explained, "The whole idea that for example, Asians are always going to do math or science. Like retrospectively, probably the reason why I am not ever going to do math and science is because, like, someone labeled my group of people." When Daphne said it would be "natural" for her to spend time with other Asian Americans, she was speaking to societal expectations as much as anything else. Preference for perceived in-group members has been documented in study after study and having same-race or -ethnicity friends has become normalized, whereas having friends of different races may still seem an oddity requiring justification.[5] But, I wondered, was participating in the Black space just a way for Daphne to satisfy a rebellious streak in distancing herself from stereotypes, inarguably harmful, of Asian Americans?

Daphne explained that her boyfriend was white, and recounted a longtime affinity for what others might label as Black culture. For example, growing up Daphne attended a local dance camp led by an African American choreographer "that was amazing for me." There she learned about dance traditions "that I couldn't have done if I had gone to like an Asian camp." Her sweeping characterizations of things along racial lines, like "Asian camp," notwithstanding, Daphne continued to discuss how participation in dance camp represented an important part of her identity that contrasted with what might be seen as a traditional Asian American orientation. She said, "I was proud to be in urban programs with other African American and Hispanic kids, because a lot of my parents' friends' daughters and sons were at camps that you had to pay for, and that you had to take an entrance exam to get into, like those sort of elitist camps." Daphne, who said of her family, "We don't have a ton of money," saw attending camps with Black and Latinx students as part of her identity growing up in a major urban center: "I was like, I'm an inner city kid." Much like Francisco who also described coming from an urban area with fewer financial resources, Daphne's experience of race was also classed. Daphne didn't find a place of belonging with her Asian American peers at "elitist camps" "that you had to pay for." Instead, conflating race and class to some degree, she found herself more at ease with Black and Latinx "urban" kids at the free dance camp.

Daphne's choice to seek out activities not typically identified with Asian American communities might have been about more than her refusal to conform to stereotypes. It might also have been due to her inability to perform certain aspects of her identity in ways expected for her to claim racial authenticity. This became apparent as I listened to Daphne comparing herself to her sister who was a few years older and who also went to dance camp. In addition to attending "urban" programs, Daphne's sister sought out more opportunities to connect with Korean and Asian American communities and was on the board of the Asian American Association at Harvard. Additionally, Daphne drew a contrast between her sister's connection with Korean culture and her own. "She knows Korean a lot better than I do, because she was born in Korea. I'm Korean by nationality. And so like she's got more of a connection to the country." It's possible that Daphne's limited knowledge of Korean and her not having been born in Korea impacted her perceived ability to claim an authentic Korean identity. I wondered whether her renunciation of cultural expectations related to an insecurity in meeting those expectations. It may have been a way for Daphne to distinguish herself from her sister, but it was equally likely that Daphne was questioning her own racial authenticity. In Kuumba these expectations didn't exist for Daphne where she said Kuumbabes "were just so nice to me . . . they were just so friendly."

Sei, who described herself as "Japanese-Chinese American," also found that she "couldn't connect" with other Asian Americans on campus in the same way that she felt she could with other Kuumbabes. Sei, whose features highlighted her East Asian heritage—broad, round face, dark olive complexion, and shoulder-length straight black hair—explained her unease with the Asian community on campus. Part of this stemmed from what Sei admitted to as having "my own stereotypes of Asian people" and never being able to imagine herself as fitting in to those stereotypes. Acknowledging that they were stereotypes, she explained, "I feel like they're, like, two kinds [of Asians] . . . really studious ones, and then the like, well my friend calls them the slutty ones but like, oh . . . I just feel like there's very rare—like I could never find one somewhere in between, and the ones that I do find, they're probably some of my closer friends. But I always felt I couldn't connect with either of them [the two stereotypes of Asians]." Sei was speaking of typecasts Asian Americans held by other Asian Americans. But these were also racist depictions perpetuated by dominant white society that framed Asians and Asian Americans as overly conscientious "model minorities" or, in the case of women, as erotic sex objects.[6]

Even before Harvard, Sei struggled with where she fit in. "I was part of the Asian American Association in my high school, but I also felt like I couldn't connect with it. . . . I guess also because they're really cliquey, I've noticed . . . in my experiences. So I've just always been like, 'No, I don't want to be part of that.'" Sei tripped over her words as she spoke to me, with many false starts and stops. I sensed that she was still working out her thoughts as we talked and that maybe this was the first time she had been able to articulate her feelings about Kuumba and her identity, which she confirmed by saying it was not something she talked about much with others.

Yet, after going on the choir's spring break tour and hearing Black Kuumbabes discuss culture and issues of import for Black students as a community, Sei longed for a similar connection with Asian Americans. As she told me, "I was like, 'Oh, I really want [that],' because [Asian Americans] seldom talk about culture. . . . I guess being . . . part of a similar culture, having similar experiences, being able to share . . . I enjoyed seeing that, but I wanted to do that, too." To explore her identity and form relationships with other Asian Americans, Sei joined an Asian American dance group at Harvard. However, she found the group limited in terms of addressing the racial authenticity issues dealt with in Kuumba. "It doesn't go as deep, I feel like, as [Kuumba] tour conversations." Sei was referring to the annual, hours-long conversation about the racial—and sometimes religious—composition of the organization Kuumbabes had while away from campus during the spring break tour. Tour conversation came up repeatedly as a practice that contributed to bridging differences within Kuumba.

Conversely, Sei suggested that the dance group had more rigidly defined parameters related to Asian American identity expression.

Prior research has suggested that non-Black students of color might seek out Black student organizations as a shared response to white racism.[7] This was a motivation for Francisco, who described the predominantly white campus of his elite university as a place where "racial tensions are high," and where there had been "incidents." Like other Black and Latinx students, Francisco expressed difficulty in replicating the types of friendships he had with white and Asian American peers prior to college. Daphne and Sei, conversely, did not describe racism as explicitly motivating them. In fact, even most Black Kuumbabes said they hadn't experienced overt racism at Harvard, if they chose to bring up racism at all in our interviews. Still, Sei and Daphne were clearly responding to stereotypes and related expectations of people of color, which is a hallmark of the normatively white space. In their own leveling of stereotypes against others with whom they share a racial or cultural background, they also demonstrate that one does not need to be white to conform to the expectations of whiteness.[8]

On the one hand, these students, especially Sei and Daphne, given that Francisco did often identify as Black, were chafing against stereotyped expectations resulting from diversity discourses in elite higher education institutions that focus on (white students') learning from difference, in that difference and identity are reduced to flat facsimiles of real-life complexity. Students of color are assumed to fulfill certain diversity roles. On the other, Daphne in particular was engaging in a similar process of objectifying the Black space and culture to some extent, by using it as a means to work through her issues. Present across these three students' stories was the desire for a broader range of identity expressions to be considered authentic both within and outside of their heritage communities.

The pressures of the white space with regard to conforming to and defying racialized expectations for the students of color contrasted with the experiences of white students in Kuumba, who did not express these same feelings of tension and resistance to stereotypes and racialized expectations; in the normatively white space, white students do not have to navigate racialized belonging in the same way. In the Black space, though, white students—or at least the white women—did have to contend with racial identity in ways that proved formidable.

My Concern Being White and in Kuumba

Emily had suffered a leg injury and was on crutches, so we chose to meet in her dorm room. From the pictures on the wall and through our conversation, it was clear that Emily lived with one Asian American woman and one African American woman. This was in keeping with the intention of Harvard's Freshman

Dean's Office to maximize diversity when assigning roommates.[9] I asked Emily, who wore her below-shoulder-length, wheat-colored hair pulled into a side pony-tail away from her round face, making her appear younger than her age, how she got involved in Kuumba. She told me that her Black roommate joined the group within days of arriving at Harvard and then got her involved at the start of the spring semester. Non-Black members regularly described being brought to Kuumba in this way. Emily's roommate invited her to a concert; that experience got Emily, like so many others, hooked on the music. "That's when I got really excited, because I have a lot of energy when it comes to music. . . . So, concert started, and we got into clapping and everything. I just loved the kind of vibrancy that Kuumba had, and the energy in their songs."

Emily did not take her participation for granted. She deliberated about what it would mean for the organization for her to join. She and her roommate discussed this at length. "Well, I wasn't sure prior to Kuumba, like prior to going, if it would be okay for me as a non-Black person to be in the group and if I would be feeling like I was intruding, or not appreciating it in the right way, or something like that. . . . It still is something that I think about." She also took issue with a point Ken Reeves had made at the introductory rehearsal in the spring, which was Emily's first time attending.

> He said, like, "Oh, it's great, Kuumba is the biggest multicultural group on campus," which, I think I understand what he was trying to say. But the way that came out, I don't know if I necessarily agree, because the way I see Kuumba, it's celebrating one culture. And I'm fine with celebrating that one culture, but it's not really a multicultural thing. I think that me viewing it as not, like, trying to bring my culture in, it's a little different. Or like, me just celebrating what Kuumba's about is what Kuumba would want in a Kuumba member.

Emily didn't "worry" about her participation in Kuumba because Reeves had "okayed and celebrated the diversity of Kuumba. . . . And Sheldon has been always welcoming with people." At the same time, in recounting her misgivings about Reeves's characterization of the group, she questioned narratives about multiculturalism that might render invisible Kuumba's specific focus on being a Black space.

At the end of each interview I asked Kuumbabes if there was anything I hadn't asked about or that they wanted to mention before we wrapped up. Emily took the opportunity to return to the point about the racial composition. She was pensive. "There is one thing that I wanted to bring up, because adding to my concern as being white and in Kuumba, I don't think Kuumba would have the same impact if it were made up of a majority of people who weren't Black. So I've thought about what would happen if, all of a sudden, more and more people of different cultures started joining, because I feel like it might lose some meaning." Without knowing it, Emily was picking up on a point Sheldon made to me when I was meeting with him one-on-one one evening to discuss his leadership of the organization. In describing challenges of non-Black Kuumbabes, Sheldon remarked that the non-Black "people who should be here" in Kuumba are precisely those who have struggled and had concerns "that their presence in this organization that they love may . . . have negative effects on it." He continued to describe the seeming contradiction that because these students loved the institution—implying that they loved and understood it as a Black space—they might, themselves, consider "that maybe they should leave," in order to preserve it.

Of the three white interview participants, this was something the women, both Emily and Anna, struggled with. Paul was an outlier among the non-Black members in not deliberating about how his presence might impact this organization. Anna and Emily thought about and grappled with their whiteness as Kuumba members, not just in terms of their decision to join, but also in terms of what appropriate participation looked like.

When I asked Emily about her discomfort as a white member of Kuumba, her voice was shaky. I wondered if Emily was uncomfortable talking about her doubts to me, a Black person, but she held my gaze as she spoke. "So I'm still a little bit uneasy about being white and being in Kuumba, because I feel like we've sang 'One by One,' and things about 'the color of my skin, I will die for it.' And that's a feeling that I can appreciate and say, 'Wow, like I've never considered myself that way.'"[10] As she performed that song, Emily realized, "Suddenly I'm taking on that role." This was an issue for her. "I don't know if that's something . . . I'm comfortable doing, because it wasn't written for me to sing." I asked if the issue was that she imagined taking on the persona of a Black person, or if it sounded wrong to her to think of a white person saying they would die for their white skin. She admitted this exact question left her in a bind. "That's what— I'm not sure which one I should do," she elaborated, "I don't think that it would be appropriate for me to change the thoughts in my mind, to be singing about, like, 'Oh, my white skin, I would die for.' But then I also don't know if it's what the song was meant for, to have someone who can't relate to the feeling of dying for your dark skin. I'm not sure. So that's been somewhat of a conflict for me." Emily never came to a conclusion, but in effect embraced the ambiguity by choosing to remain in Kuumba while actively considering her place therein. Being a white participant in a Black space provided an opportunity for Emily to learn about privilege, through the process of relinquishing some of her own. Unlike on the rest of campus, where whiteness was dominant and the norm, with Kuumba, she was no longer easy in her skin, as it were.

Anna was the only non-Black Kuumbabe to mention being described by family and friends as "white" in "the Black choir." This was a characterization with which she took umbrage and disagreed. "I remember my eighteen-year-old brother came to one of my concerts . . . and I was back at home telling a high school friend about choir. I was like, 'It's a gospel choir and it's pretty diverse in terms of like racial background and people involved.' Jake was like, 'No it's not. You're one of, like, four white kids in the whole choir.' And I was like, 'That's not true. . . . I can name all these people.' . . . Even my roommates will say that too. . . . They'll make little cracks, like, 'It won't be too hard to find you, Anna, will it?'" Though Anna laughed off this exchange, it revealed some discomfort in how she navigated being that white girl in the Black choir.

For Anna, like Emily, unease with race manifested due to the songs the group performed as well as some of the readings done at concerts. In response to a question about any struggles she had in Kuumba, Anna replied, "If I'm honest, not really." But then she went on, "Um, I think like the moments of tension especially related to me being white and the emphasis on the choir being, like, Black history, Black past. That's been, like I wouldn't say overarchingly challenging, but, again, moments of tension where it's like, okay, I love being part of this, I love celebrating this, but historically it was, like, my people who were oppressing my friends and their ancestry and their history." Anna said this was an ongoing challenge for her, but in a tone that seemed meant to assure me, she added, "I don't think it's anything anyone holds against me in the choir but it's something that I, like, is definitely on my mind, definitely not the majority of the time, but there are moments where that tension comes up." In a process like Emily's, Anna appeared to be grappling with her social position and privilege, precipitated by her choice to participate in a Black space.

Anna offered up a hodgepodge of moments, from concerts to the election of board officers to the recruitment of new members, that brought the tension of being white in a Black organization to the fore of her thinking. She reluctantly ceded that as a white person, there was a fundamental difference in how she could participate in Kuumba compared to Black members. "I'm never going to be able to participate in it to the degree that my Black friends in the choir can and I think all of us who are not Black in the choir, like that's just part of the reality." She chose the winter and spring concerts as an example to illustrate the limitations of her involvement.

> There's been all this poetry [read at the concerts] that like, Black is beautiful and like, the Black man and the Black woman. And again, I'm just like, I love that there's space for that. I get that, for that to be celebrated. And again, for me to celebrate and participate in the song to let it become a part of who I am, too. But then there are—as a non-Black member, too—I think there can be moments where—[long pause]—like when we were doing elections most recently there was a lot of talk about how are we going to reach the Black community, and like, Kuumba being very segmented and um again, I don't really know the politics of that kind of scene but a lot of the conversation kept going like that, and how do we recruit from the Black community at Harvard.

It wasn't entirely clear what Anna was trying to say here, or if she even knew what she wanted to say. The uncertainty was revealing in itself, perhaps exemplifying the inner struggles Anna grappled with regarding her participation in Kuumba. When Anna referenced "the Black community" and "Kuumba being very segmented," it was clear, though, that she was referring to the conversation about racial divisions among the Black community at Harvard. This was an ongoing discussion during the time of my ethnographic fieldwork that Black Kuumbabes spoke about as transformative in their understanding of what it meant to be Black, and the non-Black members spoke about as a conversation to which they had nothing to contribute. Though most of the non-Black members spoke about their lack of contribution to this conversation matter-of-factly, Anna spoke about it as being left out.

Anna offered that while she was "so for" Kuumba's charge to be a safe space for Black students, "as a non-Black member, like wondering, where else can you draw in people not from the Black community, but outside that, who also would get so much out of this experience? . . . I'm not really in a position of power to articulate that. I mean, I could say something to someone if I wanted to and probably have a conversation and hear what the heart of all of that is. Um, but there's just like, there are rare moments, but like, certain moments when the racial piece does become like, hmm, how do I, fit in here?" I detected apprehension in the cadence of her voice and the many qualifications she made to her claims as she continued.

> Sometimes I feel like there is a disqualification, or like, Black is better sentiment. It comes out maybe in some of the readings or an occasional song. And then in that moment like, again I don't take it personally, I don't take it to heart, but it makes me, there's a very real part of me that, I don't know if I would say I get defensive necessarily, but I don't know how to handle it or approach it. And that's when I have to remind myself, okay this moment of poetry that's being spoken, emphasizing Black is beautiful, Black is better, whatever it might sound like, how many more times have my female Black friends heard the opposite of that, you know, white is better, white is beautiful?

Learning about her privilege was painful but transformative, so much so that she wanted other non-Black people "who also would get so much out of this experience" to be actively sought out by the organization. At the end of the day, Anna reconciled this tension for herself as she came to realize that teaching white students about anti-racism was not Kuumba's purpose, and that a value for the Black members was countering harmful representations and exclusion experienced outside of the organization.

Anna and Emily viscerally experienced what it meant to be a "diversifier," an experience many of their white peers would never know.[11] For both, it was an opportunity to learn about systemic racism and allowed them to see their racial privilege anew while confronting feelings of frustration and discomfort that, for their Black peers, were just a regular part of life on Harvard's campus. This was something Emily embraced and furthered by having conversations about it outside of rehearsal with her roommate who was a Black member of Kuumba. Anna expressed more inner turmoil in making what could be described as a trade-off between relinquishing some of her racial privilege for the opportunity to participate in Kuumba, which she described as being "a home" and "a family" to her.

I'M NOT BLACK

Where Anna and Emily focused on the Black-white binary in considering their roles in the organization, Sei and Daphne framed it as a matter of either being Black or not Black. Sei put it this way: "I don't think of myself as being Asian American in the group, but just not Black. . . . Being Asian American doesn't really change anything for me, I guess. It's just that I'm not Black and I don't have that same cultural experience." No one in Kuumba or at Harvard had ever questioned their participation or made cracks about it as they did with Anna, but lacking the Black cultural experience was still a source of struggle for Sei and Daphne in figuring out their place in Kuumba. And, as with Anna and Emily, it provided the foundation for learning about race.

One thing Daphne struggled with as a freshman, non-Black member was forming relationships with Black freshmen in Kuumba. "I have freshmen friends in Kuumba," she explained. "But there are definitely some freshmen who I don't know as well because they know each other from outside of Kuumba and all these other Black organizations. So that was something I didn't even think about, the fact that there would be a little bit of a divide." This didn't dampen Daphne's interest in participating in the group, as she allowed that the dynamic might change over the coming years as members got to know each other better. Even if it didn't, and Daphne was never able to form friendships with Black members who bonded through participation in multiple racially-focused organizations, she said, "Kuumba is still Kuumba for me." Daphne didn't seek out other Korean and Asian Americans in the same way as those in a group of Black freshmen she knew, who "gravitate[d]" towards each other. "I recognize that culture is very important. Even the Asian American groups here on campus, like you can tell the first week of school, all the Asian kids will go everywhere together. . . . The reason why I'm not in an Asian group like that is because I sort of wanted to avoid that kind of thing, like avoid, because I guess my natural inclination would be to pick people who I could talk to more easily."

I considered Daphne's words and thought about the extent to which her views were wrapped up in the concerns she shared about being "grouped" with other

Asian Americans based on growing up with a large number of Black and Latinx peers. While she found a "family" in Kuumba, it seemed she still felt constrained by stereotypical expectations. She described this in terms of people assuming she was overly quiet or "not too out there" when they first meet her. Even in Kuumba, she didn't feel she could fully express her personality. "If I had just decided to be really sassy or something, people would be shocked. I don't know if they would take it the right way, you know, even though, in a lot of ways, I'm way more crazy than I think I act in Kuumba." She connected this to not being Black. "I'm not sure whether this is true or not, but I feel like maybe I have to work more to get Sheldon's attention sometimes, and get him to recognize me as a person with personality, because like, I think one thing about Black students is that they have a lot of like attitude, or whatever. People say that, they just say things. And me, I didn't grow up with that kind of—you know, I grew up to, like with my mom saying, be very careful of what you say, anything you say. . . . I feel like I have to work extra hard to get people's attention, to get people to remember, like, who I am and what I stand for, things like that." Though Daphne purported to join Kuumba to flee from the bounds of racialized expectations and stereotypes, she was nonetheless imposing analogous stereotypes on Black students and, ironically, describing Black students as a monolithic group.[12]

Participating in Kuumba did provide an opportunity for Sei and Daphne, just like Anna and Emily, to learn about more systemic issues related to race and racism both in the country and on campus. Daphne admitted that "I expected to be a minority [in Kuumba], obviously. I didn't quite expect that there was so much that I wouldn't understand." This was pronounced for her when she participated in the tour conversation. In past years, the tour conversation had considered the role of non-Black members. This year the conversation was about the dynamics among Black members of different backgrounds, such as those who were born and raised in the United States and those who were from immigrant backgrounds or were international students. This was a topic that extended beyond the tour conversation and was the one Anna described as not being able to participate in as a white person.

The tour conversation, which Daphne described as "this really great discussion," illuminated for her how the meaning of "what it means to be Black in America" was ever-changing and contested. In other words, Kuumba gave Daphne the opportunity to unlearn narratives about diversity that often lump Black students together as a group in ahistorical ways that decontextualize dynamic processes of race.[13] The conversation also gave her a chance to consider intersections between race and socioeconomic status and the legacy of slavery in the United States:

There was a lot of discussion about what it means to be African American, Black, in the sense of like homegrown [descendants of enslaved Africans in

the United States], which is the first time I've heard this phrase. . . . Whereas
the incoming [immigrant] Blacks, like . . . are, I guess, Nigerians and Kenyans,
and people who seem to be higher income, just because they had the wealth
to come here. And so there's an interesting divide that I didn't quite understand. So I guess Black Americans are traditionally poorer, or I guess that's
what the demographic seems to be labeled as. So like, some of the Black Americans [participating in the discussion] thought that being poor was a part of
living the Black tradition. And then one of the Nigerian girls was like, 'Well,
I grew up in a really low-income family' . . . talking about, basically, you don't
need to be low-income to be Black . . . It was very interesting to see how income
played into [Black students' experiences].

It is notable that Daphne needed to participate in the Kuumba tour conversation to have these realizations, given her own professed refusal to group herself
together with other Asian and Korean Americans, in part also related to socioeconomic status. Also lacking in this comment is an understanding of how systemic anti-Blackness has affected wealth and socioeconomic status of Black
Americans. Nonetheless, the conversation was formative for Daphne, though,
she concluded, "It was a conversation that I couldn't participate in, which was
fine, because I liked listening to it." Here, Daphne's response to participating in
a conversation about diversity focused exclusively on Black students' experiences
contrasted with Anna's. For Anna, the topic had felt exclusive. She felt left out.
For Daphne, she felt let in—into a world and experience that would have otherwise been inaccessible to her.

Sei, who said, "I've struggled with figuring out my place in Kuumba, if I've
had one, or like, my purpose, or why I was there," similarly expressed mostly
feeling let into instead of left out of the Black space. When I asked Sei, as I asked
all interview participants, what she contributed to Kuumba, she shared, "I feel
like I couldn't represent Kuumba, so I, in that sense I can't contribute as much.
But I think just by being there, being present, I feel like, contributes, and listening to and being part of it, and not trying to distract . . . I guess what I think
I contribute is just to not be that person they're worried about, or try not to be
that person, so like, just to be there, help out when I can." Being present and just
listening sounded to me like bearing witness. When Sei said she could "not be
that person they're worried about," she was referring to not being a non-Black
member who might try to shift the focus of the organization away from its
Black focus and intent. "The mission was and it still is to create a safe space for
Black students, where they don't have to explain themselves or like, they can
share [that] they have similar shared experiences that I don't have. . . . I'm okay
with it, and I enjoy listening to what they [Black members] have to say." She jokingly added, "I've learned a lot, definitely about hair."

For Sei, it was the opportunity to learn about Kuumba's history, and its explic-
itness about the commitment to addressing the needs and interests of Black
students, that actually solidified a sense of connection within the organization.
She explained,

> Understanding where [Kuumba] comes from and what this space originally
> was for helped me be like, 'Okay, so though I'm not these things,' still being
> aware of it, is kind of weird, but I guess being aware of it made me feel more
> connected, like just understanding where I am in relation to Kuumba or what
> my role is in Kuumba. I kind of understood it as more being part of the choir
> but also, not that I wasn't part of the choir, but just being aware that where
> Kuumba came from, it wasn't necessarily created for me specifically.

In Kuumba, the rules of engagement were not secrets that people had to hope to
navigate successfully on their own. Tensions about race and the role of non-Black
members in the Black space were made explicit, making it easier for Sei to deter-
mine where she could fit in.

I Had to Say Something

Whereas Anna and Emily, the two white women who participated in interviews,
were cautious about their participation in Kuumba, freshman Paul Dixon, the
only white man to participate in an interview, had no hesitation about showing
up and getting involved. If anything, that there were other white members
already in Kuumba suggested to him that he was entitled to join. I asked all interview participants what they struggled with as members. Each had something to
say. For Anna and Emily, the struggle was the one related to what it meant to be
white in the choir as they explored their racial privilege. But Paul did not describe
struggling with his place in the organization as a white person, or really in any
capacity. His response was anomalous. "I really can't think of anything. It's been
a completely positive experience for me so far," he said, noting only after a
moment that sometimes it was challenging for the choir to get "on point" when
rehearsing a new song. He focused on a technical aspect of the group's musicality, rather than considering race or identity.

Paul took his time speaking, though it seemed he had already thought about
many of the questions I asked. He described how he ended up joining Kuumba
after being enthralled with their freshman convocation performance. "I literally
knew nothing [about Kuumba], and the only thing I could tell is that I saw some
white people in the choir. But I had a close enough seat that I could tell it was a
predominately Black organization. But for some reason, I never had any qualms
about showing up, because I knew that other people were already there, and that
it was clearly accepted in the choir." Taking up the framing of racial diversity as

an opportunity for learning about other cultures, Paul continued, "As I went to more rehearsals and [the Kuumba president] and Sheldon talked a little bit about what Kuumba was all about, it only reaffirmed why I wanted to be there, because I think Black culture . . . like listening to the music that I listen to, it's been a big inspiration for me in years before this. . . . It was great to have an opportunity to continue to pursue, and I guess learn about Black culture."

In discussing Harvard's advertising Kuumba as a multicultural organization, Paul allowed that this wasn't the purpose of the organization and in some ways was a move by the university to pander to outsiders who might see the group and say, "Oh, look at what Harvard's doing. They have a great big group, a multicultural group on campus." Yet, picking up on the point raised by Anna about wanting to recruit more non-Black members, Paul continued, saying that the multicultural composition is "something that should be advertised, even within the Harvard student body, because there are a lot of people who really don't know anything about Kuumba, and . . . they might think of it as like the Black gospel choir, and might not have had the experience that I had where I actually saw that there are non-Black members in the choir. . . . They should make people aware at Harvard that you can join Kuumba, and your background is basically irrelevant to joining Kuumba." He then tempered this proclamation. "I guess it is an oversimplification, in the sense that, like I said, the goal is not multiculturality, or multicultural awareness, or anything like that."

Prior research on elite educational contexts repeatedly names ease—being or seeming comfortable in one's skin and finding belonging, and having this comfort and belonging be or appear natural or effortless—as a key marker of privilege and of elite identity formation.[14] This same research shows how ease is raced—and to some extent gendered. The white space that was Harvard was created for affluent white men like Paul, and often continued to operate in ways that validated the experiences and proclivities typically evidenced by this group. For Paul, the ease he might have felt elsewhere on campus seamlessly transferred to the Black space of Kuumba—though his saying that if more white students knew they could join Kuumba, they might, oversimplified the dynamics, as white students overwhelmingly socialize with other white students and do not as readily associate with Black students.[15] But, ironically due to his privileged position, Paul didn't see that. He was interested in Black culture and felt "no qualms" about participating in Kuumba, so why wouldn't others?

In addition to describing the naturalness with which he became a member of Kuumba, Paul similarly described his intentions for assuming a leadership role and for using his participation in the organization as an opportunity to demonstrate and develop his expertise as a musician. One way he did this was by creating an opportunity to play bass in Kuumba. When I asked him if he had brought his passion for playing bass to the group, he responded that "immediately" after attending an initial rehearsal, "In the back of my mind I was like, 'oh man, I would love to play bass for these guys.'" There wasn't an opportunity to play bass at his first concert. But at some point, Paul recognized a song that could include a part for bass. Paul emailed the musicians' rep, a board position responsible for liaising between the choir and the Kuumband, the instrumentalists who did not regularly attend rehearsals. "I made sure I learned [the part] well, and I showed up and played it for Sheldon. He liked it. He helped me work on [it]. But, so he liked it, and I just showed up to the rest of the musicians' rehearsals." This served as an entryway into playing bass parts in other songs Kuumba performed. Overall, Paul found the process "very inclusive" and "really low key. . . . It was a very good experience."

Another way Paul intended to demonstrate and develop his expertise was by taking on a board position in the next school year. He was aware of the norm that white members would not take on certain roles. "The upperclassmen, like they've been in Kuumba for a while, and you think they might, like in a normal organization, they might not have the right, but they have the experience needed for such positions. But they all declined, because I think they felt, they shared the same sensibilities on that issue." By declined, Paul was describing how non-Black members would be nominated for board leadership roles, but would "respectfully decline" the nomination, withdrawing themselves from consideration. It was likely an unconscious slip of the tongue to position Kuumba as not a "normal organization" as Paul did here, and I didn't stop to ask him what he meant. In any event, he found a way to take on leadership that would accord with the practices in the group. "Some of the, the lower board positions . . . it's not at all unprecedented that they're not solely Black." Just as he'd said that seeing non-Black members in the choir signaled a green light to Paul to join Kuumba, he said, "I knew that there had been white members of the choir, or non-Black members of the choir, on [the] board before, so I didn't hesitate to submit a position paper" for a board role. A "position paper" was a statement about why someone was interested in and should be considered for a board role. Submitting one was basically the equivalent of running for a position. In both of these instances it was no coincidence that Paul was demonstrating authority by speaking and conveying knowledge. Previous research has shown that white men on college campuses are permitted and encouraged to do so—if only tacitly—while women of all races and men of color are foreclosed from doing so.[16]

Paul was consistently able to navigate the Black space of Kuumba with exceeding ease, often not considering his raced and gendered privilege. This was evident in his participation in the tour conversation related to the cleavages between Black students at Harvard coming from different backgrounds. Paul's inexperience with the matter did not stop him from being one of the only non-Black members to verbally share during the conversation.

Paul set the scene for me. "For ninety-nine percent of the discussion, it had only been Black kids who were raising their hands. And not everyone had to talk.

It was all on a volunteer basis, and there were some Black kids who didn't raise their hand to talk." After acknowledging that white members did not have much they might add to the conversation, Paul still felt compelled to share his voice, to ensure that the conversation did not end without a white person saying something. "I sort of felt like I had to say something, because as it got to the end, like obviously, the white kids were all sitting there still. But, none of us felt like we had much to say. It was not startling, but it was noticeable that we each felt like this was a topic that we really couldn't add anything to because it was so, so foreign from what we had gone through as a kid. But I finally decided I had a point to make." Paul decided to contribute what he could take away from having taken part in this discussion. Building on a theme raised by one of the Black members about "What do we do coming out of this?" Paul offered an action and repeated what he had said during the actual conversation: "If I met anyone who made an ignorant comment about race who wasn't Black, I could say, 'You don't know anything about what it means to be Black, and you know how I know that? It's because I have no idea what it means to be Black, and I've sat in a room with fifty or some Black people . . . and I literally couldn't add anything, because it was just so different for me, and probably because I just didn't want to make a fool of myself.'" He continued to speak to a hypothetical white person in the future about his experience in the tour conversation and said, "There was no way for me to comment on [the discussion] aside from being an outside perspective. And I could have done that, but as far as like having a Black experience, I had had none." He summed up his contribution by saying, "So I could tell other people and pass on my experience of saying, like, 'You can't assume that this is how someone else thinks, or this is how someone else has lived their entire life.'" Paul was able to find a way to assert himself as an educator for others in a situation he described as being one he really knew nothing about.[17]

In part because he had spoken up during the tour conversation, other Kuumbabes suggested I reach out to Paul, who had not initially volunteered for an interview. When they mentioned he might have a unique perspective, they always said it with a tone of respect and not one of questioning the way in which he inserted (or asserted?) himself in the conversation. Given that I wasn't there, I have no idea how Paul's participation was received in the moment, only the meaning Paul made of it, which I did ask him to tell me more about. I asked why he had felt the need to say something. Paul responded, "Because in a sense, I didn't want it to be just a Black conversation, I guess." According to Paul, after the other Kuumbabe asked, "What do we do next?" it took him "probably a good hour and a half to . . . think inside my head, 'Okay, how do I want to phrase this? What do I want to say?' I took special care to think about it in a way that would not tick anyone off on the, like would not be misinterpreted in any way." Clearly Paul understood the delicate nature of being a white person joining this conversation. He continued, "Eventually the night was winding down, and it was well past midnight at that point. And, I felt like it needed an outside comment. But not because it was an outside comment, because it was an inside comment, because it was a member of the choir. Because there were no rules that we couldn't speak, it was like everyone was welcome to speak. . . . I thought that something had to be said, I guess, from the different perspective within the choir." That there were no rules prohibiting it meant an open invitation to Paul—or even a demand—to share his views.

Given that Paul's way of showing up in the conversation could be seen as highly raced, I wanted to know more about his thought process.

SHERRY: Tell me more about that. Something had to be said?

PAUL: I mean, it was tacitly understood, like I said, for three or some hours that we [white members] didn't really have much to add. But that wasn't a resolution for me. . . . If we had talked four hours and no white person had said a thing for the whole time, I would have gone out of the room shaking my head in some sense because, though we didn't have much to add to the conversation, I think we had an important thing to add, which was that we were coming from the opposite perspective, and we could present the opposite, the counterview, I guess. I at least wanted to get that out in the open before the discussion ended.

SHERRY: And when you say counterview, the view was counter to what?

PAUL: Well, counter as in different, or just the view of someone growing up [with] like a non-Black childhood. And though it's just ignorant to say that there's a Black experience and a white experience, there are definitely differences between the two, or between someone who's grown up like me in a predominantly white suburb and someone like any other of the Black members of the choir and their experience.

Paul described the experience of the tour conversation as transformative, saying, "It gave me the opportunity to consider things that really hadn't crossed my mind for eighteen years of my life, and to listen to stories of most of the members of the choir and say, like I've never experienced any of that . . . like how pop culture views the color of my skin or anything along those lines. . . . It's just so startling for me to think, like that's never once crossed my mind, and here's all these people saying that's been a defining experience for their life." Paul concluded talking about the tour conversation by saying, "It was the single most defining experience of my freshman year so far."

Paul was a first-year student when we spoke. It is possible that his view shifted after spending more time in the organization (as senior Leela Johnson said, for example, had happened to her in chapter 3). But this was the type of view of Black space that reinforced Kuumba's stance, explicitly discussing race and placing parameters on the participation of non-Black members. Paul, for example, who professed his love and appreciation for Black cultural expressions and for Kuumba as committed to being a safe space for Black students, saw anything, in terms of his participation, as fair game unless it was stated otherwise. Paul demonstrated how easy it could be for whiteness to encroach on the Black space and how oblivious some white students could be about the affordances of their racial privilege.

———

Kuumba as an organization was welcoming, if not to some extent indifferent, about having members of non-Black backgrounds, so long as those members could adjust to a space in which Black interests were the priority. This was a point Sheldon made as we talked one evening. He said, "I never think that there are too many other people," referring to the non-Black students. However, he went on, "We don't let [the acceptance of non-Black members] undermine the reality of who we are." To that point, he recalled a recent performance that was, in his words, "pro-Black," in which "if I was a white person in that audience, I might just be really uncomfortable. I'd be really scared." None of the white members whose voices appear on these pages were ever scared, but Anna and Emily did experience discomfort at various times as white people in the Black space. To this Sheldon would respond, "You are welcome, but know that you are being welcomed into a Black organization and what that means. . . . We can all struggle together."

The specific struggles these students negotiated reveal the workings of whiteness on campus that can influence how non-Black students end up participating in the Black space. In Paul's case there was no struggle, demonstrating the ways in which white men at elite universities are the beneficiaries of an expansive sense of ease and belonging. For Anna, Emily, Sei, and Daphne, one set of struggles included navigating their role as non-Black members of Kuumba. At times, this resulted in feeling left out and at others, feeling let in, let in on conversations about Black members' experiences they otherwise would have no access to. This represents the type of learning from "diversity" that university officials idealize. But the way in which this learning transpired in Kuumba was deeper.

Research in other predominantly white educational institutions has shown that those considered to be providing diversity—namely, Black and Latinx students as well as those of Indigenous and Asian descent—often modulate their self-presentation to fit in with or conform to unspoken expectations from the dominant culture, in this case, the culture of middle-class white students, precluding genuine learning across difference that could lead to the kind of transformation the students in this chapter experienced.[18] Yet for transformation to be possible, non-Black students in Kuumba needed to "respect" the group's mission and music, and the history and traditions that the group was built on, so much so that they did not take their welcome for granted, and indeed questioned their place in the group. For example, instead of simply watching a performance of a group mentally marked as "other," these students had the opportunity to explore issues of power relations and systemic inequality through their participation in Kuumba.[19] Further, the struggles with finding belonging in their own cultural communities that informed Francisco's, Sei's, and Daphne's decisions to join a Black student organization show how the "racialized perceptions of diversity" in predominantly white higher education pigeonholed students of color in ways that limited possibilities for them to form community.[20]

These are two sides of the same coin. The white space of the elite institution structured power relationships on campus that limited the opportunities for genuine connection across racial backgrounds. This was a structure that rewarded white students with ease and belonging, and put students of color into boxes that didn't always fit.

Chorus

LEARNING TO CARE

"Kuumba is really a come-as-you-are space. Come as you are. We'll accept you. We will genuinely care about you." —Lauren Washington, Senior

I met with Jamison Mthembu, who had held various leadership positions in Kuumba, in my windowless basement office. I offered to meet him in a more welcoming, albeit more public space, which he declined, favoring the privacy of the drab office instead. Always urbane and nonchalant, Jamison showed up wearing a crimson hooded Harvard sweatshirt, tan skinny jeans a few shades lighter than his complexion, and footwear reminiscent of boat shoes, which were popular at the time. Seated across from me at my desk—unnecessarily large, given the Lilliputian room—Jamison spoke rapidly and passionately about the community-building aspect of Kuumba. Though Jamison and I were sitting alone in my office, he was speaking as if to implore an audience of his peers. As an outgoing leader of the organization, Jamison was telling me about his message for new Kuumba board members who would pick up the mantle of the organization and to whom Jamison would be "passing on the torch" when he and his classmates graduated in a few short days. Community was embedded into the structure of the group, so much so that Jamison said, "Every board member has to understand [Kuumba's commitment to community] at some level. . . . And [that's] not to say we can't have conversation about what it means to be a community, and how we can encourage community, and how we can create it. But we have to work from the understanding that this is what we are committed to doing."

Jamison was emphatic and repeated his message. "When it comes to decision-making in the choir, we prioritize our community and our family over pretty much anything that we do." In referring to "our family," he was invoking the metaphor of Kuumba that was unanimously embraced by members and alumni. As discussed in prior chapters, Kuumbabes often used "family" interchangeably with "community," likely owing to practices of fictive kinship that are common across Black communities.[1] In this way, the connections among Kuumba members suggested something more powerful and enduring than what community might imply. For Jamison, valuing community in Kuumba and conceiving of the organization as a family was not just a feel-good gesture; he saw it as part of exposing the social order at Harvard and responding to it.

With fervor in his voice, he made his position clear. "We're a very open space, and very flexible in a lot of things. But there are some things that we're just not willing to negotiate, and community is really one of those things. And it's important to understand that we are, in a way, a political movement at Harvard." In his rapid-fire, somewhat high-pitched tenor voice, Jamison continued explaining how the founding of the organization and the emphasis on community made Kuumba a "political movement." He proceeded, "We were formed as a response to the sociopolitical—and racial, obviously—[events that were] happening at Harvard at the time. And it not only affected Harvard, but the greater Cambridge and Boston community. . . . That's how Kuumba came to be formed. And because of the principles premising our formation, we really value community beyond anything else." To Jamison, Kuumba's community-focused political work continued into the present. "It has to do with, one, mediating relationships between the different Black student organizations, but two, helping to raise the level of Black consciousness within the choir, within the Black community." Thus, coming together as a safe space for Black students in the 1970s was overtly political, but the maintenance of such a community on Harvard's campus remained an act of resistance for Kuumba, against the forces of alienation—worsened by divisions among Black students for a variety of reasons, and competing pressures on students' time—and, I inferred, subtle forces of racism that might hold Black students back from realizing their full potential on campus.

Community, therefore, was a sustaining force. It mattered more to the organization than even the group's musical excellence. Nearly everyone on campus, both in the group and otherwise, acknowledged that Kuumba's musicality was something special. But for the group, that skill, and the resulting accolades, were not enough. Rather, the organization prioritized building community and engendering a sense of connection among members. But what exactly did community mean in the Kuumba context, and what did that meaning reveal about the safe Black space? Jamison explained, "This community helps you with your mental health, your happiness, your discipline, because, as musicians, we also have to demonstrate and participate on a certain level of discipline with music. And I think you're able to kind of translate that kind of discipline into your academic discipline as well. . . . It makes Harvard easier [laughs] to deal with, right?" In listening to Jamison's descriptions of the Kuumba community, the predominant role of care became apparent. In describing the intense focus on community that was grounded in taking care of members' mental health, supporting them in meeting the rigorous demands of the choir and of being a Harvard student, focusing on their capacities—as opposed to limitations—and affirming their Blackness in this white space, Kummba was enacting "culturally relevant care."[2]

This type of race-conscious, community-centric care has a long tradition in Black activism and community organizing that has held care—for the self, for other members of the community, and for the community itself—as a centerpiece.[3] Care in these contexts is political in the ways Jamison detailed, serving a necessary function in helping build and sustain the relationships required to persist in confronting racism and in working for social justice.[4] The current resurgence in Black communal and self-care messages proliferating on social media and in popular discourse in response to Black Lives Matter protests, the 2016 and 2020 U.S. presidential elections, and the racial disparities experienced during the COVID-19 pandemic are reminders and reiterations of the importance of care in the fight against oppression.

Current messages about care in Black communities stress that becoming increasingly conscious of oppression and working to combat injustice can take a psychic toll, which can be harmful to one's health and well-being, in turn rendering it impossible to continue striving for racial justice.[5] For Black women, who comprised the majority of the Kuumba membership, communal and self-care were further imbued with political possibilities as Black women have historically been responsible for the care of others, including white families.[6] Many take inspiration from Audre Lorde's words, "Caring for myself is not self-indulgence, it is self-preservation, and that is an act of political warfare."[7] Lorde's words suggest that survival and thriving in a racist, sexist, and heterosexist society that was not set up for the survival of Black people—most especially Black and queer women—requires self-care and, therefore, self-care in and of itself is an important action in the work of social transformation.

That said, learning to care for oneself and the community was not necessarily second nature to Kuumbabes. The leadership, Jamison told me, took intentional effort to foster practices of care. As a board member, he said,

> You will learn how to create community. . . . Community happens in Kuumba, but it's oftentimes deliberate. There are a lot of structured things that might not necessarily be visible all the time that force community to happen in Kuumba. Because you are sitting in a room three hours at a time, listening to one person and learning music . . . —You don't necessarily get opportunity to actually interact with people as much. And so there are a lot of structured things in there that the administration is responsible for initiating . . . and making sure that a certain level of community is always happening in the choir.

The "deliberate[ness]" Jamison named was apparent in my research to the extent that I would describe it as Kuumba's "curriculum of care." From a sociological perspective, all institutions have a curriculum or educative element that they teach purposefully and systematically, if implicitly at times, with the goal of transmitting knowledge, skills, ways of being, and values.[8] In Kuumba, while the overall curriculum could be considered to focus on Black thriving and uplift, central to this was a culturally-grounded, community-focused ethic and practice of care. Care was the glue that held together the safe Black space.

Just as the song's chorus is sung again and again, so too the notions of community-grounded and culturally responsive care were emphasized again and again to members. Kuumbabes and their professional director, Sheldon, repeatedly emphasized the centrality of care in speaking with me, and I saw it enacted over and over in my observations. This is the "through line" of belonging to Kuumba, the part of the song that gets stuck in your head, the part of the group that stays with you long after the individual lyrics are forgotten. In this chorus chapter, then, I explore what care meant and felt like to students, why they saw it as necessary, and the ways this was enacted in the organization and among members.

As I reveal the organization's curriculum of care, the practices I share might at first seem quotidian or unremarkable. However, I interweave those with students' descriptions, contrasting Kuumba's curriculum of care with what might be characterized as Harvard's curriculum of competition and isolating individualism. This was Harvard, after all, and no matter the increasing efforts of administrators, it was not uncommon for students to feel as though everything was a competition and that in order to fit in they had to act in a certain way by focusing on how much work they had and by presenting the appearance that everything was always fine.[9] Students had to actively learn to confront this in Kuumba in order to build the type of caring community the group sought to build.

I Just Wanted to Welcome You

The hum of gospel music mingled with laughter and the chatter of voices as I stepped off the elevator and into the SOCH penthouse. Groups of students—the returning Kuumbabes—circulated to introduce themselves to unfamiliar faces. Some students were seated and appeared to be engaged in deep discussion, while others were clearly making their way around the room in attempts to meet as many new members as possible, pausing long enough in each encounter to make it feel meaningful. This was one of the first fall rehearsals. While I had attended a couple of times the previous spring to meet the group and introduce my project, now that I would be attending rehearsals regularly I had no idea where I was supposed to sit, or who I was and wasn't supposed to talk to. In an effort to be inconspicuous, I decided on a seat in the middle section, which I soon discovered was reserved for basses and tenors. I sat behind a serenely smiling man who seemed happy to be silent.

After a moment he turned around and introduced himself. The warmth of Emmanuel's ecru complexion and reddish-brown, loosely coiled hair was undiminished by the harsh overhead lighting. As we talked about his post-graduation plans, two women—one whose features matched Emmanuel's and another whose wavy, brunette hair contrasted with her pale complexion, who I later learned was Jewish—approached us. A minute later a third woman, whose name and deep mahogany skin suggested an African diasporic heritage, also joined our conversation. They each wanted to welcome me to Kuumba and find out more about who I was. I wasn't certain whether I stood out because as active group members they had a good sense of the choir membership and knew they hadn't met me before, or whether their curiosity was piqued because, being in my thirties, I didn't exactly look like a Harvard undergraduate—though there were a small number of graduate students and older community members in the choir. It may have been both and, in either case as I would learn, welcoming newcomers was part and parcel of what returning group members did, especially at the first few rehearsals each semester.

Now that I was officially starting my research, I wanted to be transparent about my intentions with everyone. I told this small group about my project; they seemed interested that I would want to do this research with Kuumba. Then I told them that I wasn't going to sing, about how I never sing in public, and how it all goes back to the trauma of being relegated to the role of "band manager" in fifth grade. My friends, Janelle and Erin, wanted to play rock star. They got to perform Natalie Cole's "Pink Cadillac" on the make-believe stage in my living room, while I listened and pretended to set up additional gigs for them. The gathered Kuumbabes laughed, but they also assured me that Kuumba was a "no-tryout group," meaning there were other voices lurking that weren't going to be Grammy Award contenders anytime soon—and that these voices were equally accepted. They also said that I might find I was so moved that I'd just have to join in. Or, they said, I could always sing along quietly to myself. Their words were gracious and sincere, and across my years conducting research, I would come to hear over and over again how Kuumba was a no-audition choir and everyone was welcome. Unconditional acceptance and welcome was a key feature of the group's curriculum of care.

Anyone who showed up to a rehearsal was given some music and expected to sing, or at least to fake it. Unlike other activities at Harvard, particularly the other musical groups, where students competed for limited and particular roles, in Kuumba there were no tryouts. In contrast, those groups referred to in campus literature as "The Harvard Choruses," which included the Harvard-Radcliffe Collegium Musicum, Radcliffe Choral Society, Harvard-Radcliffe Chorus, and the prominent and historical Harvard Glee Club—which rejected W.E.B. Du Bois when he was a student—required some combination of initial auditions, callbacks, and preliminary acceptance, or alternatively, the "Skills for Singing" class for those who were not accepted but wanted to try again.[10]

The barriers to inclusion present elsewhere on campus were actively eliminated in Kuumba. Everyone who showed up was actively welcomed, just like I was by Emmanuel and those other Kuumbabes who sought to make me feel included at that early fall rehearsal. Francisco Diaz, the senior from a nearby highly selective university, said being welcomed by group members was especially important to him given that he wasn't even a Harvard undergrad.

Francisco, like other students, remembered the specific person who greeted him and made him feel cared for. He described this encounter. "I remember Katherine Parker coming up to me and being like, 'Hey, you know, I just wanted to welcome you.' And I thought that was weird at first, but then realized that that's kind of just the norm and the standard for the group." When I asked why he found this to be weird, Francisco told me it was because coming from a big city, and being at his big university campus, "I'm not especially used to people being that friendly. And people at [my university] are very friendly. But like, my freshman year all the going up to people and saying, 'how are you doing,' meeting people for the first time, after the first week it seems very artificial." Francisco implicitly differentiated between perceived "artificial" acts of care that were the norm at his university and the sense of authentic care he felt in Kuumba, a distinction that has also been made in secondary school studies, which describe authentic care as situated in an awareness of racism, classism, and sexism in U.S. society.[11] Francisco was used to living his life as though detached from others. But, in the moment that he was greeted in Kuumba, he realized the organization was different. "The way she kind of greeted me and really welcomed me into the group without knowing who I was at all, anything about my background, I just thought that was kind of incredible. And it seems like a small gesture, but I think it really went a long way in helping me realize that Kuumba is truly family."

Small gestures of welcome formed the foundation for the caring connections that seemed abundant among and between the students in Kuumba. Francisco described another way that, at an organizational level, Kuumba embedded these practices that engendered a sense of family and care among members. "As uncomfortable as people may be with the idea, [Sheldon will say], 'Go ahead and meet somebody you haven't met' during a break." Francisco admitted that "now as somebody who's been in the group for a while, I'll go and talk to Kerry Gaspard, for example, who I go to school with." But Sheldon didn't just make this suggestion; he demonstrated the seriousness of the task by following up, making sure Kuumbabes actually did make new connections. Francisco described how on several different occasions Sheldon noticed that he was talking to people he already knew, and would "come over and be like, 'Ehh, that's not somebody new.' He's very serious, very passionate about, like, really welcoming everybody in the group."

A vignette from one rehearsal near the beginning of the school year affirmed Francisco's experience and illustrated how intentional Kuumba was in welcoming new members and building connections across choir members. On this evening, the informal chatting that opened every rehearsal had ceased and the official part of rehearsal was beginning. One of the board officers offered a reminder that the new member dinner would take place the next Tuesday prior to rehearsal at one of the dorms close to the rehearsal space where Kuumbabes regularly gathered informally for dinner before practice. A returning member raised his hand and asked, "Can old members come, too?" The board member responded, "Yes, you're going to be the ones to greet the new members." The choir laughed. The question was likely a plant, a theatrical way to remind returning Kuumbabes of their responsibility for making new members feel part of the group.

Sheldon then took the lead. He started the music section of rehearsal, as he always did, by reminding the choir to "leave the day behind you and make sure that our time together is productive. . . . Close your eyes and take a moment— you can meditate, you can pray—to remember why we're here." After a few moments before beginning the first song he asked, "Do you know the person sitting beside you? And the person behind you?" Choir members began introducing themselves to each other. Sheldon let this go on for several minutes. After going through a couple of rounds of singing, he told the choir to "Listen to each other. We have to work together. . . . tell your neighbor if they drop an octave." He also reminded choir members how they might approach a song. "How we look at things is very much a function of where we stand." Actions such as these fostered a sense of belonging among choir members by suggesting that they were or would be known in the group, that their presence and perspective mattered, and that they had to work as a cohesive group to function as a choir.

This emphasis on Kuumbabes meeting and forming relationships with one another had the intended impact of building Kuumba as an organization that was oriented towards the collective. Students came in as individuals, but developed a strong sense of group identity and commitment. Both the individual members and the organization as a whole benefited from the commitment students felt to the organization because they felt cared for and cared about by Kuumba.

WE ACCEPT YOU AS YOU ARE

Accepting members for who they were—closely related to welcoming all—was another important aspect of Kuumba's curriculum of care that kept students coming back, gave them space to explore their identities and interests, and countered feelings of alienation they might encounter elsewhere on campus— especially Black students. This was something Jason Thomas, the Black freshman who described difficulty connecting with peers of any race outside of Kuumba during his first year at Harvard, spoke with me about. When I first met Jason, we were sitting next to each other at rehearsal, this time in the SOCH Cinema, a basement theater with stadium seating. Kuumba usually rehearsed in the penthouse but moved to the basement whenever the penthouse was already booked for another event, an example of what Sheldon described as the organization "being pushed around." I sat down next to Jason, who sang bass, because he was someone I hadn't gotten to talk to yet. After introducing ourselves, I apologized in advance for my excruciating singing. Jason assured me that he had never sung before that semester, which became clear as the rehearsal progressed; Jason and I were on par with our lack of vocal skills. Curious, then, I asked what had brought him to Kuumba. He was sincere, frank, and to the point: "I wanted to meet people." Kummba was the one place where he felt like he belonged.

Later in the school year when I met Jason for a one-on-one interview, I asked him to say more about how Kuumba made him feel so welcome when he had felt so unwelcome elsewhere on campus. Jason hearkened back to that first conversation he and I had in the SOCH Cinema. "First of all, they're a singing group, but you don't have to show off, and prove that you can sing to be part of the group. So that right there is just a big, flashing neon sign that says, 'Join, join! Be a part of us!' And once you're in, you're in. No one really tells you to leave." Shortly after joining the group, he "learned the importance of the group in terms of the political atmosphere here at Harvard, and why it was a safe space, for Black students especially," which "really resonated" with him. For Jason, Kuumba was a place "Black students . . . can come and just be accepted," which was important in the "political atmosphere" of Harvard where Black students, according to Jason, had few other opportunities to make connections, even among other Black students.

The caring community of Kuumba also allowed Jason to explore his interests in ways he might never have anticipated in terms of developing his skill and confidence with singing. Though he joined Kuumba for the social aspect, lacking choir experience, by his junior year, Jason had developed his abilities and was singing solos and performing with a small, breakout male a cappella group within the choir known as "the Brothers." The Brothers wasn't something that happened every semester, but just, it seemed, when there was enough interest in putting in the extra rehearsal time to prepare additional songs.

African American senior Lauren Washington connected the group's stance of welcoming and accepting all members as they were with a sense of being cared for.

> When you're in particular groups you feel like you have to behave a certain way. But I feel like Kuumba is really a come as you are space. And we'll accept you as you are. So, whether you're a freshman, whether you're Nancy and in your sixties, whether you're Black, white, Asian, it doesn't matter.[12] The point is that . . . we accept you as you are. I think that it's really a different type of

organization because there are no requirements of us. They accept us as we are and they use what we have to do whatever we can. So, whether you can't sing, and you can dance, you can praise dance. If you can't sing, but you have a little bit of rhythm, we let you move [laughs]. . . . Kuumba has really been the only space on campus that I've experienced that really has that. Come as you are. We'll accept you. We will genuinely care about you.

While care and acceptance need not be synonymous, in Kuumba they went hand in hand. And, as both Lauren and Jason described, care and acceptance provided a foundation from which students could grow, personally, in skill, and myriad other ways.

Intertwining unconditional acceptance and care in the way Kuumba demonstrated it has roots in African American ethics of care, in which countering alienation is one aspect of care for the individual.[13] It is also grounded in Black Ivy League's students' historical resistance to being excluded from other white student organizations and campus life, resulting in Black students of past decades creating their own parallel organizations, so that they might create their own spaces in which to belong.[14] It was this overlapping sense of being unconditionally accepted and taken care of that most consistently defined members' perceptions of the organization and also separated Kuumba from the larger campus culture—that is, distinguished the safe Black space from the white space.

Circling Up

"Okay, circle up," Sheldon said, stopping rehearsal. It was near the end of the very first rehearsal I attended; I was there to present my research project. Everyone immediately began moving into one huge circle around the perimeter of the SOCH penthouse, each taking the hands of those on either side. Given that this was my very first rehearsal and I hadn't even introduced myself to the membership at large yet, just to Sheldon and the president and vice president, I thought I could stay seated, observing from my detached "researcher" position. But that was not an option. I, too, was swept into the circle—at least that was what it felt like— awkwardly mirroring what everyone else seemingly knew to do without being told. I took hold of the hands of two students I had not yet been introduced to.

We all focused on the center of the circle. At once, the circle became a point of connection, since we held hands in an unbroken chain; and a moment of exposure, as there was nowhere to hide—everyone could see and be seen in the circle. I would only realize later that this was the point. To build the kind of community that Kuumba intended, one that countered feelings of alienation on campus, required that each member learned to connect and care for others while also making oneself open to the group. I quickly learned that this was how every Kuumba rehearsal concluded—by "circling up" into a "praise and prayer circle."

But that first evening, I was taken aback. After we had all brought our attention to the center of the circle, we spent a moment in silence, staring at the people across from us. The group's president broke the silence by introducing me as a guest "who will be with us for a lot of next year." Wanting to prove I belonged—I had not yet learned that in Kuumba I had nothing to prove—I started by sharing that I was a residential advisor at Adams House. I got some "Adams!" responses. Then I said I was at the Graduate School of Education. Again, "Ed School!" Beginning to feel more and more enfolded in this community and moment, I responded, "All right, teachers!" I then told them I study culture, race, class, and gender, and some responded, "Okay, race." I finished by saying I was studying undergraduate performing arts groups with a cultural focus but members of diverse backgrounds. Some said, "That sounds like Kuumba."

After my brief introduction, the president asked for "praises" and "prayers," calling on several volunteers to share. Beginning with praises, a few remarked that their family members were coming to the big concert scheduled for that Saturday. The final sharing was a prayer request from a Black male student who said there was a murder-suicide where he was from and someone died of septic shock. He asked the group to pray for the family. This was not the kind of thing I was accustomed to hearing Harvard students talk about. At this point, students were likely tired after the three-hour rehearsal. But no one rushed the prayer request, which would be sent out by email on one of the group's lists so that individual Kuumbabes could then pray on their own or with others as they wished.

Gradually, the circle grew quiet, and the president asked for someone to lead the closing prayer. A Black woman whose picture I recognized as being included among the "Kuumba legacies"—one of her parents had been a Kuumbabe while at Harvard—volunteered. She began by asking us to bow our heads and thank the Lord for this "multicultural, multigenerational" space. I wondered whether she included this for my benefit. Her words were extemporaneous as she wove together thanks for the praises that had been offered that evening and reinforcement of the prayer requests that had been made, consistently self-assured as she spoke. We concluded in unison, "Amen."

The praise and prayer circle was another important component of Kuumba's curriculum of care that was grounded in African American ethics of care with roots in Black church traditions across the United States and West Africa.[15] However, Kuumba was not a Christian fellowship or organization. The circle and the larger curriculum of care nevertheless contributed to the sense of belonging that students across backgrounds of diverse race, ethnicity, national origin, religion, and social class experienced in the group. The lessons communicated through the circle included bearing witness to others' challenges and making oneself vulnerable to sharing in kind. But being vulnerable with peers was not automatically intuitive to Harvard students, even those drawn to an organization like this one. Instead, students learned through Kuumba.

Sophomore Bryanna Norman was one Kuumbabe who demonstrated how students learned to be in community and offer care during closing circles. In one instance Bryanna shared prayer requests for her family, including for her mother, who was caring for her terminally ill father. On a subsequent night, she was one of the first students to share a praise. "I am just grateful to be here with you and to have gotten this far in the semester." Bryanna had been able to stay at Harvard and continue to do her schoolwork because she was being bolstered by the support of her Kuumba family. She was explicit about how participating in the circle had been part of this experience for her:

> You get to a place where . . . when you're in such a community that you want to praise someone, you want to pray for them, like you see them as a part of the community. You actually start seeing yourself as a part of a group. And even if someone really outshines others . . . it's not so much about outshining you, it's like, they're a part of our group. They're an asset. There's something that's beautiful there that people can admire. That's just kind of a group dynamic that you feel eventually. You don't feel it all the time, like you don't feel joy all the time, but it's there, and you know it's there, and it's worth preserving and fighting for, and just making sure it's there for someone else.

Other students were similarly buoyed by the Kuumba family. Even Kuumbabes and alumni far away called on the choir for support. The president made a prayer request for one such alum. He explained that the alum's "father lost his job. Luckily [the alum] can support her family with her job." He asked us to keep the family in our prayers so that the father might soon find work.

But how did Kuumbabes get to this point where they were willing to share what I considered to be such personal details about their lives? This was something sophomore Claire Senai and I talked about. In response to my question about how her expectations about joining Kuumba differed from what actually happened when she showed up, Claire told me about what initially drew her to the group. She began, "It's really common for most people, because like they see Kuumba sing at something and Kuumba sounds really good, always. So, they're like, 'Oh, I just really want to be in that choir. And there are no auditions. Like, I'm gonna go do that!'" We both laughed as Claire continued, "I just primarily thought I was joining a choir and now when I talk about Kuumba, the music is usually not the thing that I talk about first. . . . I'd say, yeah, the music is not the most valuable part of Kuumba for me. It's been really good for the community and having a space where I feel very safe." Claire was raising the same points I had come to hear from Kuumbabes of all different backgrounds.

For Claire, the way this community and feeling of safety were engendered was "really hard to explain" and "not tangible," almost ineffable. But I could see its roots in how Claire spoke about coming to share in the closing circle. Perhaps speaking about Bryanna, Claire recounted a moment that opened her to the possibility of sharing in the circle.

> CLAIRE: From the beginning, you know, when you join the group people are telling you, "This is a safe space. You can always feel safe here." And, at the beginning, it's like, yeah, okay, that's cool. You can feel safe here. But, then, when you circle up for the first time after practice and someone just says to a group of one hundred people, "My father is in the hospital dying," you're like, whoa, you just said that to one hundred people. And you probably don't know a lot of their names. . . . That was a really crazy thing for me. And for the first semester of Kuumba . . . during circle, the prayer time, I was like, this is kind of weird that everyone just says these things because I don't talk about my issues with people. [We both laugh.] I'm not exactly an open book.
>
> SHERRY: Have you ended up sharing anything?
>
> CLAIRE: I have shared stuff, which is why [laughs quickly]—it's like, everyone just ends up becoming comfortable with it, because you see so many people doing it. And, you see the people—it's not like people just spit it out and that's it. People actually seem to care. And, you know, someone sends out a prayer request list over the email list after group practice. She takes notes. And I've seen people who don't know each other approach each other after practice to say, like, "Oh if you want to talk about it, I'm here," and whatever. I don't know why that is, really [laughs]. . . . Maybe Kuumba only attracts really nice people [laughs].

Claire was not the only student to comment that Kuumba must attract "nice" people, given how willing students were to share with one another and support each other. But I didn't believe that Kuumba necessarily attracted students who were naturally predisposed to being kinder than their peers; I believed that the group's curriculum of care brought this out in members. Through repeated participation in circle and witnessing their peers' reactions to sharing, students learned to disclose both triumphs and hardships and they learned how to support others. They heard collective calls for praises and prayers and stood strong for each other. This struck me as an example of what some scholars have described as "acts of reciprocal love" that are part of culturally relevant care, or what others have called "love as a form of resistance," important in Black communities for seeking to (re)unite and (re)humanize members, and it was an indispensable feature of the community Kuumba sought to foster.[16]

HOW ARE YOU *REALLY* DOING?

Beyond the circle, there were other lessons on learning to care. Sophomore Daphne Han provided an example that explicitly recognized this was a curriculum in the choir. In discussing the benefits of being a member in Kuumba, she said she had come to understand "how to take care of people. You learn on tour to ask people, like, 'Are you all right?' Or like, if your week is going badly, 'What's going on? What's up?'" I asked Daphne how she learned to do that, since asking someone how they're doing did not sound particularly revolutionary. She answered, "Well, you recognize that there's a difference in just asking someone, 'How are you doing?,' letting them say, 'Oh, it's been a rough week, I've had a lot of stuff due,' and just being like, 'Oh, me too,' and then going away. You take the time to sit down and be like, 'Well, what kinds of things? What classes?'"

Lauren also discussed the importance of asking, "How are you really doing?" Adding to what Daphne said, Lauren explained that it was expected that even outside of rehearsal, just walking across campus, Kuumbabes who passed one another would stop and take time to speak to each other. When people failed to share more than a shallow response, Lauren said, "People will really call you out." What's more, though chatting with an acquaintance as you cross campus might seem like a natural thing to do, Kuumbabes, and Harvard students more generally, complained that people walking by each other deliberately looked away so as to avoid eye contact. That was considered dehumanizing, and antithetical to Kuumba's curriculum of care.

The idea of genuinely asking, and responding, to that most generic of questions— "How are you?"—came up repeatedly in Kuumba. "How are you doing? No, how are you really doing?" were questions that exemplified to Kuumbabes learning to care and learning to transcend the competitive and alienating Harvard environment. Senior Angie Martin offered, "We don't have a lot of spaces to get real with people. Outside of Kuumba, I wouldn't have known that so many people had parents passing away, or that they were sick themselves or going through this or going through that, because we don't talk about that on Harvard's campus. So that's a really important aspect for me." By invoking the idea of "get[ting] real" Angie implied that the norm on campus was to be "fake" or present oneself as always polished. At Harvard, "You're supposed to be strong. You're supposed to handle things on your own." But she saw this as problematic. "You're away from your family, and that's not healthy. And a lot of people, they have never had to do that [deal with crises on their own] before." Angie admitted that she herself had sometimes taken this route. "I've been through quite a bit growing up. So yeah, I'll smile and move on, which, again, is not healthy." But she appreciated that, when she decided she wanted to have the support of others while she was hundreds of miles from home, she had her family at Kuumba: "If you feel like you have to go through life at Harvard alone, I can imagine that must feel absolutely terrible. So, reaching out to people like that, I think, is important in Kuumba."

Clearly Kuumba was a place where students felt they could let their guard down and let others in and this was important to them, but why weren't those conversations happening elsewhere on campus? Angie put it bluntly. "Because we're Harvard kids. You don't talk about your business like that. You keep it very, very, *very* superficial." Not only did Angie characterize the typical Harvard interaction as shallow in terms of students opening up to one another, but she suggested this was tied to competitiveness and perhaps even the ideology of meritocracy, which implied that students should be working constantly.[17] She demonstrated this by mimicking a standard conversation between two students. She began, "How are you?" Then provided a standard, albeit exaggerated, response, "Oh, I've got so much work to do. I'm really, really tired and behind, you know, like I have three finals next week and like five papers, and, you know, gotta cure cancer and all this kind of stuff. It's so intense, I actually haven't slept in the past four days." She said the student who posed the initial question would then respond, "Oh, me, too. I got like six finals next week, and you know, twenty papers, and I'm so tired. I haven't slept in a month." In this imagined conversation, the students one-upped each other in terms of who had more work to do and who was more tired. This was what Angie and other Kuumbabes referred to as the "Harvard response."

In Kuumba, the Harvard response was actively challenged. Angie clarified, "As opposed to, 'Hi, how are you doing?' it's 'Don't give me that Harvard response. How are you really doing? What's up? How's your family? How are you feeling? How's your relationship? What's going on?'" Recalling an undergraduate peer not in Kuumba who took his own life earlier in the school year, Angie lamented in a tone that sounded more contemplative than sorrowful,

> We don't really have those conversations [more broadly on campus], and thinking about what happened with [that student] . . . it bothered me, cause I know, [as if talking to the student] I've had dinner with you at least once, but for the life of me, I could not remember your name. And I know for some reason you stuck out to me. I remember seeing your face around the [residential college] House a lot. . . . And it killed me though, I'm like, why didn't I ever stop to really get to know how you were feeling or what was going on?

While choir members loved the familial aspect and focus on care in Kuumba, learning to care, disclose one's feelings, and make oneself vulnerable was hard. Sheldon's observation—"How we look at things is very much a function of where we stand"—seemed to guide many interactions; students worked to understand others' perspectives. This necessarily meant engaging in difficult conversations. Students like senior Anna Reid were willing to admit, "We get up in each other's business," meaning that students checked one another on their attitude and behavior or for not dressing appropriately for a performance. But, for Kuumbabes, this was part of being "real" and was an essential part of what it meant to be a family. Anna, laughing, explained, "People have called me out on being ridiculous. Like, I just get in a mood at rehearsals, especially if I'm tired. Or if I'm working on a paper, someone will look over and be like, 'Is that what you're supposed to be doing?'" Elsewhere on campus where appearance was paramount, such critiques or being caught not on task might seem like judgmental indictments. In Kuumba, it was seen as looking out for one another and looking out for the collective. This was how Anna saw it. "But I play that role [checking in on others] in my family, too."

The idea that it was necessary to "be real" with each other in Kuumba, and that doing so made Kuumba a unique, family-like community at Harvard, was something sophomore Takiya Moore also brought up. She described the feeling among Kuumba members as "an intense, platonic love." And, because of that "love," Takiya said people could be vulnerable and honest with each other. "People bicker and fight and stuff like that, but it's like, too, it's like there's a sense of care. So people are straight up. They will be honest with you. They'll check up on you . . . people are there for you and they have your back. You have the support of a family, basically, is the best way I can put it. It's like there's a support that's analogous to a family." Whereas some might see congenial relationships that were free of tension and challenge as being most desirable, Kuumbabes showed that caring was actually equated with being able to challenge one another. Thus, moments both big and small—from sharing the death of a loved one in circle, to learning how to ask and answer the question of "how are you doing" in a thoughtful, sincere way—formed Kuumba's curriculum of care. While members themselves were actively involved in imparting these lessons, they often took their lead from Sheldon.

They Have to Love Where They Are

"*In the valley. In the valley. Out of the valley. Out of the valley. Amen, amen, amen.*" Each "amen" was drawn out soulfully, and the richness of the choir members' mingled voices filled the cavernous space that was the SOCH penthouse. After the final note, a pause, and then the choir erupted into cheers and whistles. They had just finished a moving run-through of John P. Kee's "Lily in the Valley." Sheldon smiled and in a comical way said, "Okay, not bad." Some Kuumbabes laughed. They knew it was good, even if Sheldon wouldn't concede the point this early in the school year; there was still much work to be done, and he didn't want the group to "peak" too early on a song before it was time to perform for an audience. He wanted their best performance to be on the stage. If choir was too good at it now, the song might languish before show time.

Sheldon's faint praise wasn't fooling anyone. Daphne explained it this way: "There's a lot of Sheldon telling us that we're good without telling us that we're good. As in like, 'You guys are, you sound really good. Oh wait, no, I mean, like, you sounded not bad.' That kind of thing." But this approach, finding new ways to continually push the choir further, seemed to keep on working. So on this night, Sheldon found stylistic fixes to offer. "All you're saying is 'Amen.' Stop looking at the lyrics." Then, in a nerdy voice reminiscent of Steve Urkel, he imitated a choir member who wouldn't stop looking at the music: "I want to get the lyrics right!" The choir laughed again.

As we have seen, members continually returned to two primary explanations for what made the group special. For some Kuumbabes, like Bryanna, Kuumba was "not about the music. People will tell you that. It's about the community." However, others, like senior Leela Johnson, would tell you that there was something special about the music itself and the high-quality performances. To Sheldon, the key to the group was both. In fact, balancing the two was always foremost in his mind. He was proud that Kuumba's music was taken seriously around the University. However, he noted that a balance with the community aspects of the group was just as important and something he had "struggled with a lot." If forced to make a choice, though, his preference—like Jamison's early in this chapter—was clear. "The most important part is the community, and if that means we sacrifice some musical excellence for that, then I'm okay with that."

In his perpetual attempts to push the choir to musical excellence while also attending to the community-building aspect of the organization, Sheldon was demonstrating an aspect of culturally relevant care described in the literature as "warm demanding." Educators who demonstrate warm demanding "value interpersonal relationships between everyone within a community, demand high performance, and grapple with cultural issues."[18] These are educators who not only care for students' affective needs, but also believe in their capacities to achieve.[19] Warm demanding has been documented in studies about elementary and secondary educators of youth of color, often from disenfranchised backgrounds, and is touted as an important factor in students' success. What Sheldon demonstrated and Kuumbabes confirmed was the value of such an approach in higher education.

One of the strategies Sheldon used as a warm demander to advance the choir's musicality and community was humor—a sort that struck me as a distinctly Black form, something of a mix between *Showtime at the Apollo* and playing the Dozens.[20] During the fall near the start of my research, I noticed when students were starting to skip rehearsals to study for midterms, Sheldon used his blend of humor to give a cautionary lesson on the importance of coming to rehearsals. He described a choir member who could be seen in a video from a past concert, moving in the wrong direction during a performance of Donald Lawrence's "Stranger." Sheldon paused for dramatic effect, and then said, "Don't be that one." The choir cracked up. Then he called out Grace Carter, a Black senior, insinuating it was her. Smiling and laughing, she retorted, "I wasn't even on stage [during that song]!"

During another rehearsal, when the group was practicing an arrangement of "Amazing Grace" that Sheldon put together for the choir, the basses and tenors were singing a repeating line—"*Doo, doo.*" Sheldon interrupted, "And that's exactly what you sound like." Only some got the joke and laughed. Sheldon went on, "That'll hit some of you later." He had them start over. And at yet another rehearsal, to model the kind of subtle intensity a particular song required, Sheldon demonstrated how "it needs to be intense, but that doesn't mean *AAHHH*!" Without missing a beat, he started whispering something passionately and then broke into a hushed "*I can see it in your eyes*" from the Lionel Richie song "Hello." The choir laughed on cue.

When I ask Sheldon about his use of humor during rehearsals, it was obvious that he was intentional in his approach. He said that sometimes the choir had to work hard to nail a song and that it could be boring. "They have to want to do that. And in order to want to do that, they have to love where they are." Sheldon also wanted the choir to see that even though he was the director, they could approach him. He hoped that showing his sense of humor would make them feel safer in being able to do so. In true warm demander style, he sought to form reciprocal bonds of trust that would support the caring community in the choir and bolster the group's ability to achieve excellence. Students commented on Sheldon's humor as being a staple component of rehearsals. Takiya brought this up unprompted when I asked about what rituals took place in all or most rehearsals. "Sheldon probably will make a joke or two . . . about something. Or, he'll make fun of somebody who's not doing something right." Sheldon's humor, according to Takiya, was contagious within the choir: "Or if the altos, which we struggle a lot sometimes with singing, like, we'll get a stank face from somebody in the tenor section, like, 'What are you all doing?'" Understanding that he "can't extend rehearsals anymore," because Kuumba already took as much time as an additional course for students, if not more, Sheldon used humor to instill community accountability—a playful way to demand more and better from students—which, as Takiya showed, transferred to students doing the same among each other.[21]

Sheldon also modeled vulnerability in the group, supporting the reciprocal nature of care and trust in the organization. In one closing circle, he sorrowfully shared the story of a student at the high school where he taught, who was killed a week earlier in a drunk driving accident. At times, he infused serious moments with humor, as Leela told me. "He'll crack a joke about being Black. . . . Sheldon is notorious for talking about when he gets stopped on the street." Perhaps in these instances, in evoking laughter, he was hoping to show Kuumbabes that "under the crushing confines of racial oppression, it is possible—necessary, even—to feel more than pain," in a move to keep them invested in the important work of challenging racism and anti-Blackness.[22]

Sheldon saw part of Kuumba's charge in addressing racial injustices. This came up as he discussed the concept of the praise and prayer circle. Sheldon explained that circling up was part of the "Black spiritual tradition," allowing, though, that it may also have been part of other spiritual traditions. He then went on to say how important it was for the group to be able to share moments of both praise and struggle, connecting this practice that was derived from those in some

Black churches to political action. He said that "in the Black community, the church wasn't just the spiritual center, it was also the community center and the political center." I got the sense then and throughout my time with the choir that Sheldon was hoping some of the choir members would begin to see Kuumba in this way, if they didn't already—it was not just a musical group, but also a community, and not just a community, but also a group united in music with a political purpose.

———

Within the education literature, care has mostly been written about in K-12 schooling, and recently with an emphasis on school and community locations that serve Black and Latinx students. Current work on care in higher education suggests that women, and women of color in particular, are restricted to taking on the role of caregiver in extracurricular activities in order to be accepted by other group members and find belonging, although a tenuous sort of belonging.[23] What Kuumba showed was the power and potential of reciprocal and community-grounded care, one that all are expected to participate in, as a means of connection, self-growth, and community empowerment.

Counter to other places and organizations on campus that students described as feeling alienating and competitive, in Kuumba, many students repeated some variation of what Lauren had told me, that you could "come as you are" and be included. At a place like Harvard, one of the most elite educational institutions in the world, students did not always feel that success was possible by just coming as you were.[24] Instead, in institutions such as this, students were groomed to assume the role of being "the best of the best."[25] Students learned to put on a façade of operating with ease regardless of the social situation, and they quickly learned the social importance of distinguishing themselves by excelling in academic and extracurricular pursuits.[26] Kuumbabes, semester after semester, demonstrated that though they too could play that game, what they really desired was unconditional acceptance. This was made possible through Kuumba's curriculum of care.

This was a curriculum that students were given the power to co-create in the organization, instead of having it mostly come from the top down. While Sheldon modeled caring practices, the student board actively worked to cultivate care in the organization, and individual members also eagerly took up these practices and introduced their own. Even in the seemingly confessional practices of sharing in circle or fully responding to the question of "How are you?" disclosure was invited, but not required. Kuumbabes weren't simply trading in one type of performance for another. They were not shifting from the stoicism seemingly required elsewhere on campus to a required performance of confession.[27] Thus, the curriculum of care was intentional, but it was also something to which group members themselves committed.

Coda

LESSONS FROM THE SAFE BLACK SPACE

"In the fantasies that I dream to escape the anti-Black dysmorphia of this dystopia, I, too, create another world where, at a bare minimum, Blackness is everything—ya dig?"

—*Esther Ohito and the Fugitive Literacies Collective*

Early one evening in late October, after going to Kuumba rehearsals each week for more than a year, I was relaxing on an old, black-cushioned, wheeled desk chair in the group's office, a room that on my first visit overwhelmed me with the sheer volume of stuff that filled it. Numerous metal bookshelves containing office supplies, a few photos, and folders upon folders spilling over with the group's music took up two walls. The back wall was stacked with boxes of merchandise covered with colorful *ankara* fabric and photos of the group from past years and decades, including a bulletin board display of pictures and quotes from members and alumni. Two large and three small file cabinets, a simple table-style desk with a Mac computer, and a bulletin board covered in another wax print fabric took up an additional wall.

I looked around the room and saw the history of the organization hanging on the walls and sitting on the shelves: written words, images, and artifacts, including concert posters for bygone years, like a benefit for Hurricane Katrina, and a 1988 anti-apartheid performance, "Songs for a Free South Africa." Black and brown faces filled photos from the group's early years; men and women sported Afros and styles of the day. The first photo to show white faces looked to be from the late 1980s or early 90s, given the clothing and hairstyles the students had donned. In one black-and-white shot, I saw two women I recognized from the past couple of years—one African American and one Asian American—laughing together in their black choir robes. My eyes were also drawn to a poster that in black, red, blue, and green lettering read, "Board," and was covered with words that, I am guessing, emerged from a brainstorming session by that year's Kuumba board: "Proactive." "Sankofa."[1] "Family." "Fierce."

This space was different from the staid classrooms and offices elsewhere on campus that were adorned with images of white men or filled with books by mostly white authors, I thought. Looking around and thinking about the Black space of the Kuumba office in contrast to the white space of campus took me back to a conversation from the previous spring with Claire Senai. She told me, "A lot of people think that it's very hard to be a minority [at Harvard], which makes sense. I mean it's a white institution, basically." Claire, who identified as biracial with a white mother and Black father, preferred not to focus on the challenges and instead focus on the opportunities her elite education was affording her. I wanted to know more.

SHERRY: You said that in some ways it is hard [being a minority at Harvard]. What would those ways be?

CLAIRE: No matter how much Harvard changes—and it obviously has changed a lot and is becoming a pretty diverse place, and the university does make a lot of efforts to, like, make sure everyone is treated equally—it doesn't change the fact that for hundreds of years it was not a place that was like that. . . . I think it's especially hard for minorities who didn't go to a prep school or something because then you're just absolutely not the person who Harvard was started for.[2] This is probably true at any Ivy League or really prestigious university in the United States, where if you're a minority coming from a poor neighborhood, it's going be hard for you because you're coming to a place that's overflowing with wealth.

I still think that Harvard is [sighs] a place that is not completely defined by white privilege, but in a lot of ways kind of is still defined by white privilege because . . . like, you still can come to Harvard if you're from a certain family [legacy] and minorities don't really have that sort of long lineage that a lot of white students have because their ancestors weren't allowed to come here. So, there's still that underlying. I don't think it's hard in the sense of, like, you go to class and you're scared that someone's going call you the n-word. I don't know. . . . It's more that there's still the history of what Harvard is and that can't be erased just because of a few policy changes.

Claire was explaining what it felt like to be Black—and from a lower-income background—navigating the wealthy, white space that was Harvard. She also demonstrated how subtly whiteness works on campus: Though Claire did not have explicit experiences with overt racism, the space nonetheless felt unwelcoming and not created for her. She also hinted at the difficulties of dismantling the white space—it was not something that could be "erased just because of a few policy changes."[3] Given the perniciousness of white supremacy on campus—entangled with classism—Claire sought out a safe Black space, and found Kuumba.

Kuumba's safe Black space came about as a response to the whiteness of campus that Claire described, but was neither preoccupied with nor constrained by it. Instead, the safe Black space was grounded in an unapologetic Black autonomy, characterized by Black diasporic identification and political consciousness, supported by five pillars: authority, authenticity, acceptance, actualization, and action.[4] Upon these pillars, the organization was able to foster an environment where Black students could thrive and others were welcome to join in.

First and foremost, Black students deliberately maintained authority over the space and organization, reserving key leadership roles for Black members and operating Kuumba on their own terms, refusing to cater to white and non-Black members. This was important given that in student groups that were not racially or ethnically marked, white students often took charge and held great influence over the ways in which those organizations were run, including ways that limited Black students' participation. Even in racially diverse organizations, Black students were sometimes marginalized.[5] Further, the processes by which white students came into leadership roles on campus was usually treated as a matter of course, obscuring the way in which race mattered in who was assumed to have leadership potential.[6] Kuumba interrupted these workings of whiteness by being explicit about the importance of race, and in so doing, ensured that white interests wouldn't be able to quietly creep in and take control.

In terms of authenticity, in Kuumba, students felt seen for who they were as individuals and as Black people from different walks of life. This was achieved through the organization's practice of creating shared language around racial authenticity (i.e., what it meant to be Black) and conceptions of it that were asset-based and focused on struggle and perseverance as a community. This, in turn, acknowledged and validated the myriad Black backgrounds of members. Whereas Black students were regularly denied recognition as individuals and found their Blackness stigmatized on campus through deficit discourses, in the safe Black space, they co-created a shared vision of Blackness that affirmed their humanity and valued complexity.[7] Historically, white Americans have controlled the means by which race groups have been defined and identified, at least in terms of law and policy, doing so in ways that maintained white supremacy, which Kuumba's approach to racial authenticity rejected.[8] At a place like Harvard, where Black students were coming from a variety of disparate lived experiences, this approach to authenticity laid the foundation for students to build a type of coalitional Black identity they didn't have access to elsewhere, which led to feelings of acceptance, the third pillar.

In part because Kuumba was receptive to myriad expressions of Blackness, members felt unconditionally accepted and that they belonged. This affective state of belonging was partially achieved through institutionalized practices of caring—Kuumba's curriculum of care—and encouraged students to take the risks of trying new things and forming connections with other members. Belonging for Black students on predominantly white campuses was at a premium, but shown to be essential to students' thriving.[9] Thus, Kuumba's unqualified welcome was extraordinary and allowed students to lower their guard and take risks they otherwise might not.

Going hand in hand with acceptance, then, was actualization. Within Kuumba, there were opportunities for self-actualization, or the fulfillment of one's talents. Students were encouraged to try new things to develop themselves, which was seen as also being for the good of the group. For instance, freshman Jason Thomas came to Kuumba with no vocal skills, but a couple years in was singing solos—elevating his own skills and elevating the community as a whole. Had Jason not felt unconditionally accepted in the group, it's easy to imagine that he may never have extended himself in this way. It's also not difficult to imagine the many ways in which opportunities for Black students' self-actualization are foreclosed across campuses, owing to contexts that feel negating.[10]

Finally, everything the organization did was in the service of some greater purpose or action, primarily, the act of "leaving the space better," as stated in the mission. This was a purpose all group members were apprenticed into sharing and was realized through the collective undertaking of performing as a choir. Members were also expected to engage in collective action that would support Black peoples' thriving and perseverance on and beyond campus. In this way, the five pillars were entwined: As Black students took authority for the organization and put forward a view of Black authenticity that was expansive and strength-focused, members felt unconditionally accepted and able to self-actualize in ways that allowed Kuumba to continue to achieve excellence and engage in the collective action of leaving the space better.

Moreover, these pillars, rooted in Kuumba's unapologetic Black autonomy, enabled members to feel secure in confronting difficult issues related to race and engaging divergent views, as they could do so and still feel whole, valued, and seen, even when they disagreed with something in the group. Kuumbabes were not "snowflakes," to invoke the pejorative used to criticize calls for safe spaces on campuses.[11] Rather, challenging issues were confronted directly, and the rules of that engagement—for example, in terms of the limitations on participation for non-Black members—were made clear and explicit. Through being explicit about race, the workings of whiteness could be directly addressed in ways meant to support the thriving of Black students. This also gave non-Black students the opportunity to consider for themselves whether Kuumba's customs worked for them. If not, they were free to find some other organization in which to participate. This was a bold treatment of race at an elite institution—a context in which nonconfrontational interaction styles and "civil discourse" are typically prioritized.[12] But, in other spaces on campus where race and whiteness were not directly addressed, inequality was allowed to operate as if by natural order and run rampant.[13]

In thinking about safe space debates, then, Kuumba shows that for students to be able to challenge one another and discuss socially taboo topics, they needed to feel seen, heard, and cared about on their *own terms*. They needed to feel they could be their authentic selves and that they belonged. Kuumba would replace the idea of "comfort" that is popular in discussing safe spaces with the idea of "belonging"—in fact, they would probably say that sometimes they didn't feel comfortable at all, but that they always felt like they belonged. Kuumbabes would also refocus the purpose of taking on challenging discussions to be in the service of community progress, again, of "leaving the space better" than they found it. With this in mind, there are specific lessons to be taken from Kuumba's example for higher education more broadly.

Lessons for Higher Education

I began working with Kuumba not even a decade ago, a time that seems a world apart from where we find ourselves today. At the start of my research, a naive optimism was circulating among some that Barack Obama's election to the U.S. presidency signaled a move toward a harmonious, post-racial society, and anticipation that we were inching closer as a nation to fulfilling Dr. Martin Luther King Jr.'s "dream" of a time when people would "not be judged by the color of their skin but by the content of their character."[14] Many woke up from that dream abruptly, only to slip into a nightmare of emboldened white supremacists and ongoing acts of violence against Black people, spurred by the election of Donald Trump. Of course, post-racialism was always a myth and even during the Obama presidency, violence against Black people became more and more exposed.[15] While racism, hatred, and vitriol were always festering below the surface, they were once again on full display and amplified via the platform of the Trump presidency. This made the lessons Kuumba provided feel all the more urgent to me. Here was an organization that students of all backgrounds repeatedly described as a safe space, and one of the places where they felt most at home on campus. All the while, the organization prioritized the needs and interests of the Black students. Given how trenchant white ideology is in U.S. higher education and society, I remain convinced that this—centering Blackness and inviting others in—offers a key to true transformation.

Reorienting higher education in this way is hard work and requires a will to change. In my own teaching, in the years since I first met Kuumba, I have consistently pondered what it would mean to foster safe Black space where all could thrive because my Black students thrived. I have been met with successes and challenges in this endeavor, but have distilled three lessons from the safe Black space that might push those of us in higher education beyond merely enacting the window dressing of change, where we find ourselves implementing "diversity initiatives"—or even so-called anti-racism efforts—all the while normalizing or ignoring Black students' negative experiences and outcomes.

Lesson 1: Representation Is Necessary, But Not Enough

At one point in time, increasing representation—referring to racial diversity—on campus was a radical concept. When Kuumba began during the Civil Rights Movement, the number of Black students attending elite, historically white colleges and universities was paltry. Students protested, demanding that higher education institutions commit to admitting more Black students. On a societal level, this has had a number of positive outcomes, including supporting the growth of the Black middle class. As Black people became the beneficiaries of opportunities afforded by an elite education, they were able to contribute to expanding opportunities for others. At the campus level, increasing the percentage of Black students had the effect of creating more opportunities for connection and community and, consequently, persistence and flourishing. Research also repeatedly shows that numbers matter in terms of transforming campus cultures.[16] Without a "critical mass" of students of color, hostile and unwelcoming environments persist. Even within Kuumba, representation mattered in how the safe Black space was cultivated and maintained. Kuumbabes saw having a significant, though undefined, percentage of members who identified as Black as key to the organization's ability to continue being a safe space for Black students.

Yet, focusing on numbers alone only goes so far and can have the unintended consequence of confining students to boxes that fulfill diversity metrics. This was evident in the experiences described by the students of color who were participants in this research. When a focus on the numbers isn't backed up with a deeper commitment to ensuring positive experiences for marginalized students, stereotypes and estrangement can be the result. Moreover, focusing on numeric representation may do little to address issues of systemic racism and white supremacy.

As higher educators have come to realize that a focus on the numbers of students from racially underrepresented backgrounds is not enough to fundamentally transform campus cultures, many have argued for being more intentional in the ways students are included. In his study of belonging in campus extracurricular activities, Blake Silver argued, "If there is hope for combating the inequality that currently thrives in the college social landscape, institutions will need to be more intentional in their efforts."[17] He suggests that students need tools to resist stereotypes and inequality, which universities are, in part, called on to supply. Similarly, in her study of a deliberately diverse Intra-Varsity Christian Fellowship, Julie Park found, "intentionality was the intervention that prevented IVCF from cycling into racial homogeneity."[18] In this case, it was the organization's intention to be multiracial and to resist becoming comfortable with a solely white and Asian membership that kept them seeking counters to the forces of homogeneity—Black students' belonging in this racially diverse organization was still very much contingent, a dynamic that has led for some to critique "inclusion" as the goal.[19]

Kuumba demonstrated intentionality in terms of being deliberate about the ways in which the organization addressed racial diversity—as Sei Matsuura said, "This space was created. It doesn't just happen to be there." Indeed, Kuumba's intentionality in, for instance, having formalized discussions about the choir's racial composition and expected roles for members of different backgrounds, may be a main reason why Kuumba persisted in being a Black space despite the numbers of non-Black students that opted to participate each year. Herein lies the difference between the way intentionality and representation have been written about elsewhere in the higher education literature and what they meant in Kuumba. Elsewhere, representation and intentionality continue to operate from the assumption of white normativity, and are consequently not enough to shift institutional cultures. Focusing on representation can result in colleges taking actions we might consider to be "quick fixes" and with which white people are comfortable.

Moving beyond a focus on representation in a way that exposes the workings of whiteness on campus requires a level of sacrifice not many may be willing to make. White Kuumbabes like Anna Reid, for example, were at times uncomfortable with hearing Black students' unfiltered discussions about race, which Malik Rose said they had to deal with as participants in a Black space. One thing white people must be willing to give up, then, is their sense of entitlement or ease or authority that might be validated elsewhere, on and off campus. For instance, in order to preserve Kuumba's safe Black space, non-Black students forewent inserting themselves in leadership roles that, to use Paul Dixon's words, in a "normal organization," they might feel entitled to pursue. This shows representation and intentionality taken to the next level. White people must be willing to risk feeling left out in some ways in order to be let in to the Black space. Though other non-Black members negotiated these same issues, I focus on white members here given how whiteness works on elite campuses, offering liminal status to any non-white person.[20] It is also telling that the white participants in this research were the ones who enacted, even discursively, the centering of whiteness in the ways Kuumba attempted to combat, such as Paul and Anna suggesting a desire to actively recruit more non-Black members.

Lesson 2: Start from Black

Lesson 2 requires a move from centering whiteness to centering Blackness. To illustrate, I want to offer a turn in my own thinking that took place across the time I spent working with Kuumba. When I began this project, I was curious about the dynamic of having non-Black members participate in a Black student organization. I was focused on the non-Black students' experiences and Black students' reactions to those non-Black members. Whenever I would speak about my project with others, it was obvious this was something they, too, were interested in. I have been asked innumerable times, for example, what it is like for Kuumba to have white members. However, as I engaged in this project and got to know Black Kuumbabes, I discovered that this was not the story that most interested them. It's not that they were entirely indifferent to having white and other non-Black members. Rather, they were much more concerned with what it meant to be Black students coming together in Kuumba and at Harvard; they were more preoccupied with the diversity among Black members. At this point, I began to realize the reactions I got from others asking about white members and even my original inquiry were centering whiteness; we were starting from white. Black Kuumbabes, alternatively, were starting from Black. This is a crucial distinction if a goal of higher education is to be truly inclusive, and genuinely attempt to meet its democratic goals.[21]

Starting from Black means that Blackness is assumed as an—or *the*—essential constitutive element of a space or context. In many U.S. educational settings whiteness is the essential constitutive element. This is true even in those locations that are demographically racially diverse, or even comprised primarily of people of color, and means that ideologies and practices favoring white interests are the norm.[22] Starting from Black means assuming a Black norm. When scholar bell hooks first conceptualized choosing the margins as a place of resistance for Black folks in 1989, she wrote, "Those of us who live, who 'make it,' passionately holding on to aspects of that 'downhome' life we do not intend to lose while simultaneously seeking new knowledge and experience, invent spaces of radical openness. Without such spaces we would not survive [. . .] For me this space of radical openness is a margin—a profound edge."[23] At the time, hooks's idea was powerful and necessary. Starting from Black, however, refuses the framing of margins or counter-space, as Blackness is already at the center. Starting from Black does not ignore that the reality we live with in the United States and at many higher education institutions is one of white dominance, at least ideologically. Rather, starting from Black understands the conditions of white dominance that exist societally and how those influence conceptions of Blackness; but starting from Black is not limited by this.

Kuumba was not so much concerned with countering whiteness as it was with centering Blackness. Kuumba's safe Black space made this apparent in the explicit ways the organization unapologetically asserted its Blackness. In white educational spaces, because whiteness is normalized, racially disparate outcomes and experiences are treated as the result of race-neutral—or *natural*—policies and practices.[24] Yet, there is nothing natural or neutral about the continuing dominance of whiteness in U.S. education. When one attempts to shift from assuming whiteness to assuming Blackness this quickly becomes apparent.

One thing that came up in my research as I began to notice the ways in which Kuumba started from Black was how different the conversations about diversity were from those happening elsewhere on campus. In other spaces, when the topic of diversity came up, it was usually about how to foster more racial diversity, as in how to increase the numbers of Black and brown students in what remained a normatively white space. This was something Kuumbabes picked up on as influencing Harvard's positioning of the choir. By way of example, Jolaade Abedayo told me that the University "never say[s] we're a Black organization," instead referring to Kuumba as multicultural in a move meant to make Kuumba seem more prestigious to outside interests, such as sponsors. Kuumba's director Sheldon Reid told me that after more Black members joined, Kuumba "very quickly became Harvard's poster child for diversity." Indeed, starting sometime in the early 2000s, photos of the choir had been placed on brochures and fliers and even distributed in a video clip sent out by the admissions office to prospective students. Imitating those who might use Kuumba to peddle Harvard's diversity, Sheldon marveled facetiously, "Just look at all this color we got!"

Conversely, in Kuumba, conversations about diversity took two directions. On the one hand, Black Kuumbabes wanted to discuss diversity among Black students. Because the organization attracted Black members from a variety of backgrounds, they took advantage of the opportunity to consider the myriad ways Blackness is constructed and experienced globally. On the other hand, when I explicitly asked about the non-Black members, Black Kuumbabes continued to center Blackness in their responses, saying how the organization's racial diversity was a testament to the strength of Blackness given that non-Black students would want to participate. In the "About Kuumba" note in the 2010 fortieth anniversary concert program, the group summed it up this way: "Kuumba Singers [. . .] have always sought to leave the space called Harvard, and its surrounding community, better than we found it. The choir's current racial and ethnic diversity is both a remarkable testimony to, and a relentless test of, that noble and enduring ideal."

Lesson 3: Meaningful Change Requires Love

As I have continued to think about what would be needed to realize racial justice and eradicate anti-Black sentiment and actions on college and university campuses, I am more and more convinced that the answer lies beyond the realm of tools or best practices. I find inspiration in the words of critical educator Shamari Reid. In writing about his experience wrapping up a professional development for teachers on racial justice in education, he overheard two attendees complain that his workshop didn't offer enough tools to implement in their classrooms.

Reid didn't have the chance to directly confront these educators, but reflects,

Action plans cannot drive out hate or racism, only *love* can do that. *Love* for those who do not always look like you [. . .] *Love* for those who you have been conditioned to regard as inferior. You can acquire all the pedagogical tools in the world, but if you don't *love* your Black and Brown students [. . .] if you don't see their humanity and the systems that threaten it [. . .] those tools will do nothing but fool you into believing that you're "fighting the good fight," while your Black and Brown students continue to be sacrificed so that their *blood* may lubricate the machine that is white supremacy.[25]

I would argue the same is true in higher education. As long as historically white and elite higher education continues to focus on representational diversity and inclusion of Black bodies into the already constituted white space, Black students will continue to be dehumanized, and institutional—and societal— transformation stifled.

But what would it take to engender love for Black students at historically white colleges and universities? What would it look like? First would be a reconceptualization. By love, I draw on the definition offered by education scholar Durryle Brooks, who writes, "Love [. . .] brings back together that which oppression has sought to tear apart. Therefore, the work of love or rather a critical theory of love, both understands the innate dignity of all human life and also actively creates practices that reunites and rehumanizes."[26] Thus, love for Black students would be grounded in an acknowledgment and valuing of the dignity and humanity of those students and would be evident in the difficult, but meaningful, policies and initiatives undertaken that ask white stakeholders to trade in their comfortableness and privilege for others to thrive. For instance, it surely takes love for white and other non-Black Kuumbabes to remain in an organization that centers those who do not look like them and requires them to step back from ways they might participate and show up elsewhere in their lives.

The type of love I am calling for here is in the vein of what Dr. Martin Luther King Jr. called for in 1967 at the Southern Christian Leadership Conference. He said, "What is needed is a realization that power without love is reckless and abusive and that love without power is sentimental and anemic. Power at its best is love implementing the demands of justice. Justice at its best is love correcting everything that stands against love."[27] Love of this kind requires bold material and ideological commitments to the well-being of Black students, for instance, investing in caring and loving educators like Sheldon. A key reason for Kuumba's success at engaging sticky issues of difference is undoubtedly the legacy of visionary leadership for the organization. Sheldon was the third in a line of

successive leaders for Kuumba who have been willing to ask seemingly imperti-
nent questions about race relations on Harvard's campus and make audacious
demands, all grounded in love for Black people and Black students. These directors have also been successful in these endeavors because they have been able
to cultivate caring community, cultivating a love of Blackness among Black
Kuumbabes—and in the case of the last two directors, that includes creating
community among a multiracial membership.[28] Such leadership might be seen
as controversial and easily assailed from a certain standpoint. Colleges and universities must therefore be even more vigilant about identifying, hiring, and
supporting loving leaders who take risks as they relate to dismantling systemi-
cally racist and anti-Black practices.

I think it is no coincidence that so many Kuumbabes talked about love and
care in describing the safe Black space. There would have been no safe Black space
without love and care for Black people, history, and culture, and for the individual Black members. Elite educational institutions are generally anything
but loving, as they are defined by alienation, exclusion, and competition.[29] Nor
have I heard love spoken of much in conversations about higher education
reform. There is a missing discourse of love, a missing discourse of care in higher
education.

From Diversity to Belonging and Beyond

"Hold on just a little while longer. Fight on, fight on, just a little while longer.
Fight on, you need to fight on just a little while longer. . . . Everything will be all
right." The soloist's voice was at once imploring and reassuring, quavering
through the words of this Negro spiritual.[30] "You know you got to sing on," she
warbled, and the entire choir joined in a decrescendo, "Sing on just a little while
longer." The effect of the intermingled a cappella voices, mournful and determined, recalled the origins of this song in the experiences of slavery and Black
racial oppression. At least one Kuumbabe wept silently, tears gently streaking
her cheeks, as she continued singing and swaying in time. The sound conjured
images of the Civil Rights Movement—the era that gave rise to Kuumba—of
demonstrators walking, arms linked, into the line of fire of angry white mobs or
police in riot gear. But the time was October 2014 and the location was Harvard
University. The occasion was the I, Too, Am Harvard: Blacktivism Conference,
focused on bringing together students from various universities to explore ways
to support and advocate for Black students' interests.[31]

Kuumba co-sponsored the Blacktivism Conference, planned on the premise
that the fight for Black racial justice needed to be revived and expanded in the
hallowed halls of the ivory tower. The conference was part of the broader movement in the United States instigated by the first wave of Black Lives Matter pro-
testers taking to the streets to demonstrate for the Black lives lost at the hands

of the police. The conference was a precursor to the subsequent protests for Black racial justice that would continue sweeping the country's college campuses up to the pre-pandemic present. These protests and campaigns on campuses, which led to tangible changes in the Ivy League and elsewhere, have included students demanding more resources for those from underrepresented backgrounds, to opposing speakers they would characterize as racist and intolerant, to still others, such as students at Yale, demanding buildings be renamed to address the racist past of early contributors to these institutions.[32]

While many colleges and universities have been responsive, when I think about the Blacktivism Conference and recent campus protests for racial justice, I can't help but think to myself: Here we go again. For all of higher education's lofty intentions to support democratic goals and racial diversity through increasing numbers of students of color, there remains a grievous disconnect between espoused ideals and enacted values, and this disconnect forecloses possibilities for deeper societal change. But I remain hopeful too, given that students have raised their voices and carved out spaces like Kuumba, which can provide a path forward, if administrators, faculty members, and staff will follow their lead.

As I hear about recent initiatives in higher education to move from discussions about diversity to discussions about inclusion and belonging to ones about rightful presence, I think back to the lessons provided by Kuumba: As long as whiteness remains under- and unaddressed, and Blackness is feared or loathed far more often than loved in these contexts, I suspect such moves will remain largely semantic.[33] Diversity initiatives will continue to require Black acquiescence to white norms, which can be seen as the difference between fitting in and belonging. Social scientist Brené Brown describes this difference: "Belonging is being somewhere you want to be and they want you. Fitting in is being somewhere where you want to be, but they don't care one way or the other. // Belonging is being accepted for you. Fitting in is being accepted for being like everyone else. // If I get to be me, I belong. If I have to be like you, I fit in."[34] There is evidence, for instance, that in white educational spaces, Black women engage in maneuvering around and limiting their self-expression.[35] This is fitting in, not belonging. Privilege and being elite means being at ease in any situation, but belonging means being authentic to oneself. The two are not always compatible at a place like Harvard, and, for Black students, may be at odds and speak to strains of meritocracy—which in some senses requires that students are always trying to prove themselves worthy. Just because a student has been accepted to Harvard doesn't mean they have been accepted at Harvard.

Thinking about the safe Black space is helpful in thinking about how to foster multiracial community. For some of those doing this work, Kuumba will be inspirational, showing what is possible. This isn't necessarily replicable, but that isn't the point. That it's not simply "replicable," is part of the beauty of the thing, born of specific people in a specific time and place, carrying with them specific histories. Kuumba is also far from "perfect," as no institution is "perfect," whatever that would mean. But, from such an organizational example, there is much to learn about what might be required to dismantle the whiteness of many of the country's colleges and universities to allow the flourishing of the safe Black space, in the service of cultivating campuses where all students can belong *because* Black students belong.

Interview Participants*

Participant	Gender	Race/Ethnicity**	Born/Lived (Abroad or U.S.)	Year in College	Semesters in Kuumba	Past/Present Kuumba Officer
Jolaade Abedayo	Female	West African American	Abroad and U.S.	Junior	6	Yes
Grace Carter	Female	Black/African American	U.S.	Super Senior***	8	No
Francisco Diaz	Male	Hispanic	U.S.	Senior	6	No
Paul Dixon	Male	Caucasian	U.S.	Freshman	2	Yes
Daphne Han	Female	Asian American	U.S.	Freshman	2	No
Leela Johnson	Female	Black	U.S.	Senior	8	Yes
Allison Lawrence	Female	African American and White	U.S.	Senior	6	No
Angie Martin	Female	Black	U.S.	Senior	7	Yes
Sei Matsuura	Female	Asian American	U.S.	Sophomore	3	No
Ebony Miller	Female	Black	U.S.	Sophomore	4	No
Takiya Moore	Female	Black	U.S.	Sophomore	—	Yes
Jamison Mthembu	Male	African Descent	Abroad and U.S.	Senior	8	Yes

Bryanna Norman	Female	African American	U.S.	Sophomore	4	No
Anna Reid	Female	White/Caucasian	U.S.	Senior	3	No
Malik Rose	Male	Black/African Descent	Abroad and U.S.	Freshman	3	No
Claire Senai	Female	Caucasian and African American	U.S.	Sophomore	4	Yes
Emily Taylor	Female	White	U.S.	Freshman	1	No
Jason Thomas	Male	Black	—	Freshman	—	No
Lauren Washington	Female	African American; Native American	U.S.	Senior	2	Yes

* All information reported here is taken from a brief, online demographic questionnaire students completed prior to one-on-one interviews. Some students did not respond to all questions.

** At times in interviews or conversations, students described their race using different terminology than that shared here. For instance, students who reported "African American" here described themselves as "Black" at other times. Some responses have been modified to protect students' confidentiality.

*** Super seniors were Harvard students in their final year who had taken more than 8 consecutive semesters to complete their undergraduate degrees.

Note on Methods

"We want you to feel what we're saying."
—*Lauren Washington, senior*

When I asked African American senior Lauren Washington, "Let's say I didn't know anything about Kuumba, what would you tell me?" She responded, "Kuumba has become my home here. . . . Kuumba is a space where you can meet the most amazing people on campus. Kuumba is a space where you can recharge after a week of Harvard. Kuumba is—" She continued, working to get her words just right, "Kuumba is—It's just Kuumba. You have to see us. We can't tell you. You have to see us. And you have to engage in conversation with us." She came back to a point made by the group's professional director. "Sheldon always says when we're singing, it's not like, you're listening and then at the end you clap respectfully and then you sit back down and you listen some more. No, we're having a conversation and it's rude if you don't respond so we want you to feed off of our energy. We want you to feel what we're saying. We want you to think about the words that we're saying, and give that back to us. So, to really understand Kuumba, you have to see Kuumba."

Lauren's words encapsulated why I chose to conduct this study drawing on the social science method of portraiture. Just as Kuumba is "having a conversation" during a performance, the social science portraitist understands that, according to portraiture pioneer Sara Lawrence-Lightfoot and arts educator Jessica Hoffmann Davis, "At the heart of the aesthetic experience—a primary condition—is a conversation between two active meaning-makers, the producer and the perceiver of the work of art. This conversation results in a co-construction of meaning in which both parties play pivotal roles."[1] Portraiture recognizes that in the case of the research project, the co-construction of meaning is in fact the result of "*a series of relationships*: the relationships between the artist-researcher and the subject, the artist-researcher and the work, the perceiver and the subject of the work, and ultimately the perceiver and the producer—the two meaning-seekers interrelating through the interpretive work."[2] As a result, portraiture was poised to capture the complexity Lauren intended to convey when she said that to really know what Kuumba is, "You have to see us. We can't tell you." By employing portraiture as a methodological lens, it was my intention to show, not just *tell about,* Kuumba to the reader. I anticipated and envisaged the reader as a co-constructor of meaning, as part of the *conversation* about and with Kuumba. Furthermore, through portraiture's focus on the aesthetic whole of written research, I was able to develop an interpretive narrative of Kuumba embedded in the historical and institutional, and in the individual and group, capturing the rhythm and sequence of shifts in Kuumba's culture and inter-actions, which in turn enabled me to share my findings in such a way that, I hope, "the complex dimensions of *goodness*" shone through, rather than pathology.[3] This was essential, as I asked "what is right" here, in order to imag-ine new possibilities for social change.[4]

Seeking deep understanding of the meaning-making processes of partici-pants, and because of the uniqueness of the phenomenon of interest—few Black undergraduate student organizations with extensive multiracial memberships have been documented in the literature previously—I employed a single case study design.[5] The single case approach was compatible with portraiture, given the social science portraitist's epistemological stance that by studying and explor-ing specific instances, contexts, and so forth, we might build understandings that illuminate more universal issues and processes.[6] Case studies can be espe-cially useful in addressing "how" and "why" questions when "real-world" contexts are of interest, as with this study.

The Organization

I sought a participating undergraduate student organization that fit three crite-ria: 1) it needed to be explicitly culturally- or racially-focused; 2) it also needed to be a performing arts group, as I was curious about how the public nature of the performance and simply engaging in the collective activity of performance might impact members;[7] and lastly, 3) the organization needed to be well-known on Harvard's campus, with a history of at least ten years, so that the focus of my study would be less about a new group figuring itself out and more about a cam-pus institution in which there was a history of negotiating diversity. On top of meeting these criteria, Kuumba's many and varied components provided a rich research site with multiple opportunities for understanding the organization. For example, in addition to the functions and obligations of membership in a choir, such as practicing twice a week for 2–3 hours each time and performing at one or more small ad hoc performances ("gigs") on top of weekly rehearsals, many Kuumba members chose to go on tour together over spring break, ate meals together before rehearsals, served on committees or the board for the group, attended retreats for the group (divided by gender during the time of my research), and participated in other related endeavors. There were also two member-email listserv groups—one designated for "official" business and one for personal issues, such as prayer requests.

While there were over one hundred cultural and racial initiatives at Harvard, including twenty-eight such groups with more than one hundred members around the time of this research, few had the historical significance and present-day prominence of Kuumba.[8] In fact, Kuumba was well-known within and beyond the Harvard undergraduate community, illustrated by the fact that members hailed from the Harvard graduate schools and Extension School, Tufts University, MIT, and beyond; and that the group performed widely around the world and for visiting dignitaries at Harvard, notably the late Nelson Mandela. Perhaps more importantly, while Kuumba invited students from all racial and cultural backgrounds to be members, one of the organization's essential functions was to perform traditional and contemporary pieces from across the Black diaspora, including Negro spirituals, gospel, and songs from various African nations sung in their native tongue, such as Igbo. Therefore, not only were students of various races and cultures coming together to participate in this historically Black student organization, they were also making their participation public by performing in concerts on campus and across the globe. Consequently, though I did not initially seek out a Black student organization, research showing that Black students at predominantly white institutions report less interaction with students from other racial groups made it especially useful to focus on a site where Black students did have an opportunity to interact with both Black and non-Black peers.[9]

THE PEOPLE

Though the organization as a whole was my primary unit of analysis, individuals comprised an embedded unit of analysis for this study. An informal estimate based on the approximately sixty-six people who participated in the Christmas concert during my year of research (see Table B.1) revealed that about 18 percent (~12) identified as white, about 6 percent (~4) identified as Asian or Asian American, at least two people identified as Hispanic/Latino/a (~3%)—of the two, one identified as a Black Latino and another identified as a non-Black Latina—and at least three identified as multiracial with Black and white parents (~5%). The majority, approximately 66 percent of the choir that performed in the concert, identified as Black from across the diaspora (including African American, Caribbean, and several different African countries).[10] In terms of gender, 20 percent (~13) identified as men and the remaining majority of the choir, women; none identified as nonbinary.[11] However, many more students than captured here considered themselves members of Kuumba during this time, and participated regularly on the email listserv groups and volunteered as ushers for perfor-

TABLE B.1

ORGANIZATIONAL AND INTERVIEWEE DEMOGRAPHIC DATA

	Organization Total (n = 66*)	Interview Participants (n = 19*)
Race		
Black / African American (non-Hispanic)	65% (43)	58% (11)
Asian / Asian American	6% (4)	11% (2)
Latino/a	3% (2)	5% (1)
Multiracial	5% (3)	11% (2)
White (non-Hispanic)	18% (12)	16% (3)
Unknown / Unspecified	3% (2)	—
Gender		
Male	20% (13)	26% (5)
Female	80% (53)	74% (14)
Religion		
Christian	—	53% (10)
Buddhist	—	5% (1)
Muslim	—	5% (1)
None	—	16% (3)
Unknown / Unspecified	—	21% (4)

Note: organization-level data are based on approximations for the period explored in this research.
* The professional director is not included in either set of demographics.

mances. "Taking a semester off" from Kuumba was not an entirely uncommon practice, and many of those who did still attended at least some rehearsals, even if they could not attend the minimum number required to be eligible to participate in the concerts. This makes it difficult to provide an exact number of Kuumbabes or to provide precise information on group demographics.

From the overall membership, a subset of nineteen students and Sheldon, the director, further participated in in-depth, one-on-one interviews. The student interview participants (see Appendix A) represented a range of backgrounds reflective of the choir as a whole, with men and non-Black members together purposefully overrepresented. Five interviewees identified as men (~26%) and the other fourteen as women (~74%). Eleven (~58%) identified as Black, two (~11%) as biracial (with Black and white parents), two as Asian American (~11%), three as white (~16%), and one as Latino (racially Black) (~5%). Though my research questions did not specifically address religion, given the group's mission that includes celebrating "Black spirituality," it is important to note that one interviewee identified as Muslim (~5%), and three did not identify with any specific religious tradition (~16%). The remainder of my interviewees identified as Christian with various levels of commitment to observing their faith outside of Kuumba; these members saw Kuumba as an extension of their faith, but not a substitution for church or a Christian fellowship. At the time of this research there were also at least two known Jewish members, neither of whom volunteered to participate in an interview. Sheldon identified as a Black man of Caribbean descent and Christian faith.

Lastly, of interest to me was that interviewees represented a range of years in school and in years as Kuumba members. Therefore, interviewees ranged from first-year students to seniors, and participation ranged from one semester to four full years. Two interviewees were students at other nearby universities, which was also representative of the makeup of the Kuumba membership at large.

Data Collection and Analysis

Participant observation was a key method for answering my research questions, which relied on the documentation of the group's norms of interaction, rituals, and routines.[12] To begin building rapport with members and leaders and to gain familiarity with group practices, I began attending rehearsals and performances at the end of the spring semester in the year prior to my main ethnographic research. At the first rehearsal I attended, Sheldon and the president at the time introduced me to the choir, along with my research project. I then spent the entire subsequent school year attending weekly rehearsals, the two hallmark Christmas and spring performances, and accompanied the group on their spring break tour out of the country. I also attended several rehearsals during the fall of the following year to test emerging hypotheses and gather additional data. In total, I spent more than one hundred hours observing Kuumba. During that time, I documented the structure of rehearsals, including, for example, who led various parts, what "business" matters were discussed, and what types of formal and informal interactions members engaged in socially.

Relationships and sustained, regular interaction with participants were essential to this research approach.[13] Therefore, I participated in group activities, such as singing with the choir during rehearsal (once I built up enough courage to sing in public). I also participated in the prayer and praise circle by being present and respectfully observant, stopping short of conducting the closing prayer or making a prayer or praise request that might interject undue influence from me into the group's space.

Interviews were another key component of my research that I used as a way to invite participants to make meaning of their experiences.[14] I waited to approach the choir about formal, individual interviews until I had spent one full semester engaged in participant observation, so that I would have a better sense of group practices and norms, and so that members would be more familiar with me and my work. The president gave me time to introduce the interview component of my project at the beginning of a regular rehearsal. Though the president and Sheldon had already given me permission to observe rehearsals and receive list-serv emails prior, I sent around interview interest forms that also allowed students to opt out from having me take observation notes on them or use emails they sent over either listserv as data. This was an important reminder to participants of my presence as a researcher in the space. From there, I attempted to create a representative sample from among those who volunteered to be interviewed.[15] I approached twenty-two members by email about being interviewed, and of those, eighteen ultimately participated.[16] I also interviewed a nineteenth member, Paul Dixon, who was recommended to me by several of the other interviewees, though he had not originally volunteered.

Specifically, I conducted individual, formal, sixty- to ninety-minute, one-on-one interviews with approximately 29 percent of core, active members (including the Kuumba president and vice president at the time). Additionally, I conducted two in-depth interviews, each lasting over ninety minutes, with Sheldon. Interviewees also completed a brief demographic survey prior to participating in one-on-one interviews. Given that I interacted on a regular basis with members—and alumni—from the group through my fieldwork and my residential advising role with Harvard, informal interviews and conversations supplemented the structured, formal interviews, and allowed me to check emerging hypotheses throughout the research and writing process.

Document review was another key data collection method for this project. Documents included information shared publicly via the official Kuumba website and program materials distributed at performances, as well as other written materials distributed just to group members via email listserv groups and at rehearsals. I saved, catalogued, and analyzed these materials along with other data collected. With regard to group emails, I reviewed and categorized all list-serv exchanges during the academic year to get a sense of the topics about which group members emailed (for example, to publicize non-Kuumba specific events, to communicate logistics, or for personal issues). The categorization allowed me to sort through emails to identify data that were relevant to this study, an important task given that more than one thousand emails were exchanged collectively on the two listserv groups in the given academic year.

I approached these various forms of data with both etic codes based on themes that were prevalent in the literature on race and diversity in higher education, as well as with an emic approach allowing patterns to emerge from the data. To support my identification of emergent themes, I relied on the modes of synthesis, convergence, and contrast outlined in portraiture to reveal 1) repetitive refrains, 2) resonant metaphors, 3) cultural and institutional rituals, 4) patterns across multiple forms of data using triangulation, and 5) contrasting or dissonant patterns across perspectives.[17] I used the Atlas.ti program as a tool in the coding process, which enabled me to quickly apply codes to multiple transcripts and filter and sort data, for example by code. To keep track of emerging questions, hypotheses, and themes throughout the data collection process to support my analysis, after each observation, interview, and document review session, I wrote research memos aiming to capture rich details from my time with the group, and my developing impressions or nascent analysis.[18] By reviewing previous memos in an ongoing manner, I was further able to meaningfully guide subsequent observations, interviews, and document review.

Authenticity Considerations

Combining empirical description and aesthetic expression, portraiture makes authenticity—as opposed to validity—its standard. This principle is grounded in the understanding of the researcher as the primary research instrument. Authenticity is achieved through resonance with three audiences. "The actors who will see themselves reflected in the [portrait]," "the readers who will see no reason to disbelieve it," and "the portraitist herself [. . .] [who will] see the 'truth value' in her work."[19]

There are three ways I worked to achieve authenticity. First, given that I spent multiple academic years attending group rehearsals, meetings, performances, and other applicable events, I was able to cultivate deepening trust and rapport with members. Such relationships are foundational to deep inquiry and knowledge construction. Similarly, my professional role at Harvard offered additional insight for this study. Second, I designed this project to include triangulation of data from multiple sources. By drawing on group email communications, ethnographic fieldnotes, document review, and one-on-one interviews, I identified thematic points of convergence and divergence across multiple sources of evidence and through multiple member accounts in order to draw conclusions. Apart from that, I intermittently checked my analyses as they emerged with group members and alumni. In many cases, members and alumni agreed with my interpretations. In the instances where there was disagreement, I reconsidered my analysis, though I did not always revise my conclusions. The goal of portraiture is not to necessarily present the exact portrait that participants would themselves construct. Rather, the aim is to achieve resonance—or a "click of recognition"—with participants.[20] Finally, I worked with an interpretive community of other education scholars with whom I shared data and burgeoning analyses to help verify the authenticity of my findings. With support from these communities, I actively sought out and addressed emergent patterns and disconfirming evidence.

On Relationships and Performance

Special attention is paid to cultivating reciprocal, respectful research relationships in portraiture.[21] This is one of the reasons the methodology appealed to me. Of particular concern in terms of navigating relationships with members of Kuumba was the convergence of my work as a researcher and my work in residence with Harvard undergraduates. The crucial question for me was, where does one role end and the other begin?

This question was not only important for my own orientation to the work, but in terms of how the students perceived the relationship. For instance, a number of Kuumba members at the time of this research lived in my particular residence, meaning I had a professional responsibility as an advisor to them outside of this study, and conversations about Kuumba could happen at any time, for example in the dining hall over lunch. Most important to me was that I not violate students' trust or privacy in either role. Sociologist Shamus Khan has described this dilemma of the embedded ethnographer based on time he spent as both a teacher and researcher at the prestigious St. Paul's School. "Subjects become friends. You will tell your friend something you will not tell a researcher who is dutifully writing down everything at the end of the day. A responsible ethnographer will often remind his subjects that they are subjects—that that intimate and juicy detail that was just spilled might make its way into a book or an article."[22] To mitigate this issue, in interviews I informed students that I didn't want them to share anything they were uncomfortable sharing or felt they shouldn't share. In the end, I also chose not to write about certain topics that I thought students might not have disclosed to me were it not for my residential role on campus. While those topics could have made an interesting exploration, one that I would have liked to share because they provided valuable insight into what made Kuumba an effective organization, they did not impact the findings I ultimately reported. The potential to do harm in sharing such data outweighed the potential to do good.

Similarly, I was concerned about the possible one-sidedness of the research relationship with students readily inviting me into their Kuumba "safe space" and participating in interviews. I questioned whether some students would feel obligated to participate in my research because I had advised them or otherwise worked with them in the residence. Though many reported that they were happy to participate in my research because they loved sharing their love for the organization with a wider audience, I was aware that asking students to spend time participating in this research could mean a sacrifice in doing schoolwork or paid work. To that end, I offered to support students in several ways outside of the research. This included reading two drafts of one student's senior thesis, baking cupcakes for the Kuumba end-of-year potluck, forwarding internship, scholarship, and job opportunities for posting on the listserv groups, publicizing Kuumba concerts to my friends and colleagues who were not affiliated with Harvard or were otherwise unfamiliar with the group, providing on-the-spot interview advice to a student who was applying for a public school teaching position, and compensating students who participated in one-on-one interviews with a gift card for Amazon.com or iTunes. In the end, I hope I gave back a fraction of what I took away from the opportunity to spend time getting to know this organization and these young people.

Beyond considerations of relationship, I was also very much aware of my "performance" or presentation of self in Kuumba. Sociologist Irving Goffman defined this kind of performance as "all the activity of a given participant on a given occasion which serves to influence in any way any of the other participants."[23] He added, "When an individual presents himself before others his performance will tend to incorporate and exemplify the officially accredited values of the society, more so, in fact, than does his behavior as a whole."[24] Given my research questions, I was especially conscious of how I was presenting my race as a woman who identifies as Black-biracial, who presents phenotypically as Black or somewhat ethnically ambiguous, and of how students were interpreting my race vis-à-vis their own and their participation in a Black student organization. On at least a couple of occasions, I recall making deliberate attempts to show some knowledge of popular Black music culture. For example, when presenting my request for interview participants to the group, I commented that I had recently seen, in person, a popular Black recording artist perform a song Kuumba was also performing. I jokingly suggested the Kuumba performance blew that artist's away. Students laughed and applauded. I also questioned how my race and research interests would impact my interactions with individual members. For instance, I wondered if the white students would feel they could disclose racial tensions or misgivings to me about their participation in the group. As they all did, I feel some sense of assuredness in the strength of the relationships I built with choir members.[25]

In the end, portraiture turned out to be a particularly helpful methodology with respect to considering how my autobiography and racial identity might influence my study. Lawrence-Lightfoot and Davis explain the potential and challenge concerning the influence of a researcher's autobiography on an investigation. "The researcher brings her own history—familial, cultural, ideological, and educational—to the inquiry. Her perspective, her questions, and her insights are inevitably shaped by these profound developmental and autobiographical experiences. She must use knowledge and wisdom drawn from these life experiences as resources for understanding, and as sources of connection and identification with the actors in the setting, but she must not let her autobiography obscure or overwhelm the inquiry."[26] Thus, when appropriate, I have attempted to make explicit connections between my perspective, background, and interpretation throughout this writing. In keeping with portraiture's intent, it is my hope that readers will consider how their own histories and autobiographies intertwine with and impact their reading of the story presented in this book.

Acknowledgments

When I was in first grade, I proudly went to school one day and told my teacher I was writing a book! It was, of course, going to be my first work as an author. My teacher was encouraging and asked me about it. I explained that I was dutifully copying, word for word, a book my aunt Shirley had given me, titled *The Pony Who Couldn't Say Neigh*. To me, that was writing a book. In seeing *Black Space* come to fruition after years of effort, my six-year-old naivete is endearing. Writing a book requires so much more than putting words on a page, and writing this book would not have been possible without the support of so many others to whom I owe a debt of gratitude.

I first thank the Kuumba Singers of Harvard College, their professional director, Sheldon K. X. Reid, and those Kuumbabes who have come before, for the gifts of their song and time. Without them and their courage and imagination to create a safe space for Black students at Harvard, this project would not be. They welcomed me into the organization with complete generosity and acceptance. I am humbled by their example.

I thank my mentors for pushing me to see what was possible as I began this research. I am filled with gratitude for their indefatigable support. Sara Lawrence-Lightfoot taught me about grace and respect, and the valuable lesson of learning to ask for what I need. Her example and pioneering of the portraiture research methodology, which guided this project, showed me the beautiful possibilities of seeking out goodness in my work and of embracing scholarly life on the margins. Wendy Luttrell, for fifteen years and counting, has taught me what authentic care means through her mentorship and has shown me how it can transform research. The lessons she has provided in the classroom, conference room, and around the dinner table have been invaluable. The opportunity to collaborate on Natasha Warikoo's research in higher education and diversity laid a foundation for this project. From the beginning, Natasha was a true champion of this book, providing resources and connections that made this project a reality.

Other scholars and near-peer mentors also shaped the trajectory of this work. Rubén Gaztambide-Fernández and Carson Byrd, experts whose work is an inspiration to my own, provided invaluable feedback. OiYan Poon, in addition to providing advice and encouragement, created a physical space for me to write and a venue to develop my ideas through the women of color writing retreats she organized, where I workshopped this project. I also thank Rich Reddick for crafting a powerful foreword to this volume and for his ongoing research on Black faculty mentorship and students at predominantly white institutions; Rich's commitment to this project exemplifies the call to action presented in his research.

Across the many years of this project, I had the opportunity to work through ideas presented on these pages with several writing groups to whom I am grateful. This includes the Finer Ladies—Chantal Francois, Shari Dickstein Staub, and Anita Wadhwa—who provided consistent feedback and friendship throughout the beginning stages of this project. Chantal, more recently, has become my weekly writing check-in partner, keeping me honest about working towards my goals. I appreciate her willingness to listen, affirm my writing frustrations, and push me to keep going. Ellie Fitts Fulmer and Kathleen Riley provided a steadfast community and indispensable insights as I shaped the findings. They reread data and helped me uncover divergent perspectives. Finally, I am appreciative for the critical reading of chapters and proposal materials provided by Sabina Rak Neugebauer and Elizabeth Blair. Everyone deserves a writing group like Liz and Sabina, who combine a depth of theoretical understanding, skill at writing, and compassion in the support they provide.

This project really began to transform into this book while I was on the faculty at Ithaca College (IC). From the start, the Education Department there, under the leadership of Jeanne Copenhaver-Johnson, provided needed material resources and colleagueship. Nia Nunn provided feedback on early drafts of findings chapters, and colleagues across IC provided shared additional insights on the process of completing a book. Paula Ionide and Belisa González provided their own version of a safe space for faculty of color at IC. Paula guided my writing in generously sharing a draft of her first book proposal, as well as examples of reviewer feedback and editor comments. I will never be able to repay Paula's generosity. I only hope to pay it forward to future scholars. The book proposal workshops provided by the Center for Faculty Excellence at IC, then led by Wade Pickering and Judith Ross-Bernstein, were also essential in the development of my proposal materials.

When I transitioned to Lehman College at the City University of New York (CUNY), I found a community to support this work, including colleagues in the

Middle and High School Education Department and my two chairs, Serigne Gnigue and Wesley Pitts, and Immaculee Harushimana, who shared advice from her depth of experience working on book projects. I am especially appreciative of the feedback of the research and writers group led at the time by Gaoyin Qian, including Kenneth Schlessinger, Stacy Katz, Danielle Magaldi, Roger Peach, Jennifer Van Allen, and Rosa Rivera-McCutchen. Rosa offered input beyond the regular meetings of this group and her conceptualization of critical care was formative to the one I present in this book. Among the broader CUNY community, Debbie Sonu and I worked on a paper drawing on this research, an experience that allowed me to revisit the data with a new perspective. Warren Benfield, Charles Cange, Maggie Dickinson, David Lee, Tashana Samuel, Angelina Tallaj who were members of Anahí Viladrich's Faculty Fellowship Publishing Program group with me also provided feedback on an early draft of the prospectus for this project.

Similarly, numerous colleagues provided discerning feedback on drafts and conceptualizations of this work, including Janine de Novais, Maleka Donaldson, Jonathan Gramling, Julia Hayden, Jay Huguley, Tony Jack, Adrienne Keene, Meredith Mira, Ana Nieto, Carla Shalaby, and Nicole Simon. Helen Malone eagerly provided feedback on the publication process. I thank Jen Dorsey for not only being a part of this important network of friends and scholars, but for more recently introducing me to the Any Good Thing writing challenge (AGT) and being my accountability partner. Rebecca Barrett-Fox is a superhero for organizing and running the AGT—refusal to lose my twenty dollars as part of the AGT is the only thing that kept me working on this book some days. Jeff Imrich regularly checked in on my progress—even when the last thing I wanted was someone to ask me about my progress—and offered input as I edited this manuscript, including in-depth feedback on chapter drafts.

Additionally, I thank the communities and individuals who supported me through their consistent encouragement, including Wendy Angus, Libby and the entire Brothers family, Gretchen Brion-Meisels, CJ Crowder, Christina Dobbs, Raquel González, Betina Hsieh, Janet Kim, Jumin Kim, Te-Wen Lo, Meghan Lockwood, Kathleen Messman, Ben Moss, Tiffany Nguyen, Thomas Nikundiwe, Esther Ohito, Alison Lin, Claire Shin, Sarah Stewart Johnson, and Marcy Sutherland. The Ladies of 1410 High Rise South (and extended members) and the Toledo Lounge Collective served as inspiration for the questions I brought to this research—Neel Saxena planted a seed when he gifted me Vijay Prashad's *Everybody Was Kung Fu Fighting* for Christmas one year, way before I had ever heard of Kuumba or dreamed of writing this book.

I also had the benefit of working with two incredibly talented developmental editors, David Lobenstine and Katie Lambright. David was the only person to read and provide feedback on the entire initial draft. I had always seen myself as a "good" writer, but I am beholden to David for pushing me in new ways; I will never think about writing the same way after working with him. Katie was amazing, jumping in at the last minute to provide feedback when I realized I would need to write an entirely new chapter with an impending deadline.

In addition to the editing provided by David and Katie, August Smith was a critical reader of the entire completed draft of this manuscript. August provided a final read, offering insights and prompting me at places where my writing could be more incisive.

There would be no book without Lisa Banning's belief in this project and the support of the team at Rutgers University Press. From the beginning, Lisa was enthusiastic and receptive to my work. I am also grateful to Mary Ribesky, the production editor, and Donna Miele, the copy editor, at Westchester Publishing Services, who were both exceedingly meticulous in shepherding this work through the final stages of the production process.

Rarely do my loved ones get to be as involved in any of my research projects as Sheeba Jacob and Pia Das. Sheeba has literally been involved in this project from start to finish, first transcribing interviews and offering reflections on each, reflections that influenced what appears on these pages, and later offering feedback on my ideas and drafts of chapters. Pia, whose eagerness to always go on an adventure is something I truly admire, was willing to hop on a plane and accompany me for Kuumba's weeklong spring break trip while I was conducting ethnographic research. She traipsed across a small island-nation with me, taking a series of buses that didn't always seem to go where they were supposed to, as we attended the group's performances and social outings. To have Sheeba and Pia involved in this work in this way is a gift I can't fully articulate.

This book was finished during the dark days of the COVID-19 pandemic. If it weren't for Jen Collett and Mia Hood, I might have gone weeks without meaningful, in-person interactions, which is the lifeblood of my creative process. Not only were Jen and Mia steady presences at a time when nothing else felt steady, but they endured me going on and on about this project and provided useful input. Jen helped me realize the arc of the story and come to grips with what needed to be cut. Mia, who is a writer's writer, was also always willing to lend an ear and advice about the crafting of this book. Of course, Rigby was always by my side, too. Unfortunately, I haven't yet trained him to give feedback on writing.

Lastly, I thank my parents, siblings, and extended family, including my aunts Mae and Shirley, for instilling in me a desire to see the world as it could be, to imagine the impossible, and to believe I could never fail. My parents taught me both that love sees no color and that love definitely sees color, a useful grounding for envisioning the safe Black space. It is unfortunate that my father is not here to see that I actually have written a book. Kevin, Donna, and Tina, and all of my nieces and nephews, always show up for me when I need them most. That is the kind of love and support that makes the curiosity and tenacity needed for completing a project like this possible.

Each day as I worked on this book—even through the challenges—I had many things to be grateful for, including an inspirational project that I found fulfilling and personally meaningful, supportive mentors, and a community of family and friends who believed I was capable of achieving anything. For those I could not include here, their words of encouragement, their check-in emails and messages, and offers to be available have meant so much.

Notes

FOREWORD

1. bell hooks, "Homeplace (A Site of Resistance)," in *Yearning: Race, Gender, and Cultural Politics* (Boston: South End Press, 1990) 41–49.

2. Kimberly A. Griffin and Richard J. Reddick, "Surveillance and Sacrifice: Gender Differences in the Mentoring Patterns of Black Professors at Predominantly White Research Universities," *American Educational Research Journal* 48, no. 5 (2011): 1032–1057, https://doi.org/10.3102/0002831211405025; Veronica A. Jones and Richard J. Reddick, "The Heterogeneity of Resistance: How Black Students Utilize Engagement and Activism to Challenge PWI Inequalities," *The Journal of Negro Education* 86, no. 3 (2017): 204–219, https://doi.org/10.7709/jnegroeducation.86.3.0204; Richard J. Reddick, "Reclaiming Our Time: A 21st-Century Response to Banks' 'Afro-American Scholars in the University,'" *Urban Education* 55, no. 2 (2020): 238–266, https://doi.org/10.1177/0042085918805805.

3. Regents of Univ. of California v. Bakke, 438 U.S. 265 (1978); Grutter v. Bollinger, 539 U.S. 306 (2003); Fisher v. University of Texas, 579 U.S. ___ (2016); Fisher v. University of Texas, 570 U.S. 297 (2013).

4. See Franklin Tuitt regarding souls of Black students: "Enhancing Visibility in Graduate Education: Black Women's Perceptions of Inclusive Pedagogical Practices," *International Journal of Teaching and Learning in Higher Education* 22, no. 3 (2010): 246–257, https://files.eric.ed.gov/fulltext/EJ938560.pdf

5. Beverly Daniel Tatum, *"Why Are All the Black Kids Sitting Together in the Cafeteria?": And Other Conversations about Race* (New York: Basic Books, 1997).

INTRODUCTION: HOW DO YOU LIFT *EVERY* VOICE?

Epigraph: Lyrics originally written by James Weldon Johnson in 1899 (NAACP, "NAACP History: Lift Every Voice and Sing," Accessed November 6, 2020. https://www.naacp.org/naacp-history-lift-evry-voice-and-sing/).

1. The real names of the organization and University are used with permission.

2. I use "Black" as an umbrella term to signify people whose heritage spans the African diaspora, including African Americans and Black people from elsewhere. I use

"African American" to signify Black Americans who generally trace their heritage to enslaved Blacks in the United States. When possible, I use participants' and authors' words, which may not align with my definitions. Recognizing the ways in which power and language are entangled, "Black" as a race label is capitalized throughout, while white is not, see Esther O. Ohito and the Fugitive Literacies Collective, "'The Creative Aspect Woke Me Up': Awakening to Multimodal Essay Composition as a Fugitive Literacy Practice," *English Education* 52, no. 3 [2020]: 186–222. I defer to authors' capitalization when directly citing materials.

3. For an in-depth history of this period of Black student protest across Ivy League campuses, see Stefan M. Bradley, *Upending the Ivory Tower: Civil Rights Black Power and the Ivy League* (New York: New York University Press, 2018).

4. I distinguish "racism" from "anti-Black racism" to note the particularity of anti-Blackness in the United States, which, following from the institution of slavery, denies Black humanity and is evident in the history of indefensible violence against Black people (see Ohito and the Fugitive Literacies Collective, "Creative," 186–222; Kihana Miraya Ross, "Call It What It Is: Anti-Blackness," The New York Times, June 4, 2020, https://www.nytimes.com/2020/06/04/opinion/george-floyd-anti-blackness.html).

5. For additional context, Jamie D. Halper describes Harvard students' involvement in the 1967 Roxbury riots. See Jamie D. Halper, "With History Written in Roxbury, Harvard Remained Ambivalent," *The Harvard Crimson*, May 22, 2017, https://www.thecrimson.com /article/2017/5/22/roxbury-riots-1967/.

6. NAACP, "NAACP History: Lift Every Voice and Sing," accessed November 6, 2020, https://www.naacp.org/naacp-history-lift-evry-voice-and-sing/.

7. This was well before Beyoncé introduced "Lift Every Voice and Sing" to the pop culture canon with her 2018 Coachella performance. Ellen Reslen, "Beyoncé Reveals the Deeply Personal Story Behind Her Black National Anthem Performance at Coachella," *Harper's Bazaar*, August 6, 2018, https://www.harpersbazaar.com/culture/art-books -music/a22655019/beyonce-black-national-anthem-coachella/.

8. Marcus Granderson, "Kuumba (v., Swahili): To Create," shared on the Kuumba Singers website in 2018.

9. See Bradley, *Upending the Ivory Tower*.

10. As Harvard's oldest Black student organization, Kuumba is just around fifty years old. Compared with the Harvard Glee Club, which is the oldest college chorus in the United States founded in 1858 (Harvard Glee Club, "About Us," accessed August 30, 2018, http://www.harvardgleeclub.org/), Kuumba is a relatively young organization. While there were recognized Black student organizations on campus prior to Kuumba (dating to the mid-1960s at least), some of those were consolidated into the Harvard Black Students Association, founded in 1977 (Harvard Black Students Association, "About Us," accessed June 29, 2021, https://www.theharvardbsa.com/about-bsa-1). Referring to Kuumba as "multicultural" was from Kuumba and the University, and was suggested to mean multiracial; some members pointed out to me that Kuumba was multicultural when it was exclusively comprised of Black students, given the range of representation from the African diaspora.

11. As cited in the spring 2010 "May We Forever Stand" Kuumba concert program. Evans was the son of sharecroppers and under his tenure the Harvard Black student population multiplied more than fifteen times (Matthew S. Blumenthal, "From Share-

croppers' Son to College's Gatekeeper: During Evans' Tenure, Black Population at Harvard Multiplied 15 Times," *The Harvard Crimson*, October 17, 2005, https://www .thecrimson.com/article/2005/10/17/from-sharecroppers-son-to-colleges-gatekeeper/).

12. W. Carson Byrd, *Poison in the Ivy: Race Relations and the Reproduction of Inequality on Elite College Campuses,* edited by Harold S. Wechsler, the American Campus (New Brunswick: Rutgers University Press, 2017).

13. Wendy M. Laybourn and Devon R. Goss, *Diversity in Black Greek-Letter Organizations: Breaking the Line* (New York: Routledge, 2018), 109.

14. The first Black undergraduate from the continent of Africa, Plenyono Gbe Wolo, a male student from Liberia, earned his degree in 1917 (Kris Snibbe, "A Window into African-American History," *Harvard Gazette*, February 4, 2011, https://news.harvard .edu/gazette/story/2011/02/a-window-into-african-american-history).

15. Stephen R. Fox, *The Guardian of Boston: William Monroe Trotter* (New York: Atheneum Press, 1970), 18; Biography, "Carter G. Woodson Biography (1875–1950)," accessed November 6, 2020, https://www.biography.com/scholar/carter-g-woodson; Kimberly D. Brown, "From the Low Point of American Race Relations: Dr. Carter Woodson's Negro History Week," accessed November 6, 2020, https://americanhistory.si.edu/blog/2013 /02/what-we-know-as-black-history-month-dr-carter-woodsons-intentions-for-negro -history-week.html.

16. While I prefer Carson Byrd's rephrasing of "historically white colleges and universities" to "predominantly white" institutions (*Poison in the Ivy*, 160) to indicate that the racial histories and practices of said institutions are not neutral and consistently support the interests of white students, as they were set up to do, I use both phrases interchangeably throughout this volume for variety.

17. Shaun R. Harper, Lori D. Patton, and Ontario S. Wooden, "Access and Equity for African American Students in Higher Education: A Critical Race Historical Analysis of Policy Efforts," *Journal of Higher Education* 80, no. 4 (2009): 389–414, https://doi.org /10.1080/00221546.2009.11779022.

18. Craig Steven Wilder, *Ebony and Ivy: Race, Slavery, and the Troubled History of America's Universities* (New York: Bloomsbury Press, 2013), 3.

19. W.E.B. Du Bois, *The Autobiography of W.E.B. Du Bois* (New York: International Publishers), 1968, 124. Du Bois explained, "I was happy at Harvard, but for unusual reasons. One of these circumstances was my acceptance of racial segregation" (125).

20. Crimson Staff, "In Celebration of Black History: Harvard Has Come a Long Way from Institutionalized Prejudice, but More Needs to Be Done," *The Harvard Crimson*, February 28, 2011. Potentially revealing the university's ambivalent past of racial inclusion and exclusion, in the official history of Harvard on the university website the issue of coeducation is addressed, but this is not so much the case with racial integration (see Harvard College, "About Harvard College: A brief history of Harvard College," accessed June 4, 2021, https://handbook.fas.harvard.edu/book/brief-history-harvard-college). Yet, the university's history of excluding women is arguably more entrenched—historically speaking—than its history of excluding Black men. Women were not permitted to attend classes at Harvard until 1943. It wasn't until 1963, though, that Harvard would award degrees to then-Radcliffe women.

21. "Overseers" was also used for those who directed the work of enslaved Blacks on plantations.

22. Lauren E. Baer, "The Ku Klux Klan at Harvard," *The Harvard Crimson*, February 18, 1999, https://www.thecrimson.com/article/1999/2/18/the-ku-klux-klan-at-harvard/.

23. A *Boston Globe* survey of Black residents of eight U.S. cities found Boston characterized as least welcoming to people of color. Fifty-four percent of respondents characterized it as such (Akilah Johnson, "Boston. Racism. Image. Reality," *The Boston Globe*, December 10, 2017, https://apps.bostonglobe.com/spotlight/boston-racism-image-reality/series/image/).

24. "Third World" was the preferred terminology in the 1960s and 70s to describe university centers that focused specifically on the needs and concerns of students of color. At Harvard, this request was met with the creation of the Harvard Foundation for Intercultural and Race Relations, which focused more specifically on racial integration on campus (Shu-Ling Chen, "Debates over Third World Centers at Princeton, Brown, and Harvard: Minority Student Activism and Institutional Responses in the 1960s and 1970s" [unpublished EdD dissertation, Graduate School of Education, Harvard University, 2000]).

25. Hubert E. Walters, "Kuumba: The Early Years," the History section of the website for the Kuumba Singers of Harvard College, accessed June 6, 2021, http://kuumbasingers.org/history/.

26. Readers interested in learning more about Sheldon's leadership of Kuumba should see Deckman, in which I offer a portrait of his work with the group. Sherry L. Deckman, "Leave the Space Better than You Found It Through Song: Music, Diversity, and Mission in One Black Student Organization," *Harvard Educational Review* 83, no. 2 (2013): 279–294.

27. Harvard Gender and Sexuality Caucus, "History of the Caucus," accessed November 18, 2020, http://hgsc.sigs.harvard.edu/article.html?aid=106. In 1985, the Harvard Gay & Lesbian Caucus worked with Harvard administrators, the President and Fellows of Harvard College to create a university-wide antidiscrimination policy that included discrimination on the basis of sexual orientation, which had the effect of also prohibiting student organizations from restricting membership based on race.

28. Harvard College, "Admissions Statistics," accessed July 16, 2021, https://college.harvard.edu/admissions/admissions-statistics. See also Statistical Atlas, "Race and Ethnicity in the United States," accessed June 7, 2021, https://statisticalatlas.com/United-States/Race-and-Ethnicity.

29. For a discussion of implementation gaps in corporate diversity and affirmative action initiatives, see Alexandra Kalev, Frank Dobbin, and Erin Kelly, "Best Practices or Best Guesses? Assessing the Efficacy of Corporate Affirmative Action and Diversity Policies," *American Sociological Review* 71, no. 4 (2006): 589–617. Natasha K. Warikoo and Sherry L. Deckman also find that similar policy/structural endeavors aimed at addressing campus diversity issues at Harvard University and Brown University are experienced differently by students based on implementation, see "Beyond the Numbers: Institutional Influences on Experiences with Diversity on Elite College Campuses," *Sociological Forum* 29, no. 4 (2014): 959–981.

30. James Sidanius, Shana Levin, and Colette Van Laar, *The Diversity Challenge: Social Identity and Intergroup Relations on the College Campus* (New York: Russell Sage Foundation, 2008), 231. See also Byrd, *Poison in the Ivy*, for similar statistics on white students' membership in majority non-white student organizations on elite college campuses.

31. According to Sidanius, Levin, and Van Laar, the participation rates for other racial/ethnic groups are 28 percent Latinos, 42 percent Asians, and 60.4 percent African Americans (*Diversity Challenge*, 231).

32. See Byrd, *Poison in the Ivy*.

33. I use race, ethnicity, and culture somewhat interchangeably, as do my participants. There is much debate in the social sciences regarding differences and similarities among these constructs. This is a topic explored by expert contributors to PBS's "Race—The Power of an Illusion" discussion, some of whom argue that ethnicity is preferred to race by those who might want to obscure the impact of systematic discrimination (California Newsreel, "Race—The Power of an Illusion: Ask the Experts." accessed November 16, 2020. http://www.pbs.org/race/000_About/002_04-experts-03-02.htm). This is a distinction Stephen Cornell and Douglas Hartman also highlight, writing of the persistence of racial categorization that "it does illustrate . . . the particular power of race, which has been a foundational feature of American life in a way that ethnicity has not: the ultimate boundary between 'us' and 'them'" (*Ethnicity and Race: Making Identities in a Changing World*, 2nd ed,, *Sociology for a new century* [Thousand Oaks, CA: Pine Forge Press, 2007], 27). If and when, participants did specifically use either construct, I attempted to retain their intention. My approach to using the terms interchangeably when identifying student organizations followed Harvard's designation of such organizations. At the time when data for this research were collected, Harvard classified organizations with focuses as disparate as the Queer Students Association, the Black Men's Forum, the Korean Association, and the Texas Club as "Cultural and Racial Initiatives." In more recent years, gender and sexuality have been separated into a new category. For a list of current student organizations searchable by category, see https://dso.college.harvard.edu/list-student-organizations.

34. Byrd, *Poison in the Ivy*.

35. Du Bois, *Autobiography*; Isabel Wilkerson, *Caste: The Origin of Our Discontents* (New York: Random House, 2020).

36. The Harvard Foundation for Intercultural and Race Relations, "Expansion" Accessed June 29, 2021. https://harvardfoundation.fas.harvard.edu/expansion.

37. The term "white allies" was used in this context to signal white people who were sympathetic to and wanted to support the fight against racial injustice experienced by people of color.

38. Regarding race and performance, see E. Patrick Johnson, *Appropriating Blackness: Performance and the Politics of Authenticity* (Durham: Duke University Press, 2003).

39. Katy Perry has been criticized several times for offensively drawing on Asian and Black aesthetics and culture in her music videos and concerts (see Julee Wilson, "Katy Perry Apologizes For Cultural Appropriation, Rocking Cornrows," *Essence*, June 14, 2017, accessed June 6, 2021, https://www.essence.com/hair/katy-perry-apologizes-cultural-appropriation). Similarly, Ariana Grande has been chided for "profiting off of black aesthetics" (see Spencer Kornhaber, "How Ariana Grande Fell Off the Cultural-Appropriation Tightrope," *The Atlantic*, January 23, 2019, accessed June 6, 2021, https://www.theatlantic.com/entertainment/archive/2019/01/ariana-grandes-7-rings-really-cultural-appropriation/580978/; ¶5).

40. Further description is available at https://www.nytimes.com/2016/02/23/nyregion/off-campus-ghetto-party-condemned-by-fairfield-university.html (Kristin Hussey,

"Off-Campus 'Ghetto Party' Condemned by Fairfield University," *the New York Times*, February 22, 2016) and https://www.colorlines.com/articles/college-ghetto-themed-parties -awful-racist-idea-just-wont-die (Julianne Hing, "College 'Ghetto-Themed' Parties: The Awful, Racist Idea That Just Won't Die," *Colorlines*, February 18, 2010).

41. Natasha K. Warikoo, *The Diversity Bargain: And Other Dilemmas of Race, Admissions, and Meritocracy at Elite Universities* (Chicago: University of Chicago Press, 2016); Warikoo and Deckman, "Beyond the Numbers". Resident tutors were graduate students and professionals who lived in the twelve undergraduate houses and advised students personally, professionally, and academically. Race Relations tutors supported diversity-related programming in the houses.

42. Tatum, *Why Are All the Black Kids*.

43. Some scholars of Black and African American studies have cautioned against diasporic framings such as this, as they can both reify and obscure differences that are the result of institutional and systematic oppression (see for example, Alexander G. Weheliye, *Habeas Viscus: Racializing Assemblages, Biopolitics, and Black Feminist Theories of the Human* [Durham: Duke University Press, 2014]).

44. Evelyn Brooks Higginbotham, *Righteous Discontent: The Women's Movement in the Black Baptist Church, 1880–1920* (Cambridge: Harvard University Press, 1993). For a discussion of race and religion in higher education, see Julie. J. Park, *When Diversity Drops: Race, Religion, and Affirmative Action in Higher Education* (New Brunswick: Rutgers University Press, 2013). Park notes that church congregations and campus fellowships, like many other institutions in the United States are divided along race lines.

45. Here, I want to be explicit in acknowledging that I only interviewed those who were members and alumni of Kuumba and not those who had left the organization. It is possible or even probable that those who chose not to continue as members in Kuumba did not find it to be a safe space for reasons about which I cannot fully speculate.

46. See appendices for a detailed discussion of the research methodology, including a table of one-on-one interview participants.

47. Fannie Lou Hamer, "'Nobody's Free Until Everybody's Free': Speech Delivered at the Founding of the National Women's Political Caucus, Washington, D.C., July 10, 1971," in *The Speeches of Fannie Lou Hamer: To Tell It Like It Is*, edited by Maegan Parker Brooks and Davis W. Houck (Jackson, MS: University Press of Mississippi, 2010) 134–139, 134.

48. Wilder has written, "[. . .]Harvard's history was inseparable from the history of slavery and the slave trade" (*Ebony and Ivy*, 3).

49. Student participants were given the option of designing their own pseudonyms, which many did.

50. Sara Lawrence-Lightfoot and Jessica Hoffmann Davis, *The Art and Science of Portraiture* (San Francisco: Jossey-Bass, 1997).

51. Ibid., xvi. Emphasis in original.

52. As urged to me by Sara Lawrence-Lightfoot.

PRELUDE: (UN)SAFE SPACE AND RACIAL DIVERSITY IN THE IVORY TOWER

1. Christina Paxson, "Brown University President: A Safe Space for Freedom of Expression," *The Washington Post*, September 5, 2016.

2. See John Jay Ellison, PhD to Student of the Class of 2020, https://news.uchicago.edu /sites/default/files/attachments/Dear_Class_of_2020_Students.pdf, ¶3. Note the conflicted reception of the letter reported by Scott Jaschik in "The Chicago Letter and Its Aftermath,"

Inside Higher Ed, August 29, 2016, https://www.insidehighered.com/news/2016/08/29/u-chicago-letter-new-students-safe-spaces-sets-intense-debate.

3. Cati de los Ríos, Jorge López, and Ernest Morrell write, "Schools as racial projects operate under the assumption that the process of becoming educated is a race-neutral or color-blind experience. On the contrary, not only formal school curricula but also informal, hidden, and null curricula work to maintain economic, political, societal, and cultural order" ("Toward a Critical Pedagogy of Race: Ethnic Studies and Literacies of Power in High School Classrooms," *Race and Social Problems* 7, no. 1 [2015]: 84–96, 87).

4. Fox, Catherine, "From Transaction to Transformation: (En)Countering White Heteronormativity in 'Safe Spaces,'" *College English* 69, no. 5 (May, 2007): 496–511; Özlem Sensoy and Robin DiAngelo, "Respect Differences? Challenging the Common Guidelines in Social Justice Education," *Democracy and Education* 22, no. 2 (2014): 1–10.

5. Jennifer L. Hochschild and Nathan Scovronick, *The American Dream and the Public Schools* (Oxford: Oxford University Press, 2004).

6. Thomas J. Espenshade, Alexandria Walton Radford, and Chang Young Chung, *No Longer Separate, Not Yet Equal: Race and Class in Elite College Admission and Campus Life* (Princeton, NJ: Princeton University Press, 2009). This may be even more the case for white students, who are the most racially isolated of all groups (Sidanius, Levin, and Van Laar, *Diversity Challenge*).There is evidence that Harvard students are no different in this way. In research I conducted with Natasha Warikoo (Warikoo and Deckman, "Beyond the Numbers"), many respondents noted that Harvard is the most diverse place they have lived/attended school. This confirms that their previous living and schooling situations were primarily with people of their race background, or in the case of some students of color, primarily with white peers.

7. See Bradley, *Ivory Tower*; William C. Purdy, "Higher Education and a Living, Diverse Democracy: An Overview," *Diversity & Democracy* 21, no. 3 (2018): 4–9; Frederick Rudolph, *The American College and University: A History* (New York: Alfred A. Knopf, 1962).

8. Emphasis as cited in Bradley, *Ivory Tower,* xv.

9. See Harvard College, "Mission, Vision, & History," accessed June 10, 2021, https://college.harvard.edu/about/mission-vision-history.

10. Ibid.

11. See Wilder, *Ebony and Ivy* for further discussion of the history of exclusion.

12. Mitchell Stevens, *Creating a Class: College Admissions and the Education of Elites* (Cambridge, MA: Harvard University Press, 2007). The U.S. News & World Report university rankings, updated annually, is a prime example of this in actions (see "2021 Best National University Rankings," accessed June 10, 2021, https://www.usnews.com/best-colleges/rankings/national-universities).

13. Espenshade, Radford, and Chung, *No Longer Separate.*

14. See Harvard College, "Admissions Statistics," accessed June 10, 2021, https://college.harvard.edu/admissions/admissions-statistics.

15. Michael S. Roth, *Safe Enough Spaces: A Pragmatist's Approach to Inclusion, Free Speech, and Political Correctness on College Campuses* (New Haven, CT: Yale University Press, 2019).

16. Wendy Leo Moore, *Reproducing Racism: White Space, Elite Law Schools, and Racial Inequality* (Lanham, MD: Rowman & Littlefield Publishers, 2008); Warikoo, *Diversity Bargain.*

17. See for example, Rory Kramer, "Diversifiers at Elite Schools," *Du Bois Review* 5, no. 2 (2008): 287–307.

18. For a discussion of this phenomenon in an elite boarding high school, see Rubén A. Gaztambide-Fernández, *The Best of the Best: Becoming Elite at an American Boarding School* (Cambridge, MA: Harvard University Press, 2009) See also Stephen J. Quaye, "Facilitating Dialogues about Racial Realities," *Teachers College Record* 116, no. 8 (2014): 1–42; Stevens, *Creating a Class.*

19. Warikoo and Deckman, "Beyond the Numbers"; see also Gaztambide-Fernández, *Best.*

20. Kramer ("Diversifiers") identified a "diversifier mindset" among Black and Latino students attending elite boarding schools through the RISE program. Students in RISE— a prep school pipeline program for students of color from low-income backgrounds— were coached by program staff and older students to see themselves as, and to see value in, educating their white and privileged peers about their backgrounds.

21. Grutter, 539 U.S. 306 (2003); Fisher, 579 U.S. ___ (2016); Fisher, 570 U.S. 297 (2013).

22. Fisher, 579 U.S. ___ (2016), 12, emphasis added.

23. Grutter, 539 U.S. 306 (2003).

24. See Students for Fair Admissions, Inc., v. President and Fellows of Harvard College (Harvard Corporation) (D. Mass., filed September 30, 2019), accessed June 10, 2021, https://admissionscase.harvard.edu/files/adm-case/files/2019-10-30_dkt_672_findings _of_fact_and_conclusions_of_law.pdf.

25. See Harvard Admission Lawsuit, "The Lawsuit," accessed June 10, 2021, https://admissionscase.harvard.edu/lawsuit.

26. Lawrence Bacow, email to Alumni and Friends, October 1, 2019, ¶6. The subject line was "Admissions at Harvard College."

27. Derrick A. Bell, "*Brown v. Board of Education* and the Interest-Convergence Dilemma." *Harvard Law Review* 93, no. 3 (1980): 518–533.

28. Warikoo, *Diversity Bargain.*

29. Gaztambide-Fernández, *Best*; Shamus Rahman Khan, *Privilege: The Making of an Adolescent Elite at St. Paul's School* (Princeton, NJ: Princeton University Press, 2011); Warikoo, *Diversity Bargain.*

30. Khan, *Privilege.*

31. Warikoo, *Diversity Bargain.*

32. This is a hallmark of white supremacy in humanizing white people, in contrast to Black people (Cory Collins, "What Is White Privilege, Really?" *Teaching Tolerance* 60, [Fall 2018]:38–41).

33. Sherry L. Deckman, "Managing Race and Race-ing Management: Teachers' Stories of Race and Classroom Conflict," *Teachers College Record* 119, no. 11 (2017): 1–40.

34. W. Carson Byrd, Rachelle J. Brunn-Bevel, and Parker R. Sexton, "'We Don't All Look Alike': The Academic Performance of Black Student Populations at Elite Colleges," *Du Bois Review* 11, no. 2 (2014): 353–385; Anthony A. Jack, *The Privileged Poor: How Colleges Are Failing Disadvantaged Students* (Cambridge, MA: Harvard University Press, 2019).

35. Byrd, Brunn-Bevel, and Sexton, "Don't All Look Alike."

36. Sandra S. Smith and Mignon R. Moore, "Intraracial Diversity and Relations among African-Americans: Closeness among Black Students at a Predominantly White

University," *American Journal of Sociology* 106, no. 1 (2000):1–39; Tatum, *Why Are All the Black Kids.*

37. Byrd, *Poison in the Ivy*, 136.

38. For instance, only 56 percent of Black students' pre-college friendships were with other Black students (ibid.).

39. Gaztambide-Fernández, *Best*; Gusa; Du Bois wrote of his time as a student, "I was in Harvard, but not of it" (*Autobiography*, 126).

40. See Sara Ahmed, *On Being Included: Racism and Diversity in Institutional Life* (Durham, NC: Duke University Press, 2012), 33.

41. Ibid., 71.

42. See Liliana M. Garces and Uma M. Jayakumar, "Dynamic Diversity: Toward a Contextual Understanding of Critical Mass," *Educational Researcher* 43, no. 3 (2014): 115–124.

43. Roth, *Safe Enough*, 23.

44. Drew Gilpin Faust, former Harvard University President as cited in Presidential Task Force on Inclusion and Belonging, "Final Report," accessed July 12, 2021, https://inclusionandbelongingtaskforce.harvard.edu/files/inclusion/files/harvard_inclusion_belonging_task_force_final_report_full_web_180327.pdf.

45. Angela Calabrese Barton and Edna Tan, "Beyond Equity as Inclusion: A Framework of 'Rightful Presence' for Guiding Justice-Oriented Studies in Teaching and Learning," *Educational Researcher* 49, no. 6 (2020): 433–440.

46. Garces and Jayakumar, "Dynamic Diversity."

47. Diana Ali, "Safe Spaces and Brave Spaces: Historical Context and Recommendations for Student Affairs Professionals," *NASPA Policy and Practice Series* 2 (October 2017), accessed November 16, 2020, https://www.naspa.org/images/uploads/main/Policy_and_Practice_No_2_Safe_Brave_Spaces.pdf.

48. Laybourn and Goss, *Black Greek-Letter.*

49. Rosiline D. Floyd, "Yes We Can: The Impact Membership in Black Greek Sororities Has on the Experience and Persistence of Black Women Students at Predominantly White 4-year Institutions," unpublished PhD dissertation, Indiana State University, 2009; Douglas A. Guiffrida, "African American Student Organizations as Agents of Social Integration," *Journal of College Student Development* 44, no. 3 (2003): 304–319; Samuel D. Museus, "The Role of Ethnic Student Organizations in Fostering African American and Asian American Students' Cultural Adjustment and Membership at Predominantly White Institutions," *Journal of College Student Development* 49, no. 6 (2008): 568–586.

50. Garcia provides an example of how participation in Latina/o sororities and fraternities at predominantly white institutions contributes to students' sense of belonging. (Crystal Garcia, "Belonging in a Predominantly White Institution: The Role of Membership in Latina/o Sororities and Fraternities," *Journal of Diversity in Higher Education* 13, no. 2 [2020]: 181–193.)

51. Edward Murguía, Raymond V. Padilla, and Michael Pavel, "Ethnicity and the Concept of Social Integration in Tinto's Model of Institutional Departure," *Journal of College Student Development* 32, no. 5 (1991) 433–439.

52. Guiffrida, "African American Student Organizations."

53. Jonathan Helwink, "Safe Spaces Just Make the World More Dangerous," *the Federalist*, November 16, 2016, ¶3.

54. Roth, *Safe Enough*, 87.

55. Ibid.

56. Ali, "Safe Spaces"; Brian Arao, and Kristi Clemens, "From Safe Spaces to Brave Spaces: A New Way to Frame Dialogue around Diversity and Social Justice," in *The Art of Effective Facilitation: Reflections from Social Justice Educators*, edited by Lisa M. Landreman (Sterling, VA: Stylus, 2013), 135–150; John G. Palfrey, *Safe Spaces, Brave Spaces: Diversity and Free Expression in Education* (Cambridge, MA: MIT Press, 2017).

57. Palfrey, *Safe, Brave*, 20.

58. Ibid., 21.

59. Kristie Dotson, "Conceptualizing Epistemic Oppression," *Social Epistemology: A Journal of Knowledge, Culture and Policy* 28, no. 2 (2014): 115–138.

60. Rubén Gaztambide-Fernández and Leila Angod, "Approximating Whiteness: Race, Class, and Empire in the Making of Modern Elite/White Subjects," *Educational Theory* 69, no. 6 (2019): 719–743; Christina Sharpe, *In the Wake: On Blackness and Being* (Durham, NC: Duke University Press, 2016).

61. Morton Schapiro, "I'm Northwestern's President. Here's Why Safe Spaces for Students Are Important," *The Washington Post*, January 15, 2016, ¶10.

62. Tatum, *Why Are All the Black Kids*.

63. Elijah Anderson, "'The White Space.'" *Sociology of Race and Ethnicity* 1, no. 1 (2015):10–21.

64. Garces and Jayakumar, "Dynamic Diversity."

65. Anderson, "White Space."

66. Diane Lynn Gusa, "White Institutional Presence: The Impact of Whiteness on Campus Climate," *Harvard Educational Review* 80, no. 4 (2010): 464–489, 465; See also Moore, *Reproducing Racism*.

67. Harvard University Office of the Senior Vice President, Faculty Development and Diversity, "Faculty Demographics," accessed June 10, 2021, https://faculty.harvard.edu/faculty-demographics.

68. Özlem Sensoy, and Robin DiAngelo, "'We Are All for Diversity, but . . .': How Faculty Hiring Committees Reproduce Whiteness and Practical Suggestions for How They Can Change," *Harvard Educational Review* 87, no. 4 (2017): 557–580.

69. For example, see Jack (*Privileged Poor*), who notes that Black students from affluent backgrounds as well as those from less affluent backgrounds who attended elite secondary prep schools are also adept at these expected modes of interaction and comportment.

70. Moore, *Reproducing Racism*, 27.

71. Gusa, "White Institutional." This has been an issue in recent campus protests, where, for instance, students at Yale successfully lobbied to have the name of Calhoun College House renamed. The House's original namesake, John C. Calhoun, was a documented white supremacist and supporter of slavery (see Yale News, "Yale Changes Calhoun College's Name to Honor Grace Murray Hopper," February 11, 2017, accessed June 10, 2021, https://news.yale.edu/2017/02/11/yale-change-calhoun-college-s-name-honor-grace-murray-hopper-0).

72. Consider, for example, Harvard botanist Edward M. East's 1919 book, *Inbreeding and Outbreeding: Their Genetic and Sociological Significance* (London: Lippincott), which warned against "race mixing," stating that "the negro is inferior to the white," as cited by Adam S. Cohen, "Harvard's Eugenics Era," *Harvard Magazine*, March-April 2016, https://

harvardmagazine.com/2016/03/harvards-eugenics-era; see also Bradley 2018; Wilder, *Ebony and Ivy*.

73. Moore, *Reproducing Racism*.

74. Andrew M. Duehren, "Police Investigate Vandalism on Portraits of Black Law Professors," *The Harvard Crimson*, November 20, 2015, https://www.thecrimson.com /article/2015/11/20/law-school-vandalism-portraits/.

75. Gaztambide-Fernández and Angod, "Approximating Whiteness."

76. Ibid., 732.

77. Anderson, "White Space."

78. hooks, "Homeplace," 384. This is also similar to what Katherine McKittrick describes as a "black sense of place" ("On Plantations, Prisons, and a Black Sense of Place," *Social & Cultural Geography* 12, no. 8 [2011] 947–963).

79. hooks, "Homeplace," 385.

80. Bonilla-Silva, Eduardo. *Racism without Racists: Color-Blind Racism and the Persistence of Racial Inequality in the United States,* 2nd ed. (Lanham, MD: Rowman & Littlefield Publishers, 2006); Carmen Kynard, "From Candy Girls to Cyber Sista-Cipher: Narrating Black Females' Color-Consciousness and Counterstories in *and* out of School," *Harvard Educational Review* 80, no. 1 (2010): 30–53.

81. Garces and Jayakumar, "Dynamic Diversity"; Moore, *Reproducing Racism*.

82. Elizabeth A. Armstrong and Laura Hamilton, *Paying for the Party: How College Maintains Inequality* (Cambridge, MA: Harvard University Press, 2013); Amy J. Binder and Kate Wood, *Becoming Right: How Campuses Shape Young Conservatives* (Princeton, NJ: Princeton University Press, 2013); Warikoo, *Diversity Bargain*.

83. Binder and Wood, *Becoming Right*.

84. Moore, *Reproducing Racism*, 141.

85. Warikoo, *Diversity Bargain*; Warikoo and Deckman, "Beyond the Numbers."

86. See the introduction to this volume where I discuss Cultural Rhythms in more detail.

VERSE I: BEING BLACK

1. "We bless in the name of the Lord, in the name of the Lord are all things blessed" (translation by Kuumba). Full lyrics with translation are available at Musixmatch, "Lyrics: Hlohonolofatsa," accessed June 10, 2021, https://www.musixmatch.com/lyrics/Soweto -Gospel-Choir/Hlohonolofatsa.

2. Memorial Church, "History: World War I," accessed June 29, 2021. https://memorial church.harvard.edu/world-war-i.

3. On the first occasion, students from a Black women's group on campus were eating in the dining hall where I lived and were asked to show their campus ID cards by a white male student to prove that they were residents. Some were and others were not. There was a rule that on certain evenings, only residents could eat in the dining hall. Needless to say, the women felt they were called out because of their race, given the few Black students who lived in any residence. On the second occasion, I was waiting to attend a yoga class in one of the common spaces in my residence. A Black men's group was using the room and running late when our class was set to begin. The white woman who taught the yoga class, whose only affiliation with Harvard was teaching fitness classes, became incensed that the group was running over into her class time. When the group did not immediately disband when she informed them of her room reservation, she went to get the campus security guard—a Black man—who was always posted by

the building's main entrance, to force the group to leave. By the time the yoga teacher returned with the guard, the group was leaving. In both cases, the importance of the intersection of race and gender is glaring.

4. Gomes had been appointed minister in 1974 and was beloved and criticized, but criticized more for his sexuality and support of gay clergy than for his race (Robert D. McFadden, "Rev. Peter J. Gomes is Dead at 68; A Leading Voice Against Intolerance," *The New York Times*, March 1, 2011).

5. Peakd, "The Awesomeness of Culture in J. P. Clark's Poem, Agbor Dancer," accessed June 10, 2021, https://peakd.com/hive-148441/@gandhibaba/the-awesomeness-of-culture -in-j-p-clark-s-poem-agbor-dancer.

6. Though Kuumba was not a religious fellowship or Christian organization, a number of the group's practices, such as the closing circle, took cues from practices common across Black churches.

7. Ohito and the Fugitive Literacies Collective, "Creative," 194. Emphasis in original.

8. This phrasing is taken from the 2012 Kuumba Christmas concert program.

9. The librarian was dedicated to disseminating knowledge on the history of the organization, to remind members that Kuumba came about because of and to address Black students' struggles in a time when Harvard was much less hospitable to them. To achieve these ends the librarian would maintain archives for the organization and organize occasional "historical moments" during rehearsals to share snippets of the organization's history. The librarian was also instrumental in determining each concert's theme and wrote a welcome letter for each concert program.

10. For a critical perspective on the erasure of structural violence from such romanticizing, see Saidiya V. Hartman, *Scenes of Subjection: Terror, Slavery, Self-Making in Nineteenth-Century America* (New York: Oxford University Press, 1997).

11. John S. Rosenberg, "Harvard Explores Slavery Connections Further," *Harvard Magazine*, November 22, 2019, https://www.harvardmagazine.com/2019/11/harvard-slavery -links-initiative; note also the point made by Gaztambide-Fernández and Angod ("Approximating Whiteness," 741): "[O]ne cannot hold elites accountable for their historical implication in slavery while at the same time becoming *one of us* with global elites and moving with ease through the world by feeling at home everywhere."

12. See E. Johnson, *Appropriating*; Ohito and the Fugitive Literacies Collective, "Creative"; Baratunde Thurston, *How to Be Black* (New York: Harper, 2012). Furthermore, scholars of Black studies have long argued that we live in the "afterlife" or "wake" of slavery. Christina Sharpe has asked unsettling questions that illuminate the presentness of the legacy of slavery in the lives of Black Americans: "Might we [. . .] understand the absence of a National Slavery Museum in the United States as recognition of the ongoingness of the conditions of capture? Because how does one memorialize the everyday? How does one, in the words often used by institutions, 'come to terms with' (which usually means move past) ongoing and quotidian atrocity?" (*In the Wake*).

13. Sandra S. Smith and Mignon R. Moore, "Intraracial Diversity and Relations among African-Americans: Closeness among Black Students at a Predominantly White University," *American Journal of Sociology* 106, no. 1 (2000):1–39.

14. Anthony A. Jack, *The Privileged Poor: How Colleges Are Failing Disadvantaged Students* (Cambridge, MA: Harvard University Press), 2019.

15. Ohito and the Fugitive Literacies Collective, "Creative."

16. For robust discussions on racial performativity through music, see David Grazian, *Blue Chicago: The Search for Authenticity in Urban Blues Clubs* (Chicago: University of Chicago Press, 2003) and E. Johnson, *Appropriating.*

17. See The Guardian, "Africa Is Not a Country," January 24, 2014, https://www.the guardian.com/world/2014/jan/24/africa-clinton.

18. Angie was referring to the song "Jordan River."

19. "Been in the Storm So Long" is a Negro spiritual about metaphorically weathering a storm, a period of challenge and tribulation.

20. Gaztambide-Fernández and Angod, "Approximating Whiteness."

21. For the clip, see "Lebo M—One By One," YouTube, accessed June 10, 2021, http://www.youtube.com/watch?v=QQCjmI4MW-E.

22. For the full translated lyrics, see lionking.org, "One By One Lyrics," accessed June 10, 2021, http://www.lionking.org/lyrics/OBCR/OneByOne.html.

23. This type of use of humor is something Ohito also observed in her practice of a Black critical pedagogue in centering Blackness in her higher education teaching practice (Esther O. Ohito, "'I Just Love Black People!': Love, Pleasure, and Critical Pedagogy in Urban Teacher Education," *The Urban Review* 51 [2019]: 123–145).

24. The students also engaged in student-led discussions, which is explored further in chapter 3.

25. "Super seniors" were uncommon among Harvard students, as students typically finished their degrees within the standard four years. However, Grace and others like her opted to take time off while at Harvard and required extra time to finish.

26. Given the documented marginalization of Black students on elite campuses, this is not unwarranted.

27. Spike Lee, dir., *School Daze* (N.p.: 40 Acres and a Mule Filmworks, 1988), (Burbank, CA: RCA/Columbia Pictures Home Video, 1988. DVD); Thurston, *How to Be Black*; Elaine Welteroth, *More Than Enough: Claiming Space for Who You Are (No Matter What They Say)* (New York: Viking, 2019).

28. Thurston, *How to Be Black*, 11.

29. Signithia Fordham, and John U. Ogbu, "Black Students' School Success: Coping with the Burden of 'Acting White,'" *Urban Review* 18 (1986): 176–206.

30. See for example, André Robert Lee, dir., *The Prep School Negro* (N.p.: Point Made Films, 2012), DVD; Sarah Susannah Willie, *Acting Black: College, Identity, and the Performance of Race* (New York: Routledge, 2003).

31. Signithia, Fordham, "Passin' for Black: Race, Identity, and Bone Memory in Postracial America," *Harvard Educational Review* 80, no. 1 (2010): 4–30, 4. In this article, Fordham implicitly draws on the image of "passing for white" in discussing Black identity, referring to the historical practice of light-skinned Blacks to sometimes live in white society as white people, not revealing their African descent.

32. Ibid., 5.

33. There is evidence that this tension, feeling excluded by white peers and predominantly white institutions while also feeling a distance and lack of acceptance by Black peers and Black communities outside of the university more broadly, is nothing new. Stephen Bradley (*Ivory Tower*) demonstrates how historically this has been an issue for Black students attending Ivy League institutions.

34. Kiratiana Freelon et al., *Black Guide to Life at Harvard* (Cambridge, MA: Harvard Black Students Association, 2002), 234.

35. Ibid.

36. Kimberlé Crenshaw. "Mapping the Margins: Intersectionality, Identity Politics, and Violence against Women of Color," *Stanford Law Review* 43, no. 6 (1991): 1241–1299.

37. Byrd, Brunn-Bevel, and Sexton ("Don't All Look Alike") and Jack (*Privileged Poor*) provide recent examples of how predominantly white colleges and universities continue to problematically treat Black students as a monolithic group.

38. Du Bois, W.E.B., *The Souls of Black Folk* (New York: Penguin Books, 1996), 3.

39. Opportunity Insights (https://opportunityinsights.org/) has conducted some of the most recent and encompassing research demonstrating the ways race mitigates social mobility.

40. Danielle S. Allen, *Cuz: The Life and Times of Michael A.* (New York: Liveright, 2017).

41. See Warikoo, *Diversity Bargain*.

42. Students for Fair Admissions, Inc., v. President and Fellows of Harvard College (Harvard Corporation) (D. Mass., filed September 30, 2019), accessed June 10, 2021, https://admissionscase.harvard.edu/files/adm-case/files/2019-10-30_dkt_672_findings_of_fact_and_conclusions_of_law.pdf.

43. See Jack, *The Privileged Poor*, in which he describes Black students from backgrounds of lower socioeconomic status who did not attend prep schools prior to college as the "doubly disadvantaged," to sum up their lack of understanding of how to navigate the elite college environment and their lack of financial resources.

44. See Tatum (*Why Are All the Black Kids*) for additional discussion of this phenomenon.

45. Only Kuumbabes from backgrounds of lower socioeconomic status said anything about "embarrassing us." Maybe they had to contend with the atmosphere of respectability politics in a different way (see Higginbotham, *Righteous Discontent*).

46. Byrd, *Poison in the Ivy*, 136.

47. Gaztambide-Fernández, *Best*.

48. This is a dynamic also discussed by Guiffrida ("African American Student Organizations") with undergraduate students at a predominantly white institution.

49. Although in a much graver context, this idea of a caricatured performance of Blackness for an unsuspecting white audience is reminiscent of Hartman's "puttin' on." Hartman describes "puttin' on" as the enslaved person's performance of contented subjection. This performance was, in part, a subversive act. But it simultaneously reinforced the system of racial domination and oppression. Hartman writes, "since acts of resistance exist within the context of relations of domination and are not external to them, they acquire their character from these relations, and vice versa" (*Scenes of Subjection*, 8).

50. In her research at a predominantly white university, Winkle-Wagner demonstrates in detail the ways the Black women in her study chose to limit what and how much they shared with classmates due to perceived racialized expectations (Rachelle Winkle-Wagner, *The Unchosen Me: Race, Gender, and Identity Among Black Women in College* [Baltimore: Johns Hopkins University Press, 2009]). See also Gaztambide-Fernández and Angod, "Approximating Whiteness"; Rachelle Winkle-Wagner et al., "Authentically Me: Examining Expectations That Are Placed Upon Black Women in College," American Educational Research Journal 56, no. 2 (2019): 407–443.

51. The U.S. Black population in 2019 was 13.4 percent (U.S. Census Bureau, "QuickFacts," accessed June 29, 2021, https://www.census.gov/quickfacts/fact/table/US/PST045219). In contrast, the percentage of enrolled Black or African American undergraduates at Harvard College in 2011 was about 6.8 percent of the population (Harvard College, President and Fellows of, *Harvard University Fact Book 2011–12* [Cambridge, MA: The Office of Institutional Research, 2012], https://oir.harvard.edu/files/huoir/files/harvard_fact_book _2011-12_final.pdf). Though the College had been admitting greater numbers of African American students, 11.8 percent for the class of 2015 (Jeevan Vasagar, "Harvard Admits Record Numbers of African-American and Latino Students," *The Guardian*, April 12, 2011), the matriculated population remained relatively low.

52. Without offering specifics, the Freshman Dean's Office has noted that housing assignments were set up to be "as diverse as possible" so that "students 'learn from all kinds of people with different kinds of interests'" (Adam M. Guren, "Freshman Roommates, Meet Your Makers," *The Harvard Crimson*, August 12, 2005, https://www.the crimson.com/article/2005/8/12/freshman-roommates-meet-your-makers-it/). Anecdotally through this research, speaking with other Harvard undergraduates, and through my own observations, it was quite common to encounter freshmen rooming groups with compositions similar to Jason's, with, say, one Black roommate, one white roommate, and one Asian or Latinx roommate. Warikoo also discusses how Harvard's assignment of first-year roommates impacts students' experiences and understandings of diversity (*Diversity Bargain*).

53. Race may still have played a part unconsciously, given the documentation of implicit bias in educational contexts (see Mark J. Chin et al., "Bias in the Air: A Nationwide Exploration of Teachers' Implicit Racial Attitudes, Aggregate Bias, and Student Outcomes," *Educational Researcher* 49, no. 8 [2020]: 566–578).

54. Kristen A. Clayton has documented how Black students develop identity differently based on attending either historically white or historically Black colleges and universities. On historically white campuses, like Harvard's, biracial students demonstrate feeling excluded from whiteness and being viewed as non-white. ("Biracial Identity Development at Historically White and Historically Black Colleges and Universities," *Sociology of Education* 93, no. 3 [2020]: 238–255.)

55. See Warikoo and Deckman, "Beyond the Numbers," for a discussion of how institutional context impacts students' experience of diversity initiatives.

56. Rubén A. Gaztambide-Fernández, "Bullshit as Resistance: Justifying Unearned Privilege among Students at an Elite Boarding School," *International Journal of Qualitative Studies in Education* 24, no. 5 (2011): 581–586.

57. The importance of this function of the organization shouldn't be underestimated, as research shows that a positive Black identity can contribute to students' thriving in college (Sabrina Zirkel, and Tabora Johnson, "Mirror, Mirror on the Wall: A Critical Examination of the Conceptualization of the Study of Black Racial Identity in Education," *Educational Researcher* 45, no. 5 [2016]: 301–311).

58. Bradley illuminates this dynamic historically: "Black students in the Ivy League have always been marginalized to some degree. From the 1800s to the present, they have been something of a spectacle even as they gained greater access to the eight elite institutions. Because of their race, they stood apart from their school peers, and because of their opportunity to enroll, they were unique among their racial peers" (*Ivory Tower*, 374).

VERSE II: STAYING BLACK

1. This research took place before the country reeled from the scandals of Rachel Dolezal and Jessica Krug, two women who admittedly were born into white families, but chose to live as Black women (see Decca Aitkenhead, "Rachel Dolezal: 'I'm not going to stoop and apologise and grovel,'" *The Guardian*, February 25, 2017 https://www .theguardian.com/us-news/2017/feb/25/rachel-dolezal-not-going-stoop-apologise -grovel; Michael Levensen, "Professor Investigated for Posing as Black Has Resigned, University Says," *The New York Times*, September 9, 2020, https://www.nytimes.com /2020/09/09/us/jessica-krug-george-washington-university.html). It would be interesting to consider how those stories might impact the characterization presented here.

2. Erica R. Meiners, "Disengaging from the Legacy of Lady Bountiful in Teacher Education Classrooms," *Gender and Education* 14, no. 1 (2002): 85–94.

3. E. Johnson, *Appropriating*, 4.

4. See Warikoo, *Diversity Bargain*.

5. See Warikoo and Deckman, "Beyond the Numbers."

6. See Anderson, "White Space."

7. Elizabeth Calvert Fine, *Soulstepping: African American Step Shows* (Urbana: University of Illinois Press, 2003); Helen Gilbert, and Joanne Tompkins, *Post-colonial Drama: Theory, Practice, Politics* (London: Routledge, 1996).

8. See Maya Angelou, "Still I Rise," *poemhunter.com*, accessed June 11, 2021, http://www.poemhunter.com/poem/still-i-rise/.

9. Yet, at the same time, students saw forming an intentional Black community as necessary to the organization's mission of creating a safe space for Black students. As another Kuumbabe told me, part of Kuumba's work involved getting members out to other Black students' shows (theater, dance, music, etc.); emails promoting such events were one of the most typical kinds of postings to listserv groups.

10. See Park, *When Diversity Drops.*

11. Binder and Wood found this same sort of dispassionate approach to engaging in political discussions among conservative students at one elite university. They suggest that this discourse style is influenced by institutional norms around what constitutes preferred "civilized discourse" (*Becoming Right,* 157).

12. See the introduction to this volume for an explanation of this policy and its origins.

13. Sociologists of elite education have described how multicultural experiences are seen as an essential part of elite identity formation (Gaztambide-Fernández, "Bullshit"; Khan, *Privilege*; Warikoo, *Diversity Bargain*).

14. Assistant directors—there were more than one for this given academic year—helped Sheldon by, for instance, running warm-ups for the choir, playing the piano during that time, and leading the group in practicing scales. This position was viewed by some Kuumbabes like Daphne as being more about the choir's musicality than racial history.

15. While the choir did some a cappella work, the Kuumband accompanied the choir at the Christmas and spring concerts and on the spring break tour. However, band members did not attend the majority of the regular rehearsals. Here it is also interesting to note that expertise in music seemed to create another kind of authenticity for Kuumbabes, particularly those of non-Black backgrounds. This may have connections

with Gaztambide-Fernández's (*Best*) conception of elitism as encompassing excellence in extracurricular activities.

16. Regarding opportunity hoarding, see John B. Diamond, and Amanda E. Lewis, "Opportunity Hoarding and the Maintenance of 'White' Educational Space," *American Behaviorial Scientist* (forthcoming); and regarding accumulation by dispossession, see Kristen L. Buras, "Race, Charter Schools, and Conscious Capitalism: On the Spatial Politics of Whiteness as Property (and the Unconscionable Assault on Black New Orleans)," *Harvard Educational Review* 81, no. 2 (2011): 296–331.

17. See Harvard University, "Harvard College Handbook for Students: Policy Regarding Undergraduate Student Organizations," accessed June 11, 2021,https://handbook.fas.harvard.edu/book/policy-regarding-undergraduate-organizations.

18. Anderson, "White Space," 10.

19. Ibid., 15–16.

BRIDGE: NON-BLACK MEMBERS IN THE BLACK CHOIR

1. See Harvard College Dean of Students Office, "Student Organization at Hilles (SOCH)," accessed June 11, 2021, https://dso.college.harvard.edu/soch.

2. Here, Francisco is contending with the racialization of Latinx people in the United States, which further reveals the social construction of race. For a more substantive discussion, see Douglas S. Massey, "The Racialization of Latinos in the United States," in *The Oxford Handbook of Ethnicity, Crime, and Immigration*, edited by Sandra M. Bucerius and Michael Tonry (Oxford: Oxford University Press, 2014), 21–40.

3. Sunaina Maira referred to this as an "authenticating framework" ("Ideologies of Authenticity: Youth, Politics, and Diaspora," *Amerasia Journal* 25, no. 3 [1999]: 139–150, 141).

4. Mary C. Waters, *Black Identities: West Indian Immigrant Dreams and American Realities* (Cambridge, MA: Harvard University Press, 1999).

5. See David Myers, *Exploring Social Psychology* (Boston: McGraw-Hill, 2007), for a synthesis of this research in social psychology. However, Todd L. Pittinsky has challenged this view, arguing that throughout time there have been people who have "loved" cultures they perceived to be different from their own, which he terms "allophilia" (*Us Plus Them: Tapping the Positive Power of Difference* [Boston: Harvard Business Review Press, 2012]). Nonetheless, Daphne's view that having an affinity for one's own race/ethnicity was "natural" remains widely held.

6. See, for example, Stacey J. Lee, Eujin Park, and Jia-Hui Stefanie Wong, "Racialization, Schooling, and Becoming American: Asian American Experiences," *Educational Studies* 53, no. 5 (2017): 492–510; Shruti Mukkamala and Karen L. Suyemoto, "Racialized Sexism/Sexualized Racism: A Multimethod Study of Intersectional Experiences of Discrimination for Asian American Women," *Asian American Journal of Psychology* 9, no. 1 (2018): 32–46.

7. Laybourn and Goss, *Black Greek-Letter.*

8. Diamond and Lewis, "Opportunity Hoarding."

9. Guren, "Freshman Roommates."

10. Perhaps in a twist of irony, "One by One" was a song made popular in the Disney Broadway musical *The Lion King* (see lionking.org, "One By One Lyrics," accessed June 10, 2021, http://www.lionking.org/lyrics/OBCR/OneByOne.html). It was performed in a non-English language spoken in South Africa that did not make the message of the lyrics widely accessible to a predominantly English-speaking audience.

11. Kramer, "Diversifiers."

12. For instance, in her book, *Pushout: The Criminalization of Black Girls in Schools* (New York: The New Press, 2016), Monique Morris problematizes describing Black girls as "sassy" or having "attitude."

13. Gaztambide-Fernández and Angod, "Approximating Whiteness."

14. Gaztambide-Fernández, *Best*; Gaztambide-Fernández and Angod, "Approximating Whiteness"; Khan, *Privilege*.

15. Byrd, *Poison in the Ivy*.

16. Blake R. Silver, *The Cost of Inclusion: How Student Conformity Leads to Inequality on College Campuses* (Chicago: University of Chicago Press, 2020).

17. Ibid.

18. See Gaztambide-Fernández, *Best*; Kramer, "Diversifiers"; Winkle-Wagner, *Unchosen Me*.

19. This is what Warikoo and Deckman describe as a "power analysis frame" (see *Diversity Bargain*).

20. Debbie Sonu and Marissa Bellino, "Stranger-Making as Difference: Childhood Memories of Belonging and Exclusion by Undergraduates of Color," *Race Ethnicity and Education* 23, no. 4 (2020): 563–580.

CHORUS: LEARNING TO CARE

A version of the section "They Have to Love Where They Are" appears in Deckman, "Leave the Space."

1. See for example, Bradley, *Ivory Tower*; Fordham, "Passin'"; Vanessa Siddle Walker and John R. Snarey, eds., *Race-ing Moral Formation: African American Perspectives on Care and Justice* (New York: Teachers College Press, 2004).

2. Wanda Watson, Yolanda Sealey-Ruiz, and Iesha Jackson, "Daring to Care: The Role of Culturally Relevant Care in Mentoring Black and Latino Male High School Students," *Race Ethnicity and Education* 19, no. 5 (2016): 980–1002.

3. Walker and Snarey, *Race-ing Moral Formation*; Audrey Thompson, "Caring and Colortalk: Childhood Innocence in White and Black," in *Race-ing Moral Formation: African American Perspectives on Care and Justice*, edited by Vanessa Siddle Walker and John R. Snarey (New York: Teachers College Press, 2004), 23–37.

4. Shawn A. Ginwright, *Black Youth Rising: Activism and Radical Healing in Urban America* (New York: Teachers College Press, 2010).

5. Bedford Palmer, "Self-Care for #BlackLivesMatter Activists!" accessed November 16, 2020, https://medium.com/@DrBFPalmer/tips-for-self-care-in-activism-and-the-blacklivesmatter-movement-b501052d6379.

6. Evette Dionne, "For Black Women, Self-Care Is A Radical Act: Not Placing Ourselves First is Costing Black Women More Than Peace of Mind," *Ravishly*, March 9, 2015; hooks, "Homeplace."

7. Lorde is cited, for example, by Kali Robinson in "When Self-Care is Radical: the Importance of Black Joy," *Blackboard: Northwestern's Black Student Magazine*, accessed June 11, 2021, http://blackboardmag.com/when-self-care-is-radical-the-importance-of-black-joy/.

8. Lawrence Cremin, *Public Education* (New York: Basic Books, 1976).

9. Aria N. Bendix, "Stress in a 'Type A' Environment," *The Harvard Crimson*, January 24, 2013; Gaztambide-Fernández, *Best* and "Bullshit." Around the time of this research,

this idea of the need to present an unflappable self-image while experiencing tremendous amounts of stress and distress was the topic of an article by Anonymous, "I Am Fine," that appeared in *Fifteen Minutes: The Magazine of the Harvard Crimson* on February 17, 2011. The article, which was considered controversial at the time, was written in first-person by a student who described an ongoing battle with suicidal ideation, all the while acting outwardly as though everything was fine, responding to perceived social pressures on campus.

10. Kuumba, the University Choir, and the Harvard Summer Chorus are noted as "Other Choral Groups at Harvard," suggesting less prominence (Harvard Choruses, "Harvard Choruses Auditions Process," accessed June 29, 2021, https://www.singatharvard .com/audition.html). See Bradley (*Ivory Tower*) regarding Du Bois's rejection from the Glee Club.

11. See for example, Marnie W. Curry, "Will You Stand for Me? Authentic Cariño and Transformative Rites of Passage in an Urban High School," *American Educational Research Journal*, 53, no. 4 (2016): 883–918.

12. Nancy was an older white woman from the community who had been in Kuumba for a few years. She came to the organization after her daughter was a member.

13. Siddle Walker and Snarey, *Race-ing*.

14. Bradley, *Ivory Tower*.

15. Siddle Walker and Snarey, *Race-ing*.

16. Respectively: Watson, Sealey-Ruiz, and Jackson, "Daring to Care," 982; Durryle N. Brooks, "(Re)conceptualizing Love: Moving Towards a Critical Theory of Love in Education for Social Justice," *Journal of Critical Thought and Praxis* 6, no. 3 (2017): 102–114, 108.

17. See Khan (*Privilege*) for an example of how the ideology of meritocracy led students at St. Paul's school to put on the façade that they were constantly engaged in doing schoolwork, even though they were not.

18. Watson, Sealey-Ruiz, and Jackson, "Daring to Care," 984.

19. Rosa L. Rivera-McCutchen, "Caring in a Small Urban High School: A Complicated Success," *Urban Education* 47, no. 3 (2012): 653–680.

20. The Dozens is a form of playful "ritual insult" common within the African American community. For a fuller discussion see, for example, Django Paris, "'They're in My Culture, They Speak the Same Way': African American Language in Multiethnic High Schools," *Harvard Educational Review* 79, no. 3 (2009): 428–448.

21. Watson, Sealey-Ruiz, and Jackson ("Daring to Care") documented this sort of community accountability among students in their study on culturally relevant care in a high school mentoring program for Black and Latino youth.

22. Ohito, "I Just Love Black People!," 139.

23. Blake R. Silver, *The Cost of Inclusion: How Student Conformity Leads to Inequality on College Campuses* (Chicago: University of Chicago Press, 2020).

24. Recent rankings by *U.S. News and World Report* list Harvard as the number one university in the world. See U.S. News and World Report, "Harvard University, #1 in Best Global Universities," accessed June 11, 2021, https://www.usnews.com/education/best -global-universities/harvard-university-166027.

25. Gaztambide-Fernández, *Best*.

26. Anonymous, "Fine"; Gaztambide-Fernández, *Best*; Khan, *Privilege*. These are hallmarks of the new meritocracy in which students are continually working to prove

they belong and are meritorious enough for the privileged position they have earned at an exclusive institution like Harvard.

27. See Michel Foucault, *The Will to Knowledge (The History of Sexuality Volume 1)* (London: Penguin Books, 1998).

CODA: LESSONS FROM THE SAFE BLACK SPACE

Chapter epigraph from Ohito and the Fugitive Literacies Collective, "Creative," 216 (emphasis in original).

1. Sankofa is often associated with the Akan proverb that roughly translates to "It is not wrong to go back for that which you have forgotten." See https://www.adinkrasymbols .org/symbols/sankofa/.

2. Jack, *Privileged Poor*.

3. For a discussion on the limitations of policy in bringing about meaningful change related to diversity in U.S. higher education, see Jones and Reddick, "Heterogeneity of Resistance."

4. My findings echo and expand on the five characteristics of places of belonging that Garcia, in "Belonging," found among Latinx participants at predominantly white colleges.

5. Julie J. Park, "'Man, This is Hard': A Case Study of How Race and Religion Affect Cross-Racial Interaction for Black Students," *Review of Higher Education* 35, no. 4 (2012): 567–593.

6. See Silver, *Cost of Inclusion*.

7. See Byrd, Brunn-Bevel, and Sexton, "Don't All Look Alike."

8. Wilkerson, *Caste*.

9. See Silver, *Cost of Inclusion*.

10. Ibid.

11. See Madison Gesiotto, "Facts, Not Feelings: Snowflakes, Safe Spaces, and Trigger Warnings," *Washington Times*, March 2, 2017.

12. Binder and Wood, *Becoming Right*.

13. See Wilkerson, *Caste*.

14. See https://www.npr.org/2010/01/18/122701268/i-have-a-dream-speech-in-its-entirety.

15. Consider, for example, that it was during the Obama presidency that the country saw Trayvon Martin, Sandra Bland, and Tamir Rice perish at the hands of a civilian vigilante and the police.

16. See, for example, Garces and Jayakumar, "Dynamic Diversity"; Park, *When Diversity Drops*.

17. Silver, *Cost of Inclusion*, 157.

18. Park, *When Diversity Drops*, 147 (emphasis in original).

19. Barton and Tan, "Beyond Equity as Inclusion."

20. Gaztambide-Fernández and Angod, "Approximating Whiteness."

21. I thank Esther Ohito who used this phrase, "starting from Black," in a presentation to my class. The idea was one which Tarilyn Little further developed by rethinking Black as being on the margins to being in the center.

22. Diamond and Lewis, "Opportunity Hoarding."

23. bell hooks, "Choosing the Margin as a Space of Radical Openness," *Framework: The Journal of Cinema and Media* 36 (1989): 15–23, 19.

24. Diamond and Lewis, "Opportunity Hoarding."

25. Shamari K. Reid, ". . . pedagogical tools cannot drive out darkness, only love can do that," Shamari K. Reid, August 13, 2018, accessed November 15, 2020, https://www .shamarireid.com/pedagogicaltools, ¶8. Note that in the original, "love" is bolded and "blood" is written using red font. I have substituted italics here to maintain the intended emphasis.

26. Brooks, "(Re)conceptualizing," 108.

27. Martin Luther King, Jr., *Where Do We Go From Here: Chaos or Community?* (Boston: Beacon Press, 2018), 38.

28. For a discussion of love of Blackness, see Bettina L. Love, *We Want to Do More than Survive: Abolitionist Teaching and the Pursuit of Educational Freedom* (Boston: Beacon Press, 2019).

29. See Gaztambide-Fernández, *Best*; Gaztambide-Fernández and Angod, "Approximating Whiteness."

30. "Hold On Just A Little While Longer" is a spiritual of unknown origin.

31. The Blacktivism Conference came about on the heels of the 2014 Black Arts Festival, also cosponsored by Kuumba, which featured Kuumbabe Kimiko Matsuda-Lawrence's play, "I, Too, Am Harvard" (see Bethonie Butler, "'I, Too, Am Harvard,': Black Students Show They Belong," *Washington Post*, March 5, 2014, https://www.washingtonpost.com/blogs/she -the-people/wp/2014/03/05/i-too-am-harvard-black-students-show-they-belong/).

32. For a timeline of related demonstrations, see Alia Wong and Adrienne Green, "Campus Politics: A Cheat Sheet," *Atlantic,* April 4, 2016, https://www.theatlantic.com /education/archive/2016/04/campus-protest-roundup/417570/.

33. See Barton and Tan, "Beyond Equity as Inclusion," regarding "rightful presence."

34. Brené Brown, *Braving the Wilderness: The Quest for True Belonging and the Courage to Stand Alone* (New York: Random House, 2017), 160.

35. Danielle Apugo, "A Hidden Culture of Coping: Insights on African American Women's Existence in Predominantly White Institutions," *Multicultural Perspectives* 21, no. 1 (2019): 53–62; Winkle-Wagner, *Unchosen Me.*

APPENDIX B: NOTE ON METHODS

1. Lawrence-Lightfoot and Davis, *Art and Science of Portraiture,*10.

2. Ibid., 30–31. My emphasis.

3. Ibid., xvi. Emphasis in original.

4. Ibid., 10.

5. Robert K. Yin, *Case Study Research: Design and Methods.* 4th ed. (Los Angeles: Sage Publications, 2009). Park's research on a "multiethnic" campus religious organization (*When Diversity Drops*) is one that comes close to addressing this issue and informs my study. However, in the case of Park's work, the organization had an explicit focus on fostering a multicultural membership without focusing on one specific race or ethnicity as central to the organization. Laybourn and Goss similarly studied the experiences of non-Black members of Black Greek-letter organizations, though their work focuses on student participants across a variety of organizations and campuses (Laybourn and Goss, *Black Greek-Letter*).

6. Lawrence-Lightfoot and Davis, *Art and Science of Portraiture.*

7. See E. Johnson (*Appropriating*) for a nuanced discussion of the complications of performing race, particularly when the "performer" does not identify as being a member of

the race being performed. For instance, Johnson led an undergraduate course in which, at least on one occasion, a white student performed the part of a Black person in an excerpt from a theatrical production. There was backlash from the Black students in the class.

8. Harvard College Dean of Students Office, "List."

9. Espenshade, Radford, and Chung, *No Longer Separate*.

10. To respect students' confidentiality, exact numbers of students and research years are obscured. However, the information provided presents an accurate picture of the organization during the early 2010s. Data on race for two students (~3%) was either unspecified or unavailable.

11. The percentage of men and women in the choir has fluctuated. Even in my years of attending concerts, there have been times where the numbers were closer to equal. Lower numbers of men in the choir may be related to slightly lower numbers of Black men attending Harvard compared to women. In 2011, of 474 African American undergraduate enrollees, 201 (~42%) were male and 273 (~58%) were female (Harvard College, *Fact Book*). It is also possible that this trend is reflective of attitudes about singing and gender, as one male member indicated to me when asked. However, there is no comparison group at Harvard, given that the next largest choral groups are divided by gender or require tryouts for a set number of voice parts. In general, when I asked Kuumba alumni and participants about this gender disparity, they didn't seem to make much of it; it was unremarkable to them. A few mentioned that in past years there had been more charismatic male student leaders who were able to recruit more men to the group.

12. Robert M. Emerson, Rachel I. Fretz, and Linda L. Shaw, *Writing Ethnographic Fieldnotes,* Chicago Guides to Writing, Editing, and Publishing (Chicago: University of Chicago Press, 1995); Lawrence-Lightfoot and Davis, *Art and Science of Portraiture*.

13. Emerson, Fretz, and Shaw, *Writing*, 2.

14. Irving Seidman, *Interviewing as Qualitative Research: A Guide for Researchers in Education and the Social Sciences*, 3rd ed. (New York: Teachers College Press, 2006).

15. Robert Stuart Weiss, *Learning from Strangers: The Art and Method of Qualitative Interview Studies* (New York: Maxwell Macmillan International, 1994), 17.

16. Of the four who didn't participate, timing at the end of the semester did not work for three, and one was unresponsive to my emails.

17. Lawrence-Lightfoot and Davis, *Art and Science of Portraiture*.

18. Wendy Luttrell, *Qualitative Educational Research: Readings in Reflexive Methodology and Transformative Practice* (New York: Routledge, 2010).

19. Ibid., 247.

20. Ibid.

21. Ibid., 136.

22. Khan, *Privilege*, 202.

23. Erving Goffman, *The Presentation of Self in Everyday Life* (Garden City, NY: Anchor, 1959), 15.

24. Ibid., 35.

25. While some could argue that students might have shared what they thought I wanted to hear, I believe they were being sincere in what they shared as various sources of data converged around the same findings.

26. Lawrence-Lightfoot and Davis, *Art and Science of Portraiture*, 95.

Selected Bibliography

Ahmed, Sara. *On Being Included: Racism and Diversity in Institutional Life.* Durham: Duke University Press, 2012.

Ali, Diana. "Safe Spaces and Brave Spaces Historical Context and Recommendations for Student Affairs Professionals." *NASPA Policy and Practice Series* 2 (October 2017). Accessed November 16, 2020. https://www.naspa.org/images/uploads/main/Policy _and_Practice_No_2_Safe_Brave_Spaces.pdf.

Allen, Danielle S. *Cuz: The Life and Times of Michael A.* New York: Liveright, 2017.

Anderson, Elijah. "'The White Space.'" *Sociology of Race and Ethnicity* 1, no. 1 (2015):10–21. https://doi.org/10.1177/2332649214561306.

Anonymous. "I Am Fine." *Fifteen Minutes: The Magazine of the Harvard Crimson*, February 17, 2011.

Apugo, Danielle. "A Hidden Culture of Coping: Insights on African American Women's Existence in Predominantly White Institutions." *Multicultural Perspectives* 21, no. 1 (2019): 53–62. https://doi.org/10.1080/15210960.2019.1573067.

Arao, Brian, and Kristi Clemens. "From Safe Spaces to Brave Spaces: A New Way to Frame Dialogue around Diversity and Social Justice." In *The Art of Effective Facilitation: Reflections from Social Justice Educators*, edited by Lisa M. Landreman, 135–150. Sterling, VA: Stylus, 2013.

Armstrong, Elizabeth A., and Laura Hamilton. *Paying for the Party: How College Maintains Inequality.* Cambridge, MA: Harvard University Press, 2013.

Baer, Lauren E. "The Ku Klux Klan at Harvard." *The Harvard Crimson*, February 18, 1999. https://www.thecrimson.com/article/1999/2/18/the-ku-klux-klan-at-harvard/.

Baldwin, James. *The Fire Next Time.* New York: Vintage International, 1993. Originally published in 1963 by The Dial Press (New York).

Barton, Angela Calabrese, and Edna Tan. "Beyond Equity as Inclusion: A Framework of 'Rightful Presence' for Guiding Justice-Oriented Studies in Teaching and Learning." *Educational Researcher* 49, no. 6 (2020): 433–440. https://doi.org/10.3102/0013189X20927363.

Bell, Derrick A. "*Brown v. Board of Education* and the Interest-Convergence Dilemma." *Harvard Law Review* 93, no. 3 (1980): 518–533. https://doi.org/10.2307/1340546.

Bendix, Aria N. "Stress in a 'Type A' Environment." *The Harvard Crimson*, January 24, 2013. https://www.thecrimson.com/article/2013/1/24/stress-type-a/.

Binder, Amy J. and Kate Wood. *Becoming Right: How Campuses Shape Young Conservatives*. Princeton, NJ: Princeton University Press, 2013.

Biography. "Carter G. Woodson Biography (1875–1950)." Accessed November 6, 2020. https://www.biography.com/scholar/carter-g-woodson.

Blumenthal, Matthew S. "From Sharecroppers' Son to College's Gatekeeper: During Evans' Tenure, Black Population at Harvard Multiplied 15 Times." *The Harvard Crimson*, October 17, 2005. https://www.thecrimson.com/article/2005/10/17/from-sharecroppers-son-to -colleges-gatekeeper/.

Bonilla-Silva, Eduardo. *Racism without Racists: Color-Blind Racism and the Persistence of Racial Inequality in the United States*. 2nd ed. Lanham, MD: Rowman & Littlefield Publishers, 2006.

Bradley, Stefan M. *Upending the Ivory Tower: Civil Rights, Black Power, and the Ivy League*. New York: New York University Press, 2018.

Brooks, Durryle N. "(Re)conceptualizing Love: Moving Towards a Critical Theory of Love in Education for Social Justice." *Journal of Critical Thought and Praxis* 6, no. 3 (2017): 102–114. https://doi.org/10.31274/jctp-180810-87.

Brown, Brené. *Braving the Wilderness: The Quest for True Belonging and the Courage to Stand Alone*. New York: Random House, 2017.

Brown, Kimberly D. "From the Low Point of American Race Relations: Dr. Carter Woodson's Negro History Week." Accessed November 6, 2020. https://americanhistory.si.edu /blog/2013/02/what-we-know-as-black-history-month-dr-carter-woodsons-intentions -for-negro-history-week.html.

Buras, Kristen L. "Race, Charter Schools, and Conscious Capitalism: On the Spatial Politics of Whiteness as Property (and the Unconscionable Assault on Black New Orleans)." *Harvard Educational Review* 81, no. 2 (2011): 296–331. https://doi.org/10.17763/HAER.81 .2.6L42343QQW360J03.

Byrd, W. Carson. *Poison in the Ivy: Race Relations and the Reproduction of Inequality on Elite College Campuses*. The American Campus, edited by Harold S. Wechsler. New Brunswick, NJ: Rutgers University Press, 2017.

Byrd, W. Carson, Rachelle J. Brunn-Bevel, and Parker R. Sexton. "'We Don't All Look Alike': The Academic Performance of Black Student Populations at Elite Colleges." *Du Bois Review* 11, no. 2 (2014): 353–385.

California Newsreel. "Race—The Power of an Illusion: Ask the Experts." Accessed November 16, 2020. http://www.pbs.org/race/000_About/002_04-experts-03-02.htm.

Chen, Shu-Ling. "Debates over Third World Centers at Princeton, Brown and Harvard: Minority Student Activism and Institutional Responses in the 1960s and 1970s." Unpublished EdD dissertation, Graduate School of Education, Harvard University, 2000.

Chin, Mark J., David M. Quinn, Tasminda K. Dhaliwal, and Virginia S. Lovison. "Bias in the Air: A Nationwide Exploration of Teachers' Implicit Racial Attitudes, Aggregate Bias, and Student Outcomes." *Educational Researcher* 49, no. 8 (2020): 566–578. https:// doi.org/10.3102/0013189X20937240.

Clayton, Kristen A. "Biracial Identity Development at Historically White and Historically Black Colleges and Universities." *Sociology of Education* 93, no. 3 (2020): 238–255.

Collins, Cory. "What Is White Privilege, Really?" *Teaching Tolerance* 60, (Fall 2018): 38–41. https://www.tolerance.org/magazine/fall-2018/what-is-white-privilege-really.

Cornell, Stephen, and Douglas Hartmann. *Ethnicity and Race: Making Identities in a Changing World.* Sociology for a New Century. 2nd ed. Thousand Oaks, CA: Pine Forge Press, 2007.

Cremin, Lawrence. *Public Education.* New York: Basic Books, 1976.

Crenshaw, Kimberlé. "Mapping the Margins: Intersectionality, Identity Politics, and Violence against Women of Color." *Stanford Law Review* 43, no. 6 (1991): 1241–1299. https://doi.org/10.2307/1229039.

Crimson Staff. "In Celebration of Black History: Harvard Has Come a Long Way from Institutionalized Prejudice, but More Needs to Be Done." *The Harvard Crimson*, February 28, 2011.

Curry, Marnie W. "Will You Stand for Me? Authentic Cariño and Transformative Rites of Passage in an Urban High School." *American Educational Research Journal*, 53, no. 4 (2016): 883–918. https://doi.org/10.3102/0002831216660380.

De los Ríos, Cati, Jorge López, and Ernest Morrell. "Toward a Critical Pedagogy of Race: Ethnic Studies and Literacies of Power in High School Classrooms." *Race and Social Problems* 7, no. 1 (2015): 84–96. https://doi.org/10.1007/s12552-014-9142-1.

Deckman, Sherry L. "Leaving the Space Better than You Found It Through Song: Music, Diversity, and Mission in One Black Student Organization. *Harvard Educational Review* 83, no. 2 (2013): 279–294. https://doi.org/10.17763/haer.83.2.48577681047466w6.

———. "Managing Race and Race-ing Management: Teachers' Stories of Race and Classroom Conflict." *Teachers College Record* 119, no. 11 (2017): 1–40.

Diamond, John B., and Amanda E. Lewis. "Opportunity Hoarding and the Maintenance of 'White' Educational Space." *American Behavioral Scientist*, forthcoming. Accessed November 16, 2020. https://www.johnbdiamond.com/uploads/6/5/0/7/65073833/american _behavioral_scientist_paper_opportunity_hoardingfinal_7-27-20.edited.pdf

Dionne, Evette. "For Black Women, Self-Care Is A Radical Act: Not Placing Ourselves First is Costing Black Women More Than Peace of Mind." *Ravishly*, March 9, 2015. http://www.ravishly.com/2015/03/06/radical-act-self-care-black-women-feminism.

Dotson, Kristie. "Conceptualizing Epistemic Oppression." *Social Epistemology: A Journal of Knowledge, Culture and Policy* 28, no. 2 (2014): 115–138. https://doi.org/10.1080 /02691728.2013.782585.

Du Bois, W.E.B. *The Autobiography of W.E.B. Du Bois.* New York: International Publishers, 1968.

———. *The Souls of Black Folk.* New York: Penguin Books, 1996.

Emerson, Robert M., Rachel I. Fretz, and Linda L. Shaw. *Writing Ethnographic Fieldnotes.* Chicago Guides to Writing, Editing, and Publishing. Chicago: University of Chicago Press, 1995.

Espenshade, Thomas J., Alexandria Walton Radford, and Chang Young Chung. *No Longer Separate, Not Yet Equal: Race and Class in Elite College Admission and Campus Life.* Princeton, NJ: Princeton University Press, 2009.

Fine, Elizabeth Calvert. *Soulstepping: African American Step Shows.* Urbana: University of Illinois Press, 2003.

Fisher v. University of Texas, 579 U.S. ___ (2016). https://www.supremecourt.gov/opinions /15pdf/14-981_4g15.pdf.

———. 570 U.S. 297 (2013).

Floyd, Rosiline D. "Yes We Can: The Impact Membership in Black Greek Sororities Has on the Experience and Persistence of Black Women Students at Predominantly White 4-year Institutions." Unpublished PhD dissertation, Indiana State University, 2009.

Fordham, Signithia. "Passin' for Black: Race, Identity, and Bone Memory in Postracial America." *Harvard Educational Review* 80 no. 1 (2010): 4–30. https://doi.org/10.17763/haer.80.1.u5232230430716w2.

Fordham, Signithia, and John U. Ogbu. "Black Students' School Success: Coping with the Burden of 'Acting White.'" *Urban Review* 18, (1986): 176–206. https://doi.org/10.1007/BF01112192.

Foucault, Michel. *The Will to Knowledge (The History of Sexuality Volume 1).* London: Penguin Books, 1998.

Fox, Catherine. "From Transaction to Transformation: (En)Countering White Heteronormativity in 'Safe Spaces.'" *College English* 69, no. 5 (May, 2007): 496–511. .

Fox, Stephen R. *The Guardian of Boston: William Monroe Trotter.* New York: Atheneum Press, 1970.

Freelon, Kiratiana, Marques J. Redd, Toussaint G. Losier, and Harvard Black Students Association. *Black Guide to Life at Harvard.* Cambridge, MA: Harvard Black Students Association, 2002.

Garces, Liliana M., and Uma M. Jayakumar. "Dynamic Diversity: Toward a Contextual Understanding of Critical Mass." *Educational Researcher* 43, no. 3 (2014): 115–124. https://doi.org/10.3102/0013189X14529814.

Garcia, Crystal. "Belonging in a Predominantly White Institution: The Role of Membership in Latina/o Sororities and Fraternities." *Journal of Diversity in Higher Education* 13, no. 2 (2020): 181–193. https://doi.org/10.1037/dhe0000126.

Gaztambide-Fernández, Rubén A. "Bullshit as Resistance: Justifying Unearned Privilege among Students at an Elite Boarding School." *International Journal of Qualitative Studies in Education* 24, no. 5 (2011): 581–586. https://doi.org/10.1080/09518398.2011.600272.

———. *The Best of the Best: Becoming Elite at an American Boarding School.* Cambridge, MA: Harvard University Press, 2009.

Gaztambide-Fernández, Rubén, and Leila Angod. "Approximating Whiteness: Race, Class, and Empire in the Making of Modern Elite/White Subjects." *Educational Theory* 69, no. 6 (2019): 719–743. https://doi.org/10.1111/edth.12397.

Gesiotto, Madison. "Facts, Not Feelings: Snowflakes, Safe Spaces and Trigger Warnings." *The Washington Times*, March 2, 2017. https://www.washingtontimes.com/news/2017/mar/2/facts-not-feelings-snowflakes-safe-spaces-and-trig/.

Gilbert, Helen, and Joanne Tompkins. *Post-colonial Drama: Theory, Practice, Politics.* London: Routledge, 1996.

Ginwright, Shawn A. *Black Youth Rising: Activism and Radical Healing in Urban America.* New York: Teachers College Press, 2010.

Goffman, Erving. *The Presentation of Self in Everyday Life.* Garden City, NY: Anchor, 1959.

Grazian, David. *Blue Chicago: The Search for Authenticity in Urban Blues Clubs.* Chicago: University of Chicago Press, 2003.

Griffin, Kimberly A., and Richard J. Reddick. "Surveillance and Sacrifice: Gender Differences in the Mentoring Patterns of Black Professors at Predominantly White Research Universities." *American Educational Research Journal* 48, no. 5 (2011): 1032–1057. https://doi.org/10.3102/0002831211405025.

Grutter v. Bollinger, 539 U.S. 306 (2003).

Guiffrida, Douglas A. "African American Student Organizations As Agents of Social Integration." *Journal of College Student Development* 44, no. 3 (2003): 304–319. https://doi.org/10.1353/csd.2003.0024.

Guren, Adam M. "Freshman Roommates, Meet Your Makers." *The Harvard Crimson*, August 12, 2005. https://www.thecrimson.com/article/2005/8/12/freshman-roommates-meet-your-makers-it/.

Gusa, Diane Lynn. "White Institutional Presence: The Impact of Whiteness on Campus Climate." *Harvard Educational Review* 80, no. 4 (2010): 464–489. https://doi.org/10.17763/haer.80.4.p5j483825u110002.

Halper, Jamie D. "With History Written in Roxbury, Harvard Remained Ambivalent." *The Harvard Crimson*, May 22, 2017. https://www.thecrimson.com/article/2017/5/22/roxbury-riots-1967/.

Hamer, Fannie Lou. "'Nobody's Free Until Everybody's Free': Speech Delivered at the Founding of the National Women's Political Caucus, Washington, D.C., July 10, 1971." In *The Speeches of Fannie Lou Hamer: To Tell It Like It Is*, edited by Maegan Parker Brooks and Davis W. Houck, 134–139. Jackson, MS: University Press of Mississippi, 2010.

Harper, Shaun R., Lori D. Patton, and Ontario S. Wooden. "Access and Equity for African American Students in Higher Education: A Critical Race Historical Analysis of Policy Efforts." *Journal of Higher Education* 80, no. 4 (2009): 389–414. https://doi.org/10.1080/00221546.2009.11779022.

Hartman, Saidiya V. *Scenes of Subjection: Terror, Slavery, Self-Making in Nineteenth-Century America*. New York: Oxford University Press, 1997.

Harvard Black Students Association. "About Us." Accessed June 29, 2021. https://www.theharvardbsa.com/about-bsa-1.

Harvard Choruses. "Harvard Choruses Auditions Process." Accessed June 29, 2021. https://www.singatharvard.com/audition.html.

Harvard College. "About Harvard College: A Brief History of Harvard College." Accessed June 4, 2021. https://handbook.fas.harvard.edu/book/brief-history-harvard-college.

Harvard College Dean of Students Office. "List of Student Organizations." Accessed June 6, 2021. https://dso.college.harvard.edu/list-student-organizations.

Harvard College, President and Fellows of. *Harvard University Fact Book 2011–12*. Cambridge, MA: The Office of Institutional Research, 2012. https://oir.harvard.edu/files/huoir/files/harvard_fact_book_2011-12_final.pdf.

Harvard Gender and Sexuality Caucus. "History of the Caucus." Accessed November 18, 2020. http://hgsc.sigs.harvard.edu/article.html?aid=106.

Harvard Glee Club. "About Us." Accessed August 30, 2018. http://www.harvardgleeclub.org/.

Helwink, Jonathan. "Safe Spaces Just Make the World More Dangerous." *The Federalist*, November 16, 2016. https://thefederalist.com/2016/11/16/safe-spaces-make-world-more-dangerous/.

Higginbotham, Evelyn Brooks. *Righteous Discontent: The Women's Movement in the Black Baptist Church, 1880–1920*. Cambridge, MA: Harvard University Press, 1993.

Hochschild, Jennifer L., and Nathan Scovronick. *The American Dream and the Public Schools*. Oxford: Oxford University Press, 2004.

hooks, bell. "Choosing the Margin as a Space of Radical Openness." *Framework: The Journal of Cinema and Media* 36 (1989): 15–23. http://www.jstor.org/stable/44111660.

———. "Homeplace (A Site of Resistance)." In *Yearning: Race, Gender, and Cultural Politics*, 41–49. Boston: South End Press, 1990.

Jack, Anthony A. *The Privileged Poor: How Colleges Are Failing Disadvantaged Students.* Cambridge, MA: Harvard University Press, 2019.

Johnson, Akilah. "Boston. Racism. Image. Reality." *The Boston Globe*, December 10, 2017. https://apps.bostonglobe.com/spotlight/boston-racism-image-reality/series/image/

Johnson, E. Patrick. *Appropriating Blackness: Performance and the Politics of Authenticity.* Durham: Duke University Press, 2003.

Jones, Veronica A., and Richard J. Reddick. "The Heterogeneity of Resistance: How Black Students Utilize Engagement and Activism to Challenge PWI Inequalities." *The Journal of Negro Education* 86, no. 3 (2017): 204–219. https://doi.org/10.7709/jnegroeducation.86.3.0204.

Kalev, Alexandra, Frank Dobbin, and Erin Kelly. "Best Practices or Best Guesses? Assessing the Efficacy of Corporate Affirmative Action and Diversity Policies." *American Sociological Review* 71, no. 4 (2006): 589–617. https://doi.org/10.1177/000312240607100404

Khan, Shamus Rahman. *Privilege: The Making of an Adolescent Elite at St. Paul's School.* Princeton, NJ: Princeton University Press, 2011.

Kramer, Rory. "Diversifiers at Elite Schools." *Du Bois Review* 5, no. 2 (2008): 287–307. https://doi.org/10.1017/S1742058X0808017X.

Krammer, Donna, and Rosemarie Mangiardi. "The Hidden Curriculum of Schooling: A Duoethnographic Exploration of What Schools Teach Us about Schooling." In *Duoethnography: Dialogic Methods for Social, Health, and Educational Research*, edited by Joe Norris, Richard D. Sawyer, and Darren E. Lund, 41–70. Walnut Creek, CA: Left Coast Press, 2012.

Kynard, Carmen. "From Candy Girls to Cyber Sista-Cipher: Narrating Black Females' Color-Consciousness and Counterstories in *and* out *of School.*" *Harvard Educational Review* 80, no. 1 (2010): 30–53. https://doi.org/10.17763/haer.80.1.4611255014427701.

Lawrence-Lightfoot, Sara, and Jessica Hoffmann Davis. *The Art and Science of Portraiture.* San Francisco: Jossey-Bass, 1997.

Laybourn, Wendy M., and Devon R. Goss. *Diversity in Black Greek-Letter Organizations: Breaking the Line.* New York: Routledge, 2018.

Lee, André Robert, dir. *The Prep School Negro.* N.p.: Point Made Films, 2012. DVD.

Lee, Spike, dir. *School Daze.* N.p.: 40 Acres and a Mule Filmworks, 1988. Burbank, CA: RCA/Columbia Pictures Home Video, 1988. DVD.

Lee, Stacey J., Eujin Park, and Jia-Hui Stefanie Wong. "Racialization, Schooling, and Becoming American: Asian American Experiences." *Educational Studies* 53, no. 5 (2017): 492–510. https://doi.org/10.1080/00131946.2016.1258360.

Luttrell, Wendy. *Qualitative Educational Research: Readings in Reflexive Methodology and Transformative Practice.* New York: Routledge, 2010.

Maira, Sunaina. "Ideologies of Authenticity: Youth, Politics, and Diaspora." *Amerasia Journal* 25, no. 3 (1999): 139–150. https://doi.org/10.17953/amer.25.3.q917482qqn305u56

Massey, Douglas S. "The Racialization of Latinos in the United States." In *The Oxford Handbook of Ethnicity, Crime, and Immigration*, edited by Sandra M. Bucerius and Michael Tonry, 21–40. Oxford: Oxford University Press, 2014.

McFadden, Robert D. "Rev. Peter J. Gomes is Dead at 68; A Leading Voice Against Intolerance." *The New York Times*, March 1, 2011. https://www.nytimes.com/2011/03/02/us/02gomes.html.

McKittrick, Katherine. "On Plantations, Prisons, and a Black Sense of Place." *Social & Cultural Geography* 12, no. 8 (2011): 947–963. https://doi.org/10.1080/14649365.2011 .624280.

Meiners, Erica R. "Disengaging from the Legacy of Lady Bountiful in Teacher Education Classrooms." *Gender and Education* 14, no. 1 (2002): 85–94. https://doi.org/10 .1080/09540250120098861.

Memorial Church. "History: World War I." Accessed June 29, 2021. https://memorialchurch .harvard.edu/world-war-i.

Moore, Wendy Leo. *Reproducing Racism: White Space, Elite Law Schools, and Racial Inequality*. Lanham, MD: Rowman & Littlefield Publishers, 2008.

Morris, Monique W. *Pushout: The Criminalization of Black Girls in Schools*. New York: The New Press, 2016.

Mukkamala, Shruti, and Karen L. Suyemoto. "Racialized Sexism/Sexualized Racism: A Multimethod Study of Intersectional Experiences of Discrimination for Asian American Women." *Asian American Journal of Psychology* 9, no. 1 (2018): 32–46. http://dx.doi.org/10.1037/aap0000104.

Murguía, Edward, Raymond V. Padilla, and Michael Pavel. "Ethnicity and the Concept of Social Integration in Tinto's Model of Institutional Departure." *Journal of College Student Development* 32, no. 5 (1991) 433–439.

Museus, Samuel D. "The Role of Ethnic Student Organizations in Fostering African American and Asian American Students' Cultural Adjustment and Membership at Predominantly White Institutions." *Journal of College Student Development* 49, no. 6 (2008): 568–586. https://doi.org/10.1353/csd.0.0039.

Myers, David. *Exploring Social Psychology*. Boston: McGraw-Hill, 2007.

NAACP. "NAACP History: Lift Every Voice and Sing." Accessed November 6, 2020. https://www.naacp.org/naacp-history-lift-evry-voice-and-sing/.

Ohito, Esther O. "'I Just Love Black People!': Love, Pleasure, and Critical Pedagogy in Urban Teacher Education." *The Urban Review* 51 (2019): 123–145. https://doi.org/10 .1007/s11256-018-0492-7.

Ohito, Esther O., and the Fugitive Literacies Collective. "'The Creative Aspect Woke Me Up': Awakening to Multimodal Essay Composition as a Fugitive Literacy Practice." *English Education* 52, no. 3 (2020): 186–222. https://library.ncte.org/journals/ee/issues /v52-3/30596.

Palfrey, John G. *Safe Spaces, Brave Spaces: Diversity and Free Expression in Education*. Cambridge, MA: MIT Press, 2017.

Palmer, Bedford. "Self-Care for #BlackLivesMatter Activists!" Accessed November 16, 2020. https://medium.com/@DrBFPalmer/tips-for-self-care-in-activism-and-the-blacklives matter-movement-b501052d6379.

Paris, Django. "'They're in My Culture, They Speak the Same Way': African American Language in Multiethnic High Schools." *Harvard Educational Review* 79, no. 3 (2009): 428–448. https://doi.org/10.17763/haer.79.3.64j4678647mj7g35.

Park, Julie. J. *When Diversity Drops: Race, Religion, and Affirmative Action in Higher Education*. New Brunswick, NJ: Rutgers University Press, 2013.

Paxson, Christina. "Brown University President: A Safe Space for Freedom of Expression." *The Washington Post*, September 5, 2016.

Pittinsky, Todd L. *Us Plus Them: Tapping the Positive Power of Difference*. Boston: Harvard Business Review Press, 2012.

Purdy, William C. "Higher Education and a Living, Diverse Democracy: An Overview." *Diversity & Democracy* 21, no. 3 (2018): 4–9. https://www.aacu.org/diversitydemocracy /2018/summer/purdy.

Quaye, Stephen J. "Facilitating Dialogues about Racial Realities." *Journal of College Student Development* 116, no. 8 (2012): 542–562.

Reddick, Richard J. "Reclaiming Our Time: A 21st-Century Response to Banks' 'Afro-American Scholars in the University.'" *Urban Education* 55, no. 2 (2020): 238–266. https://doi.org/10.1177/0042085918805805.

Reid, Shamari K. ". . . pedagogical tools cannot drive out darkness, only love can do that." Shamari K. Reid, August 13, 2018. Accessed November 15, 2020. https://www .shamarireid.com/pedagogicaltools.

Rivera-McCutchen, Rosa L. "Caring in a Small Urban High School: A Complicated Success." *Urban Education* 47, no. 3 (2012): 653–680. https://doi.org/10.1177%2F00420 85911433522.

Ross, Kihana Miraya. "Call It What It Is: Anti-Blackness." *The New York Times*, June 4, 2020. https://www.nytimes.com/2020/06/04/opinion/george-floyd-anti-blackness .html.

Ross, Lawrence C. "Harvard Has More Black Students Than Ever, But Are They African-American?" *The Grio*, April 21, 2011. http://thegrio.com/2011/04/21/harvard-has -more-black-students-than-ever-but-are-they-african-american/.

Roth, Michael. S. *Safe Enough Spaces: A Pragmatist's Approach to Inclusion, Free Speech, and Political Correctness on College Campuses*. New Haven, CT: Yale University Press, 2019.

Rudolph, Frederick. *The American College and University: A History*. New York: Alfred A. Knopf, 1962.

Schapiro, Morton. "I'm Northwestern's President. Here's Why Safe Spaces for Students Are Important." *The Washington Post*, January 15, 2016.

Seidman, Irving. *Interviewing as Qualitative Research: A Guide for Researchers in Education and the Social Sciences*. 3rd ed. New York: Teachers College Press, 2006.

Sensoy, Özlem, and Robin DiAngelo. "Respect Differences? Challenging the Common Guidelines in Social Justice Education." *Democracy and Education* 22, no. 2 (2014): 1–10. https://democracyeducationjournal.org/home/vol22/iss2/1.

———. "'We Are All for Diversity, but . . .': How Faculty Hiring Committees Reproduce Whiteness and Practical Suggestions for How They Can Change." *Harvard Educational Review* 87, no. 4 (2017): 557–580. https://doi.org/10.17763/1943-5045-87.4.557.

Sharpe, Christina. *In the Wake: On Blackness and Being*. Durham: Duke University Press, 2016.

Sidanius, James, Shana Levin, and Colette Van Laar. *The Diversity Challenge: Social Identity and Intergroup Relations on the College Campus*. New York: Russell Sage Foundation, 2008.

Siddle Walker, Vanessa, and John R. Snarey, eds. *Race-ing Moral Formation: African American Perspectives on Care and Justice*. New York: Teachers College Press, 2004.

Silver, Blake R. *The Cost of Inclusion: How Student Conformity Leads to Inequality on College Campuses*. Chicago: University of Chicago Press, 2020.

Siskind, Sarah R. "Affirmative Dissatisfaction: Affirmative Action Does More Harm Than Good." *The Harvard Crimson*, 2012 November 2, 2012. https://www.thecrimson .com/column/the-snollygoster/article/2012/11/2/Siskind-affirmative-action/.

Smith, Sandra S., and Mignon R. Moore. "Intraracial Diversity and Relations among African-Americans: Closeness among Black Students at a Predominantly White University." *American Journal of Sociology* 106, no. 1 (2000):1–39.

Snibbe, Kris. "A Window into African-American History." *Harvard Gazette*, February 4, 2011. https://news.harvard.edu/gazette/story/2011/02/a-window-into-african -american-history/.

Sonu, Debbie, and Marissa Bellino. "Stranger-Making as Difference: Childhood Memories of Belonging and Exclusion by Undergraduates of Color." *Race Ethnicity and Education* 23, no. 4 (2020): 563–580. https://doi.org/10.1080/13613324.2018 .1497960.

Stevens, Mitchell. *Creating a Class: College Admissions and the Education of Elites* Cambridge, MA: Harvard University Press, 2007.

Tatum, Beverly Daniel. *"Why Are All the Black Kids Sitting Together in the Cafeteria?": And Other Conversations about Race*. New York: Basic Books, 1997.

Thompson, Audrey. "Caring and Colortalk: Childhood Innocence in White and Black." In *Race-ing Moral Formation: African American Perspectives on Care and Justice*, edited by Vanessa Siddle Walker and John R. Snarey, 23–37. New York: Teachers College Press, 2004.

Thurston, Baratunde. *How to Be Black*. New York: Harper, 2012.

Tuitt, Franklin. "Enhancing Visibility in Graduate Education: Black Women's Perceptions of Inclusive Pedagogical Practices." *International Journal of Teaching and Learning in Higher Education* 22, no. 3 (2010): 246–257. https://files.eric.ed.gov/fulltext /EJ938560.pdf.

U.S. Census Bureau. "QuickFacts." Accessed June 29, 2021. https://www.census.gov /quickfacts/fact/table/US/PST045219.

Vasagar, Jeevan. "Harvard Admits Record Numbers of African-American and Latino Students." *The Guardian*, April 12, 2011.

Walters, Hubert E. "Kuumba: The Early Years." The History section of the website for the Kuumba Singers of Harvard College. Accessed June 6, 2021. http://kuumbasingers .org/history/.

Warikoo, Natasha K. *The Diversity Bargain: And Other Dilemmas of Race, Admissions, and Meritocracy at Elite Universities*. Chicago: University of Chicago Press, 2016.

Warikoo, Natasha K., and Sherry L. Deckman. "Beyond the Numbers: Institutional Influences on Experiences with Diversity on Elite College Campuses." *Sociological Forum* 29, no. 4 (2014): 959–981. https://doi.org/10.1111/socf.12128.

Waters, Mary C. *Black Identities: West Indian Immigrant Dreams and American Realities*. Cambridge, MA: Harvard University Press, 1999.

Watson, Wanda, Yolanda Sealey-Ruiz, and Iesha Jackson. "Daring to Care: The Role of Culturally Relevant Care in Mentoring Black and Latino Male High School Students." *Race Ethnicity and Education* 19, no. 5 (2016): 980–1002. https://doi.org/10.1080/13613324 .2014.911169.

Weheliye, Alexander G. *Habeas Viscus: Racializing Assemblages, Biopolitics, and Black Feminist Theories of the Human*. Durham: Duke University Press, 2014.

Weiss, Robert Stuart. *Learning from Strangers: The Art and Method of Qualitative Interview Studies*. New York: Maxwell Macmillan International, 1994.

Welteroth, Elaine. *More Than Enough: Claiming Space for Who You Are (No Matter What They Say)*. New York: Viking, 2019.

Wilder, Craig Steven. *Ebony and Ivy: Race, Slavery, and the Troubled History of America's Universities*. New York: Bloomsbury Press, 2013.

Wilkerson, Isabel. *Caste: The Origin of Our Discontents*. New York: Random House, 2020.

Willie, Sarah Susannah. *Acting Black: College, Identity, and the Performance of Race*. New York: Routledge, 2003.

Winkle-Wagner, Rachelle. *The Unchosen Me: Race, Gender, and Identity Among Black Women in College*. Baltimore: Johns Hopkins University Press, 2009.

Winkle-Wagner, Rachelle, Briget Turner Kelly, Courtney L. Luedke, and Tangela Blakely Reavis. "Authentically Me: Examining Expectations That Are Placed Upon Black Women in College." American Educational Research Journal 56, no. 2 (2019): 407–443. https://doi.org/10.3102/0002831218798326.

Yin, Robert K. *Case Study Research: Design and Methods*. 4th ed. Los Angeles: Sage Publications, 2009.

Zirkel, Sabrina, and Tabora Johnson. "Mirror, Mirror on the Wall: A Critical Examination of the Conceptualization of the Study of Black Racial Identity in Education." *Educational Researcher* 45, no. 5 (2016): 301–311. https://doi.org/10.3102/0013189X16656938

Index

About the Author

Sherry L. Deckman is an associate professor in the School of Education at Lehman College, the City University of New York and an affiliated faculty member with the PhD program in urban education at the Graduate Center, the City University of New York. She is a former undergraduate advising coordinator and residential advisor at Harvard University, where she received her doctorate from the Graduate School of Education. Her research addresses issues of race, class, gender, and sexuality equity in education.

Available titles in the American Campus series

A. Fiona Pearson, *Back in School: How Student Parents are Transforming College and Family*

Adrianna Kezar and Daniel Maxey, eds., *Envisioning the Faculty for the Twenty-First Century: Moving to a Mission-Oriented and Learner-Centered Model*

Barrett J. Taylor and Brendan Cantwell, *Unequal Higher Education: Wealth, Status, and Student Opportunity*

Dana M. Malone, *From Single to Serious: Relationships, Gender, and Sexuality on American Evangelical Campuses*

Derrick R. Brooms, Jelisa Clark, and Matthew Smith, *Empowering Men of Color on Campus: Building Student Community in Higher Education*

Gordon Hutner and Feisal G. Mohamed, eds., *A New Deal for the Humanities: Liberal Arts and the Future of Public Higher Education*

James M. Thomas, *Diversity Regimes: Why Talk Is Not Enough to Fix Racial Inequality at Universities*

Jillian M. Duquaine-Watson, *Mothering by Degrees: Single Mothers and the Pursuit of Postsecondary Education*

Kirsten Hextrum, *Special Admission: How College Sports Recruitment Favors White Suburban Athletes*

Nathanael J. Okpych, *Climbing a Broken Ladder: Contributors of College Success for Youth in Foster Care*

Nolan L. Cabrera, *White Guys on Campus: Racism, White Immunity, and the Myth of "Post-Racial" Higher Education*

Ryan King-White, ed., *Sport and the Neoliberal University: Profit, Politics, and Pedagogy*

Scott Frickel, Mathieu Albert, and Barbara Prainsack, eds., *Investigating Interdisciplinary Collaboration: Theory and Practice across Disciplines*

Sherry L. Deckman, *Black Space: Negotiating Race, Diversity, and Belonging in the Ivory Tower*

Vicki L. Baker, Laura Gail Lunsford, and Meghan J. Pifer, *Developing Faculty in Liberal Arts Colleges: Aligning Individual Needs and Organizational Goals*

W. Carson Byrd, *Poison in the Ivy: Race Relations and the Reproduction of Inequality on Elite College Campuses*